PRAISE FOR *The Tail on*

"I was mesmerized by *The Tail on my Mother's Kite* ... finished it in two sittings ... it is the most touching memoir I have ever read."
— DOROTHY NELSON, J.D.

"I've interviewed authors for 35 years; this memoir takes the cake. It starts with a bang and stays that way: Maralys Wills, part of an extraordinary "ordinary" family, lived a yo-yo life, growing up in fourteen different locations. Before she was an adult she'd experienced wealth and deprivation, moments of warm hugs and seasons of stunning neglect. At the center of the story is her loving, impetuous, generous, selfish, oversexed, often-absent Mother, a woman lucky enough to raise—or sometimes raise—two brilliant children. Necessarily an adult before her teens, Maralys is now a full-time author with a marvelous memory, a wise but childlike sense of humor, a chronic lust for adventure, and a lasting trust in the ultimate good. It's a life lesson. And it's GOT to be a movie!"
— STEPHANIE EDWARDS
Emmy-Winning TV/Radio Commentator

"Maralys Wills' entertaining memoir ranges from laugh-out-loud funny to very touching. This book is hard to put down because I found myself relating to so many of Maralys' experiences. Many of us have had lives that are just as unlikely, and this candid book illustrates again that truth is stranger than fiction. "
— IRENE BERARDESCO, B.A.

"This is Maralys Wills' recollection of her mercurial childhood: a capricious adventure lived on the coattail of her beautiful, charismatic, and unpredictable mother. A life which afforded, on one hand, a multitude of privileged experiences ... and on the other, kids left unattended, lonely, and in the care of strangers. The book is a page-turner. I could not wait to start each new chapter, wondering what could possibly happen next, and always curious to see how the children would weather the never-ending storm that was their life. "
— BERNARDINA WILCOX, B.S.

"Not only the tail on her mother's wild kite, but Maralys was also her mother's tall baggage, set down in strange places way too often. The story is so engrossing, so poignantly rendered without any mawkish sentiment, that I read it in almost one sitting. It touched me in ways unexpected."

— LINDA MEIER
Co-owner, Wills Wing

PRAISE FOR *Higher than Eagles*

"A gripping tale of transformation and redemption."

—*Kirkus*

"This well-written story of a family that loses children to the sport they love is recommended."

—*Library Journal*

"Maralys Wills and Chris Wills have given us earthbound parents a soul-lifting image of how to let go. I am in awe of their courage and eloquence."

—ELIZABETH FORSYTHE HAILEY
AUTHOR, *A Woman of Independent Means*

"This is a beautiful story. This is about real kids doing what real kids do … It's a book you will remember for a long, long time."

—VELMA DAVIS
Winter Haven News Chief

PRAISE FOR *A Circus Without Elephants*

"… wonderful, funny, sad, and uplifting book"

—*Writer's Digest*
(AWARD WINNER FOR LIFE STORIES)

"A beautifully-written family saga. Maralys Wills' deeply moving story of her family's triumphs and tragedies is a page-turner that I couldn't put down."

—JOAN DIAL
Author of *Roses in Winter*

"Wills' memoir is as warming as a pot of good coffee shared by old friends. Wise and loving, it's a celebration of the joys and heartbreak of parenthood that ought to be required reading for every dewy-eyed young couple contemplating marriage."

—MELISSA MATHER
Author of *One Summer in Between*

PRAISE FOR *A Clown in the Trunk*

"Maralys Wills ... she is clearly a force to be reckoned with."

—SIDNEY SHELDON
AUTHOR OF *The Other Side of Midnight*

"Maralys Wills proves that humor can be found anywhere—from a hospital bed to a tree full of ripening plums. This second book proves that the comic wellsprings in her family never run dry."

—PATRICIA TEAL
Literary Agent

"*A Clown in the Trunk* sparkles with wit and nostalgia. Wills' memories of life with a rambunctious family range from the absurd to the poignant and her reader is constantly howling with laughter, sympathizing with an outnumbered mother, or wiping a responsive tear. Writers will particularly enjoy this book. If Wills could write under these circumstances, no writer has an excuse for not doing so."

—JAN MURRA
Author, *Castoff*

The Tail on my Mother's Kite

a memoir

Maralys Wills

To Denny —

The Tail on my Mother's Kite

Nice to meet you!

a memoir

Maralys Wills

Maralys Wills

Lemon Lane Press • Santa Ana, California

ISBN 978-0-9859426-7-0 (print)

ISBN 978-0-9859426-8-7 (eBook)

Lemon Lane Press
1811 Beverly Glen Drive
Santa Ana, CA 92705
(714) 544-0344

To contact the author: maralys@cox.net

Cover design: Suzanne Campbell

Dedicated to my daughter, Tracy, who
understands bravery better than any of us.

CONTENTS

Acknowledgements

IF IT TAKES A VILLAGE TO RAISE A CHILD, IT ALSO TAKES A village to create a book. Few of us can do it without help. At the very least, somebody has to fill in and do the jobs we normally do. For me that would be Rob, my husband. He does the gardening, runs errands, gives me time I don't have to account for, and offers plenty of dinners out. He's also the one who allows me to read chapters hot off the computer and often says, "It's perfect, Babe. Don't change a word." I couldn't be an author without him.

A HUGE THANKS GOES TO MY SON, CHRIS, WHO NOT ONLY IN-sisted I write this book in the first place, but encouraged me with positive reinforcement as I churned it out.

Others, mainly my critique group, offered vital insights, chapter by chapter. Barbara French, P.J. Penman, Allene Symons, Pam Tallman, Erv Tibbs, and Terry Black saw glitches or made suggestions that improved the story. Friend and fellow author Dorsey Adams gave me hours, with margin notes that had a huge impact.

Special thanks to Allene Symons, who presided over the completed book in myriad, creative ways.

A writer also needs readers who grasp the bigger picture. Among them were family members Ken Wills (who can spot a typo or misspelling from three states away), Lauren Zeffaro, Betty-Jo Wills, Christy Pierce, and Tracy Hagen.

Other readers added comments for which I'm grateful: Writer Bob Ernst, who painstakingly did a line-by-line critique, plus friends Jevelyn Yonchar, Stephanie Edwards, Linda Meier, Irene Berardesco, and Bernie Wilcox, all of whom said things that made me glad I'd put in the work.

Some authors claim they go it alone. I'd like to meet even one and ask how he does it.

A Word to the Reader

Why would anyone want to write four memoirs? Surely three should be plenty, a whole lifetime's worth.

In the beginning, I never planned to write more than one. Back in the late Seventies, I saw our family's hang gliding years as special, a time set apart ... an era that brimmed over with drama, and yes, the ultimate in tragedy.

Once I realized the book should be about our oldest son, Bobby, I knew I had a dramatic arc, even an emotional rags-to-riches tale. Everyone who read it said, "This should be a movie." And indeed, that may yet happen. When, in 1992, *Higher Than Eagles* finally found a publisher, I imagined my memoir-writing years were over.

I was by then an author, and clearly my destiny was to keep writing. There came a moment in 2001 when, after my ninth book, I asked myself, What shall I write next? Something I make up? A novel? Another techno-thriller?

Then something occurred to me: maybe I already have a next book.

For forty years, around Christmas, my husband Rob had been mailing out to friends what he called our Annual Report. The thing was actually a booklet: a middle section with pictures, a few pages of news/philosophical musings by Rob, then another few pages by me—whatever I thought was the funniest or zaniest event of the year.

I wondered, *How many people have forty years worth of humorous vignettes already written? And how many are lucky enough to have an earlier, never-published manuscript to draw from?*

Voila! With a lot of polishing, I soon had a tenth book, titled by Rob, *A Circus Without Elephants*. But wouldn't you know, the material couldn't be contained in one volume. So there was my second light-hearted memoir: *A Clown in the Trunk*.

Okay, then. Memoirs over.

It was our son, Chris, who later demanded I write the story of my growing-up years.

"But there's not much to say," I protested. "Not enough material, not enough plot."

"Start writing," he said. "You'll see what you have."

Eventually I did as I was told and sure enough, I finally saw what Chris saw, a tale with fascinating threads woven among the characters: my brother and I, raised on-and-off by an oversexed, highly educated Bohemian, a mother who created drama wherever she went—and only partly because she chose to be married seven times; our astonishing grandfathers, one rich and one poor, whose destinies merged with the union of their two remarkable offspring; my brother and I repeatedly dropped off to live with surrogate parents in settings that ranged from bucolic to privileged ... and how, in spite of our crazy upbringing, we both managed to become successful adults.

With the mere act of creating scenes, I re-lived moments I'd left on a forgotten back burner. As my earliest years unfolded I discovered I did, after all, have a fourth memoir, the story Chris wanted.

CHAPTER ONE

Mt. Shasta, California

AFTER THE FIRE, NOTHING WAS EVER THE SAME.

Even to our mother who, like Elizabeth Taylor, was destined by her own choice to have seven husbands, nothing was more life-changing than the Siskiyou County forest fire.

Like a cougar stalking its prey, the fire crept down the ridges of Mount Eddy and arrived in full destruction mode at our family's virgin guest ranch, a 320-acre property with two houses—one wrinkled and old, the other newly framed, barely roofed. The year was 1939.

In the distance Mount Shasta still rose above the clouds, lofty and gleaming white, disdainful in its splendor as though such devastation a mere seven miles away was beneath its notice.

Unlike the grownups, I hadn't seen the fire coming. As I stood in the dirt road with our mile-away neighbors, I watched in awe as one by one, flames shot up the pines on a distant hill. We'd never seen anything like it. In unison, Alice Deetz and her three boys and I all shouted, "Oooh! There's another one!" "Oh … wow!" "A big one! Look at that!" We were spectators at a shocking, living event, thrilled but not afraid. The sparking hill was far away, across a vast meadow—as all of us knew, in its own universe.

I thought, *Wait 'til I tell people about this! They won't believe what I'm seeing.*

But then a wind came up, and with it the pungent odor of burning wood … and soon, carried on warm currents, a couple of charred twigs that whirled past, above our heads.

Suddenly, without a word to any of us, eight-year-old Jimmy Deetz grabbed a shovel and ran to a nearby patch of grass and beat out tiny flames.

Flames? But from where? I wondered. No flames had come near us, only a few blackened twigs.

Then Laddie, seven, found a discarded broom and pounded another sparking weed. I stared at them, amazed. Two farm boys used to hard work. *Nobody asked you to do this. But you found them all*, I thought, *there won't be any more.*

For a moment part of me backed away and in my imagination I saw the fire as a drama, a story I would write someday. Even as I envisioned words on paper, the truth dawned, hit me so hard I gasped: *This is how fire travels.*

Sure enough, the boys beat down more tiny flames, then ran with their tools to pound others.

I looked around. *Oh God, tiny flames are everywhere, like a swarm of mosquitoes.* Suddenly their efforts seemed futile. *What's the point of what they're doing?* I thought. *They'll never stop the fire with a broom.*

Yet there they were, two kids imprinted on my memory.

The wind blew ever harder. When smoking embers landed at my feet, my mood changed. The fire had crept closer, and now here it was, circling like a panther, threatening to end my ten-year-old life.

A hot ember landed on my arm and I panicked, logic and selfishness coalescing into stark terror. *We're going to die. Right here on this road.*

Like me, the oldest boy, Charlie, stood motionless and pale. *I have to get out of here.*

Suddenly one of our hired hands careened down the road from our ranch. I ran to intercept the truck, waving my arms. "Please. Please! Take me to town."

I wasn't thinking about my mother, back on the ranch, or my stepfather, or whoever else might be there. I was intent on escaping the fire, desperate to save my own life.

Charlie, too, begged to be taken away. As though we were already ablaze, we jumped into the truck and the man roared down the road.

NOT SO MY MOTHER. SHE LINGERED ON THE RANCH AS LONG as she dared. At the last second, her pickup loaded with family possessions from our 100-year-old house, she rocketed down the dirt road between towering pines sparking like Roman candles. Nothing short of a tree toppling on the car could have stopped her.

Sadly, she rescued the wrong house.

Her faulty choice was symbolic of her life.

ONE DAY AFTER THE FIRE, ALICE DEETZ, WHO SOMETIMES felt like my mother, drove me back to the ranch. Through the windows of her jalopy I stared left and right. The horror out there, the claustrophobic sense that you dared not breathe the air because it was full of particles and dangerous, the awfulness of our once-majestic pines and firs reduced to blackened, smoking spires, some of them still sizzling near the ground. So this was the aftermath of all those brilliantly-lit trees! Part of me withered as I looked, for I'd loved the majesty, the multi-hued greens that lined the dusty road I'd long considered my own. This was my path—my private route to a larger world, and the trees were my friends. Once, they'd touched fingers overhead as though forming an arch for a cathedral.

"It's pretty sad," Alice said, taking a quick sideways look. "I'm glad your brother missed this. Allan was better off at camp." She paused. "I feel sorry for your mother, though. I don't know what Virginia will do with the guest ranch."

"Won't the trees grow back?" *Surely, surely, in a few years …*

Alice shook her head. "Not soon enough, Maralys. Not nearly soon enough. I hope this won't mean …" She broke off, leaving the rest unsaid.

I tried to grasp where she'd been headed, the deeper meanings she understood but wouldn't express to such a young girl.

I knew my mother liked her, respected her. I knew she confided in Alice, her only neighbor, sometimes for hours. Nobody ever told me, but I guessed how much Mom relied on Alice—for her innate common sense, her stability.

What I didn't know was that Alice could perceive all too well what the fire would do to her best friend.

After several bends in the road, one depressing, black-tree vista after another, we arrived at the clearing where, to our right, a long-ago family from the eighteen hundreds had chosen to settle and build a great, two-story home.

Yet that's not where I looked.

The first thing I saw to the left of our dirt turnaround was the cement foundation laid by my stepfather, most of it charred and grimy, where three days ago I'd had the makings of a room ... a bed, clothes, a bureau. In the unfinished house, my brother and I were more or less camping out. The fresh, newly-hewn wood framework was gone—and with it, the roof. Instead, with no walls in sight, two sturdy brick chimneys stood there alone, poking at the sky.

I sucked in my breath. *Where were all my things?*

Eventually I looked to the right, and there stood the old house. The pines and cedars that framed it were as fresh, as green as before. Like an island in the midst of a vast, blackened ocean, the house stood as it had for those hundred years, solid, unspoiled, untouched.

It was Alice's turn to gasp. "I've heard the legends in town," she muttered. "The old Metcalf house would never burn, they said, because for some reason the winds part around it in strange ways. In ways that keep forest fires away. Which is why the Metcalfs built the house there." She shook her head. "I never believed those tales, of course." Together we stared at this strange monument to a piece of "common knowledge," to the town's enduring folklore.

"Well," she said, "at least Virginia still has this. I guess your mother will figure out something." She didn't even mention my stepfather, Hans.

It's not enough for me, I thought.

"I hope it will ..." she began and paused. "I hope this place will ... that the house that didn't burn will keep your mother sane."

CHAPTER TWO

Los Angeles, A Year Earlier

IN THE DAYS BEFORE THE RANCH, ALLAN AND I, AGES NINE AND seven, were city kids—or so we thought. Our house was quaint, like an artist's studio, with imaginative angles and little setouts that passed for bedrooms—but it was ours and it was bright and it was nestled in La Cañada, just outside Los Angeles.

"I'm going to live here until I'm old," Allan announced one day, shortly after we moved in. The house had yellow bedrooms and an orange living room with mullioned windows. He plopped down onto Mother's newly-acquired purple couch.

"Why until you're old?" I asked.

"Because I'm tired of moving," he said. "If she moves again I'm not going with her."

"Me too," I said, mostly because he'd said it first. But I was also tired of moving. "I'm not going either."

Our colorful house might have been the perfect place to linger and let a few years pass, and Allan and I could have grown up without our farm-kid attitudes and our scant attention to manners; we wouldn't have known about cow cakes or barn spiders. We'd never have been forced to push a car to get to school.

If things hadn't changed, we would have been like the other children in La Cañada, kids whose mothers drove on cement instead of dirt … and we'd never have found ourselves staring in horror at endless blackened trees and a burned-down house.

But we were unrealistic. Though we only sensed it, staying in one place could never happen. Our mother was a gypsy—a restless soul who couldn't live long without a man (even when it wasn't always the same man), and we were the gypsy's children. Though we didn't know it then, our home near Los Angeles was simply one of our many stopping-off places.

WE'D ONLY BEEN IN LA CAÑADA A FEW MONTHS WHEN Mother disappeared and a nanny named Bridget moved in. We'd learned to tolerate our mother's absences, never felt like lost children as long as she left us snug and together and wrapped in the arms of a home. But there was more. Unlike Mom, Bridget walked us to school each day and she asked what we wanted for dinner—and then, to our surprise, she cooked it.

Our Grandmother Alice, Mom's mother, dropped by one afternoon to explain. "Your mother has gone to Europe," she said, "but I think she'll be back soon."

She sat stiffly on the purple couch, her unlined face stern and queenly under a tiara of white hair, a cluster of diamonds on her ring finger. "Virginia deserves some joy in her life," she added, "because lately she has suffered needlessly." Abruptly her mouth tightened and her eyes burned through us. "There's not much tolerance in this family. I'd put a stop to this if I could—to this constant abuse from a hypocrite who pretends he loves her. But at least she has me."

Who is she talking about? I wondered. For a cool and formal person like her, it seemed odd—that Grandma Alice worried more about her grown daughter than our mother worried about us.

"Well, then." Her expression softened. "Virginia has left Austria and gone on to Switzerland. She cabled me to come look after you."

"All the time?" I asked, "instead of Bridget?" and Allan asked, "Will you sleep here?"

"Oh no," said Alice, "I won't sleep here. I'll stay where I am—the Beverly Hills Hotel." She paused at a rap on the door. "My driver's here. You will have lunch with me on Saturday. Please be ready at eleven, because Henry will come get you and you must be prompt."

On Saturday as promised, Henry rapped again, and in her black limousine he swept us away to the Beverly Hills Hotel.

As Grandma opened her door, Allan and I drew in quiet breaths and shamelessly gawked. It wasn't a room, but a palace. Deep blue Persian rugs covered the floors, and across the room two, high-backed tapestry couches, cream-colored with a gold thread, touched elbows at right angles.

Grandma waved us in. "Lunch will arrive soon," she said.

We ate in Grandma's spacious dining room—a meal brought to us on rolling carts and silver trays. As Allan and I gobbled our food, Grandma explained, "Your mother left because she needed to escape. Your Grandfather Russell has made me ashamed I was ever married to him. Mortified, in fact. For months he's been at her. Creating misery. Jabbing her constantly."

"With a hot poker?" Allan asked.

Grandma stared at him.

I stifled a grin, deciding Allan had been reading too many cowboy books. At least now we knew the mean person was Russell.

Grandma continued to frown. "He poked her with his mouth," she said. "With ugly words. Even as far away as New York he's been calling your mother names. He told her she'd done nothing but disappoint him."

"But what did she do?" Allan asked.

"To start with, she married Walter Ellsberg," Grandma said. "For Russell, that was a mortal sin."

"Like fornication?" Allan asked, and Grandma gasped. "Mind your mouth," she said.

To me, Allan *was* minding his mouth. He had dredged up something we'd both heard once in church—he just didn't know what it meant.

"That will end this conversation," Grandma Alice said tartly. "If you've finished eating, we'll have dessert."

MOTHER WAS FINALLY BACK—AND WITH A NEW LIGHTNESS, A gaiety that hadn't been there before she left on her trip.

With Mom once more at home we saw a difference in everything she did. I didn't know about Allan, but I could feel the change, even in my stomach. Mom smiled more. She frequently laughed—the big, explosive laugh that was so loud it was embarrassing in public, where people turned around to look. But a sound we never minded at home.

"Mom's really happy," Allan observed matter-of-factly one

morning as he pulled down a box of cereal. We mostly made our own breakfast.

I nodded. "Grandma Alice said the same thing. She told me over the phone that Mom finally found what she needs—and now Russell will leave her alone." An image flicked through my mind. "Do you remember Russell?"

"No."

"I barely remember him." I stirred the mixture in my bowl … crumbled shredded wheat and sugar and milk. I was thinking about the one time I'd met my grandfather, and how we kids all used his first name, because he'd once told our mother, "Your children must call me Russell. Grandpa sounds like an old man—and I'm not old."

"Russell is bald," I said now. "And he doesn't talk much. He acts kind of mysterious."

Allan was only half listening.

"Grandma Alice told me more stuff. She says Russell can be cruel … like when he divorced her. Or last month, when he took Mom out to fancy dinners in New York and sat there saying every mean thing he could think of—yelling at her for marrying a slimy Bohemian."

Allan was listening now.

"Some nights before she left," I said, "the phone woke me up. Must've been Russell, 'cause afterwards I heard her crying." I didn't tell him I felt like crying too.

"I heard her every time." Allan stared into his bowl. "I tried not to listen, I tried plugging my ears and—"he broke off, picked up his spoon. "When she cried like that I couldn't sleep."

ONLY A FEW DAYS LATER, AS WE WERE HUNCHED OVER OUR cereal bowls, Mother suddenly appeared in the doorway. "We're leaving, kids. We're moving away."

We stared at her, astonished as she walked off.

Allan looked at me. "Yesterday I saw her opening my bureau drawers. I told her I didn't want to go anywhere."

"What did she say?"

He shrugged. "Nothing. She just laughed and kept pulling out shirts. She wouldn't look at me. Then she said, 'Never? … in your life?' She thought if she patted my shoulder I wouldn't care." He laid down his spoon, his face stubborn and serious. What he said next came out slowly. "Mom doesn't care whether I care."

Having no answer, I just told him to hurry, we'd be late.

THAT AFTERNOON WHEN WE ARRIVED HOME, MOM WAS AL-most running through the house. Everything about her was joyous, her touch quick and firm as she packed my clothes, the way she said, "You kids can bring whatever toys you want. Just tell me, I'll help you gather them," her steps light as she darted into the living room.

Allan said in a monotone, "I don't want to bring toys. I want to stay here."

Mother ignored him. She began pulling shutters closed, blocking out the sun. Our house, for all its smallness, was so full of bright yellows and oranges and purples splashing across couches and throw rugs, so blatant about its wild colors, that it must have been ideal for her—a haven for a Bohemian.

Mom was hurrying, all right, but it was an excited hurrying, toward something instead of desperate to leave something.

In the kitchen I watched her pack up a few pots, a few bright-ly-colored dishes. "Los Angeles is nice, honey …" she swiveled to give me a look, "but wait till you see where we're going."

She turned fully and smiled, and in her eyes I saw the happiness she wanted to share with me and I felt little flakes of love showering down all around. A mother's love.

If anything else went wrong, at least I had that.

Mom and her beloved Hans. Wedding picture.

CHAPTER THREE

Enroute to Mt. Shasta, 1938

THE NEXT DAY THE THREE OF US—ALLAN RELUCTANT IN THE back seat—were in the car, the first time in years we'd all gone anywhere important. Mom's light and happy mood filled all the empty spaces, and I could sense my brother coming around.

It was late June, starting to get hot in Los Angeles. I never liked heat so I hoped we were headed someplace cool, but when I thought about it, Mother never seemed to notice that I was sweltering, or even whether there was heat outside or no heat.

She hadn't given a thought to the thermometer the day in early June that she left me in the desert with a cultish sun-lover, a woman who fed me pumpkin seeds and carrot juice and then made me stay several hours in the baking sun. "The sun is good for you, dear," the woman said, pushing me outside. She closed the door. I was trapped by a dilapidated metal fence and ugly dirt and no shade, and I felt like the woman's dog. The sun was relentless. I wanted to peel off my skin to get cooler. But there was no escape, not until I pounded the door and she finally let me in.

I'm not sure the woman ever told my mother. Anyway, Mom was a people person, not a temperature person.

On the outskirts of the city, she began driving faster.

After all the years Allan and I and mother had lived in places where we weren't together ... sometimes separate boarding schools for us, sometimes, like the Barton School, where Allan and I were together but not with her, sometimes living with relatives and not even knowing where our mother was ... this car, now that all three of us were in it, felt like an extension of our home.

After a while I stopped thinking about where we were going, whether cold or broiling hot, because for once in a long time it felt like we'd be moving there together, that wherever it was, we'd still be with her, we'd still be a family.

I imagined as well that once we got there we'd surely have a house.

UNDER HER BREATH, MOTHER WAS HUMMING. IT WAS SOFT, the small notes of someone who didn't know she was doing it. But then she stopped and the tune drifted away. Briefly she turned her head. "Kiddies, you don't know where we're going, do you?"

"You didn't tell us," said Allan.

"Well, I'll tell you now." Mom's tone abruptly became dramatic. "You really haven't an inkling, do you? Not a clue. Not the slightest thought. Really." She said it in a voice so full of mystery and innuendo she sounded like an actress on the radio. I thought, *She's trying to give us shivers.*

Then she paused, building up the suspense. "We're going to Mount Shasta!"

If she expected us to react, to change expression or say anything, she failed to notice that we didn't. As an actress she created her own world, her own audience.

We'd never heard of Mount Shasta, so all her drama flew right over our heads. We just waited to hear more.

"Mount Shasta," she repeated, "the most beautiful place in the world."

"Is it big?" Allan asked innocently, because one of us had to say something.

"Very big. You'll see."

"So where is it?" I asked, but Mom just threw me a sideways look.

"Honey, you wouldn't know if I told you."

Mom drove north and then, with no warning, she began singing in a different voice, loud enough for all of us, but pausing between stanzas so we could fix the tune in our heads—so we could sing it back to her.

Singing took us part way through the long, hot flat country, and up to a spot south of Redding. I could have gone on singing forever.

She got us onto Highway 99, and finally we sailed past Redding, past Red Bluff, and started up a long, winding valley with a river at the bottom and steep banks on both sides, slopes thick with pine and fir and cedar and flowering dogwood—though at age nine I couldn't have named any of them. I only knew the view outside my window was a banquet of color, so many shades of green that I was dazzled and couldn't stop staring.

Mom finally said, "You don't know anything about Northern California, do you?"

We admitted we didn't.

"We'll be in Siskiyou County," she explained as she navigated the curves. "It's cooler up there. Mount Shasta is both a town and a mountain. You will love the way it looks, kiddies, popping straight up from nowhere. The most beautiful mountain formation I've ever seen. In another hour we'll see it from the road. Two peaks, and they're always white."

Allan and I had no idea what to say, so we listened.

"The ranch is different from any place you've lived before," she added after a while. "The house is old, so it has no electricity."

No electricity?

I turned to look at Allan, who shrugged. Neither of us were sure what that meant.

"At night we'll use kerosene lamps."

Lamps? To read by?

"And there's no bathroom. At least not yet."

"Where do we … ?" Allan began.

"There's an outhouse," Mom responded gaily, "the good news being, it's already there. You won't love it, I'm sure, but you'll get used to it."

From the backseat I could feel the questions Allan wasn't asking.

"We'll be farmers," Mother said with a laugh. "For awhile we'll live like the pioneers who inhabited this country years ago. It'll be okay because it's summer."

Farmers, I thought, and my mind drifted off. *What do girls wear on a farm?* I wasn't sure. But I knew I'd have to figure it out and find the right clothes. Unlike Allan, I cared how I looked. *And it won't be a dress,* I thought, *like the ruffled blue one I'm wearing now.*

"It'll be an adventure, children, nothing you've ever done before," Mother added later. "You'll see … you'll learn about nature, you'll love camping out. We'll live on a ranch with 320 acres—the most beautiful spot in Siskiyou County. In a few hours you'll know what I mean, that there's no place more gorgeous. Hans is up there now, putting up two big tents. He'll take care of us."

Hans, I thought. *The man we've never met.*

"Hans will be your new father," she said. "He knows all about you kids. And he'll love you," a pause, "the way we love each other."

My feelings darkened. How did she know he'd love us? We'd already had two fathers—our own, whom I didn't remember, and the second I'd only just met, a man who didn't love us at all. Once I accidentally saw Walter Elsberg and Mom in bed together. As I stood in the doorway he suddenly noticed me and his mustache rose and he lifted his head off the pillow and shouted, "Get out!"

I felt like I'd been slapped. My stomach lurched as I turned and ran.

Mom promptly enrolled me in a boarding school.

Now from the backseat Allan said, "I need a father." He was matter-of-fact about it, just letting her know what he thought.

"Well now you'll have one," said Mom. "You'll see, Allan. This will be a new life for all of us. A better life."

I need a father too, I thought, *but it probably won't be Hans.*

All at once I wasn't sure about what was coming, had no illusions that life would be better than it had been so far. *But we'll be living with Mom,* I thought. *Maybe this time she won't go away.*

The curving road continued, and suddenly there it was, looking down at us through a break in the trees: the whitest, most spectacular mountain I'd ever seen, its twin peaks gleaming in perfect symmetry, the whole mountain staring at us from afar, as though it commanded the world.

It did seem that important. Allan and I gasped, because it was so big and so white and so everywhere.

"You see?" Mom chortled. "You see? Here's why we've come. That mountain. Everything about it is perfect. Once I found the mountain I knew I had to live here. Or live nearby. You can see it from the ranch. I love it. And Hans loves it too. He's from Switzerland, you know. This is his kind of country. He said to me one day, "Zis mountain is ze best I've seen."

She laughed. "He doesn't pronounce *th* very well. Which makes him charming."

Well, I loved the mountain right away. But I wasn't at all sure I'd love Hans.

Chapter Four

Mt. Shasta, 1938

Before we even arrived at the ranch, I learned a small thing about dirt roads and dust. As long as you're moving, the cloud cheerfully trails along in the rear, rolling and churning, but the minute you stop you give it permission to keep right on going, a filthy cloud that rolls on past and envelops the car. Merely opening the door makes you feel like an elephant taking a dust bath.

Dust was the first element in our new lives. Not something I cared about then one way or another, just something I noticed.

Hans was the second element. I saw him hurrying toward the car, a tall man with an open, handsome face, and the hair of a German General, slicked straight back. He was smiling, striding fast. Within seconds he'd opened Mother's door, pulled her out and cried "Ginny! Ginny!" He kissed her passionately.

As though forgetting we were there, he eased her away from the cloudy air and kissed her again.

We kids didn't watch them kissing; it didn't seem like something you'd want to see. Instead, Allan and I fanned away the dirt, which had caught up and was swirling past, stinging our eyes.

Our car had stopped in the center of a large turn-around, next to a small and sorry wooden fence. The whole thing leaned toward the house, as though any minute its posts would buckle and the slats would sink to the ground.

I turned to look back, saw the meadow we'd just passed—an open space so large and grassy I imagined myself running across it barefoot. It was like one of the lawns that belonged to rich people—except this one went on and on, a dozen lawns all joined together. Across the lush expanse from where we stood, a forest rose upward from the far edge, a hill we could climb.

Mom turned away from Hans and pointed. "That meadow is ours," she said, her voice rich with pride. "And so is that hill."

Here we were, just the four of us, with a meadow and a hill, but no sign anywhere of other people.

"And there's the house," Mom said, nodding to our right, but of course we'd noticed. A tired-looking, two-story place with a steep roof covered in dark shingles and the front faced with dark, stained wood. Even its few windows seemed half-closed, as though the house was trying to sleep.

I gave it a second look. "It's older than Grandma Alice," I said.

"Hans will fix it up," Mom said, and I glanced at the decrepit place again, then at Hans, who stood there smiling and nodding. "Zis will be much work. But I'll do it."

"And these are my children, honey," Mom said, gently pushing us forward. "Allan and Maralys. Allan is just past seven and she's eight, almost nine. We're all glad to be here,"

"Ah … yes. I too am glad." He gave a little bow, first to Allan, then to me. Stiff and formal, but then he held out his hand. Tentatively, Allan touched his fingers, and then so did I, both of us unsure about what we should be doing. You could see by his face he wasn't sure, either. Still, he had a good smile, which helped.

"Well," Hans said. "We should go see your new home. Yah?" But he didn't head toward the house, he grabbed two of our suitcases and led us toward two enormous tents set up beyond the turnaround.

He threw open the flap on the nearest one, and stood aside to let us see. On a fresh, new wooden floor sat two small beds, each covered with some kind of puffy green comforter. He pushed our suitcases into an empty space and backed out again. *So this is home,* I thought, confused and bewildered, thinking only, *I'm glad the floor looks new.* The clean wooden floor seemed to make up for the rest: the funny smell which I came to recognize as Tent Smell. The sense that you could only stand up straight if you happened to be exactly in the middle.

As I eased out of my new bedroom, Mom was waiting with a smile. "Well, how do you like this, Kiddies? Isn't it fun? Camping out?"

Allan merely looked at her. "Where do we go to the bathroom?"

"Over there." She pointed to a structure off to the left of the house, a humble building we hadn't noticed earlier because it was small and crouched behind some bushes, hiding. A building that pretended it wasn't there.

"Oh," said Allan.

"It's called an outhouse," Mom said, "like I told you in the car. We'll use it this summer, until Hans builds us a bathroom."

I looked at this man with new eyes. First a tent with a nice wooden floor, then a bathroom. Some men, it seemed, could do anything. I began to like him.

Allan and I quickly discovered a world unlike any we'd ever known. Neither of us had ever seen an outhouse. We'd never laid eyes on a kerosene lamp, much less put a match to one. We'd never slept in a tent. We'd never known you could keep bottled milk outside in a "cooler," which was basically just a wire-enclosed window sill. Neither of us had ever lived on a dirt road or knew anyone who owned a cow. We'd certainly never milked one. When Mom's first hired hand said, "Look out for the cow pies," we didn't know what he was talking about.

Yet with all the places we'd been left, separately or together, the ranch had the greatest feel of being a home. In the first place, it was big—and our mom owned it all. In every direction, wherever we looked, the world belonged to us: meadows and trees and fences and a huge barn and an old house ... and yes, even the outhouse. Sometimes in early evening deer came to our meadow; they simply leaped over the distant fence and flew lightly into the grass.

"Deer!" Allan cried. "Look, Maralys. Three of them!" We watched the graceful creatures in awe.

We used the outhouse ... because we had to. We never got used to it. "I hate that place," Allan said. The dark, stagnant interior, the Montgomery Ward catalogs. The cold wooden seat. The smell. None of us stayed inside a second longer than we had to.

At night we used a kerosene lamp to illuminate the tent—again because we had no choice. On the first night, bringing us a glass bowl filled with fluid and topped by a glass chimney, Hans showed us some tricks. "First you pull off ze glass, but be careful. It breaks." He laid the chimney aside. "With a match, light this little wick. Then put za glass back on and turn up ze wick." He turned a knob and elevated the thin, clothlike structure. "If the flame is too high, you'll smoke up ze chimney. Zen you can't see."

He set the lamp on the old trunk between our beds. "Here, Allan, you do it."

"It's easy," Allan said. Within a few minutes, the two of us became competent Kerosene Lamp Lighters.

We soon discovered a user's chief objection. Once you blew out the flame you were through for the night; for at least twenty minutes, the glass chimney was too hot to touch.

I'd never have dreamed that for the next four years I'd do all my nighttime reading by kerosene lamp.

For a couple of months, Allan and I were free to do whatever we pleased. When you live in a tent and sleep in a sleeping bag, life is uncluttered. Sometimes I hung around upstairs in the dark old house and watched Mom peel wallpaper off the bedroom walls. Dust flew everywhere, but the oddest things were the sewing needles—one after the other, all stuck into the wallpaper as if the whole room was nothing but a pincushion. "Here's another one, honey," Mom said and handed it to me. Her head was up under a slanted ceiling and bent at an odd angle.

I laid the needle on the floor with all the others. "Who lived here before us?" I asked. "They must have done nothing but sew."

"I met the matriarch once," Mom said. "When I bought the place, old Mrs. Metcalf still lived here. She had scraggly gray hair and the deepest wrinkles you ever saw, like valleys in her face, and she sat in a rocking chair downstairs. I never saw her do anything but sit." Mom stopped briefly to straighten up, out from under the room's steep slant. "The Metcalfs were famous around here. I'm not sure for what." With a grin she added, "We'll be famous too, honey. Just wait and see."

She went on with her work—more ripping, more needles,

more dust. "We're going to make this a guest ranch, you know. The Luginbuhl Ranch."

"We are? How will people pronounce it? Luginbuhl?"

"You just did, Honey. It's easy." She laughed. "No place on earth is more beautiful. We're fixing it up so people will come from everywhere, from Los Angeles and San Francisco, just to be here for a few days. Hans will teach skiing on the mountain." She turned to smile at me. "You'll be part of the excitement, Maralys. You and Allan will help us."

How my life had changed! Mom had just made me part of a special team. A famous team. The Luginbuhl Ranch team.

She extended her hand. "Here's another needle."

THE WORK WENT ON DAY AFTER DAY, HANS ALWAYS BUSY. We could hear pounding as he dug into a closet.

Within a few weeks he had cut out a section of roof and began enlarging the floor space, so it became a room that stuck out from the house—a new bathroom with a dormer window and its own peaked roof.

One day I looked into the miracle he had created. Here was a generous floor with new linoleum. Hans was on his knees, sealing up a giant tub.

Allan came upstairs to look. "A bathroom!" he crowed. I swear, Allan was the happiest of us all.

TWO MONTHS LATER ALLAN AND I STARTED SCHOOL. THE FIRST day, Mom drove us into town to meet the principal. Allan would be in second grade, but for some reason, perhaps because Mom had started me early, my old school had left me wedged between grades, not quite fourth or fifth. We all sat down in Mr. Conrad's office, where Mom introduced Allan and me. "My daughter's name is Maralys … rhymes with careless."

The principal looked me over and grinned. "Careless," he said. "I'll remember that." Then he turned serious. "What do you think, Mrs. Luginbuhl? Do we move Maralys back half a grade, or propel her ahead, into fifth?"

Mom couldn't decide.

The principal squinted in my direction. "She's a large girl, and probably smart. My guess is, she'll do just fine in fifth grade."

And thus it was decided, a decision that affected the rest of my life. From then on, I was taller than everyone else, but also younger. Psychologically, I never quite fit with my peers, and feelings of being unsophisticated, of never quite belonging, began to haunt me.

STARTING SCHOOL MEANT ALLAN AND I FINALLY MET OUR nearest neighbors, the Deetzes.

Well, our only neighbors. Beyond them lived nobody, not for another two miles.

As our road emerged from the forest, there, to the right, sat a tiny, unpainted wooden house perched on a small plateau, as though the structure had long ago slid off the side of the road and settled a few feet down.

With no trees shielding the house, the place had a look of barrenness, of desolation … made worse by the accumulation, left and right, of broken-down plows and old engines and rusted farming implements.

I stared at the place in horror. *How does anyone live here?*

Mother seemed not to notice. She jumped from the car and ran down the three railroad ties that led to the front door. "Alice!" she called gaily. "Alice Deetz, come out! Meet my children!"

The door opened. A small woman with a bright smile, as inquisitive and lively as a chipmunk, came out. Behind her lingered three boys—two nearly identical in size, the oldest a tad taller.

"Virginia!" cried Alice. "Wonderful to see you again!" Beaming, she held out her hands to us. "Maralys and Allan. Of course. Your mother told me so much about you." She turned and signaled to her boys. "Come here and meet our neighbors!"

Shyly, they edged forward. Three sets of overalls. Thumbs in the straps. All three boys with handsome faces, though the oldest face was long, a tad awkward. "Charlie, Jimmy, and Laddie," Alice Deetz explained, "in that order. I think Charlie may be a year younger than you, Maralys. Jimmie and Allan will be in the same grade. Laddie will

35

tag along behind. Well." She paused. "I've just made some cookies. Jimmie, go get some for everyone."

I noticed she didn't ask us into the house; I thought I knew why. But I was starving, and cookies sounded marvelous.

When Jimmie came out again, he had exactly one cookie for each of us. For as long as I lived near the Deetzes, and during those moments after school when we arrived at their home literally famished, I would never see more than one cookie apiece. In their own way the cookies defined what it meant to be poor.

"Wonderful," said Mom. "Our kids will all be going to school together. My two will walk to your house."

Allan and I looked at each other. *We will?*

"The school bus stops here," she said. "Doesn't it?"

With a look of regret, Alice shook her head. "Once it did. Not anymore. It only comes to the Four Corners."

Allan and I exchanged glances. Another mile and a half.

"If they're early enough," Alice said, "the kids can walk. "If not … She broke off, leaving the rest unsaid.

"Perhaps you can drive them?" Mother asked anxiously. "I'll pay for the gas."

"If the car runs, I can. Well. We'll see."

This time I didn't look at Allan. It seemed neither mother was prepared to ferry us the seven miles to town. On further thought, it appeared that somehow we five kids and our five sets of legs and maybe Alice's car (but maybe not), all had to get ourselves to the Four Corners.

No Four Corners. No bus. No school.

Allan and I had just learned another of the vital lessons about living in the country. School did not come to you—or work very hard at coming after you. The school bus was a privilege you had to earn. If you wanted to go to school you had to gather your willpower and your walkingest shoes and figure out how to get to wherever the bus came.

Our helpful Mt. Shasta neighbor, Alice Deetz.

Mt. Shasta and Black Butte, seen from our meadow.

The ancient Mt. Shasta house, still alive.

CHAPTER FIVE

Mt. Shasta, Fall 1938

FOR OUR FIRST THREE DAYS OF SCHOOL, ALICE DEETZ'S JA-lopy—she called it Izzy—graciously agreed to run. Of course we kids didn't know willingness was involved. Lulled into complacency when the vehicle sputtered and backfired, we thought the car was simply waking up. Anyone could see it was trying.

Alice knew better, knew Izzy had an attitude: *I'm not hauling five brats to the Four Corners.*

Each school day she did what she had to do, hauled back on the choke and pumped the gas. On some deeper level she recognized that her auto had become a stubborn old mule with a bad disposition, and now required goosing before it eventually snorted, spewing out brown smoke.

Those first days we five kids waited with keen interest as the 1929 black Chevy made its distinctive noises, until it finally sounded fully alive, with Jimmie yelling, "It's going! It's going! Hey, quick everyone, jump in!" which we all did, scrambling aboard and landing wherever we could, mostly on top of each other.

Alice usually laughed. "How do you like that, kids?"

"Hey! Yeah!" we shouted, and from both sides we hung out the windows as the overburdened car, belching and groaning, chugged a mile and a half to the Four Corners.

On the fifth day the Chevy balked. Alice said, "Now you know why it's called Izzy. Izzy gonna run or izzy not?"

Try as she could, Alice couldn't persuade the tired old machine to make the slightest effort. She pumped the gas pedal, pushed the choke in and out, then pressed on the clutch as she moved the stick shift in every direction—all futile. Izzy wasn't going anywhere.

She shook her head sadly. "Everybody out!"

Optimism had put us all in the jalopy prematurely, expecting what the car realized it couldn't deliver, so now Izzy just sat there, lumpish and still, as though determined to die.

"You have to push!" Alice cried, and we jumped out and began. All five of us shoved the thing around a curve on the dirt road, because Alice had wisely chosen an alternate route—the one with a slight downhill tilt.

"Push faster!" she yelled, "it's coming to!" and so we redoubled our efforts, hands on the stubborn, dusty rear and toes digging into the dirt. In unison we grunted and shoved, until finally a moment arrived when Izzy obstinately stopped … coughed … and then sent out its familiar plume of brown smoke. With that came little farty sounds from the rear.

"Get in!" Alice shouted. "Hurry!"

This time we had to chase our ride and throw ourselves aboard at five miles an hour. Luckily, Izzy was going only four.

Away we chugged once more, the five of us trying to recover our breaths, which didn't happen much before the Four Corners.

There sat the yellow bus. Another minute and we'd have missed a day of school.

DURING OUR FIRST YEAR AT THE MT. SHASTA ELEMENTARY School, the Deetz jalopy required kid power about as often as it didn't. Some days it refused to budge, and then we all cried, "Run, Jimmy!" and the fleetest of our group, the light-legged Jimmy trailed by his brother, Laddie, sprinted ahead of us to flag down and hold the bus.

For Allan and me, the bus trip was more than a ride to town, it was a curtain pulled aside to reveal a world even poorer, more destitute than what we saw at Deetz's.

At the Four Corners stop, a flock of children poured down the aisle, numerous members of two families, the Smalls and the Stiers, seemingly unlimited in numbers. With them came strange odors and dirty faces and torn clothes. Never-mended overalls competed with stained shirts from which poked grimy elbows. The smell that permeated the bus was unlike any I'd ever experienced, whether from garlicky cooking odors or worse—who knew?

Only nine myself, I stared shamelessly, not feeling the compassion that would later develop. I'd never seen the houses from which they came, never given a thought to what must have been homes as ragged as those shirts. Had I ever summoned the question, Where do they bathe? I would have known the answer. They didn't.

One day Allan shared a secret. "Hans drove me past the Small house. Part of it's falling down. We could see right inside, and I could tell, Sis—there's only one room."

I stared at him. "That's so sad," I said. I tried to picture the house, but couldn't

He added as an afterthought, "Yesterday I gave Wayne Small my sandwich."

"Weren't you hungry?"

He just looked at me and didn't answer.

I'd never wanted to sit next to those children. But it wasn't an issue, because Allan always shared my seat. One day he remarked offhandedly, "If you weren't here, Sis, I'd be over there." He pointed to Juanita Small. "She needs someone to sit by her." Beyond his natural compassion, my brother seemed to sense our family's destinies were linked … though he'd never have guessed in what way.

Neither of us would know until years later.

CHAPTER SIX

Mt. Shasta, Fall 1938

FROM MY FIRST DAY AT MT. SHASTA ELEMENTARY, school-work came easily, but socializing didn't. With the kids around me all older, I never knew how to interact. Most had quicker tongues than mine; their witticisms seemed to whiz by while I was still collecting my thoughts. *Hey, I have something to add*, I'd think, but by then the others were on to new topics … which meant they motored right over the top of anyone still in first gear. That skipped grade had turned into a liability, a huge mistake. My brain had jumped ahead of my hormones.

One day I was sent out, by accident, to play with the other nine-year-olds. How I puffed around the playground that day, and how quickly I rose to the top of their social ladder … merely because I felt smarter and funnier and yes, even older than the rest.

Kids compensate. And so did I—with books. My desk, with its lift-up lid and hidden cubbyhole, became my world. Deep inside I kept my private stash, a Bambi and an Alice in Wonderland. Books became a way of controlling the days.

Yet often enough my books stayed put.

When Miss Tilly lectured on the Constitution, I listened avidly. "A Congressman must be 25, and serves for two years. Senators are at least age 30, with a term of six years …"

The deeper we got into checks and balances, the more sense the document made. With its inherent logic and overriding brilliance, the Constitution fascinated me in Fifth Grade and remained on a pedestal all through grammar school and beyond into college.

And then there was math. Meaning, of course … numbers. Numbers without personality or nuance, without color or zest, with no tolerance for even the smallest mistake. Math was harsh and unforgiving, and long-division was worse—not only intolerant but endless and boring.

All those exercises you were forced to do, and for what purpose?

With math, the chair became harder, the half-hours dragged into hours, the air turned stifling. You couldn't get away, nobody would let you leave. So I stopped listening, and escaped my usual way … into books.

How cleverly I learned to dodge my enemy by slipping a volume onto my lap!

In a small town like Mount Shasta where nothing much ever happens, it was big news when somebody like the Nesbitts blew in to spend a weekend at Abrahms Lake. We'd all heard of the famous soft drink, Nesbitt's Orange, and some of us had even tried it.

That first day the wife announced imperiously to the lake's proprietor, "I'm Mrs. Nesbitt—of Nesbitt's Orange," words later repeated in every corner of town. Had she wired the mayor in advance, she wouldn't have attracted greater notoriety. I kept hearing it at school. "Did you know the Nesbitts of Nesbitt's Orange were here?" For that weekend, Mt. Shasta, in its own eyes, became famous.

Outside of a few happenings like the Nesbitts—plus some exciting radio shows and for me, books, movies were everyone's escape. Still vivid are the shows we Luginbuhls saw at the Mt. Shasta Cinema, especially the way our emotional depths were plumbed by the coal miners in "How Green Was My Valley." Even as I tried not to, I found myself sniffling. *I hope nobody hears me.*

Above all, our theater featured Shirley Temple! With Mother and Allan on either side, I sat in the darkened picture house bursting with excitement as she shook her curls, curtsied, sang, and tap danced. Afterwards, Allan and I found we could sing back every word of "Animal Crackers."

Deep in my psyche, Shirley Temple became my imaginary twin. The prior year, Grandma Alice had twice taken us to the cinema to see her. And once Grandma walked me down a rich person's street in Beverly Hills, and there, by lucky accident, I'd seen the young star in person! She stood next to a private horse stall, feeding somebody's rich brown thoroughbred. With what excitement and awe I lurked behind the cameras, filling my eyes with that golden-haired vision. One of the cameramen saw me and leaned close. "She's only eight," he said, and I whispered back, "So am I."

A year later, now in Mount Shasta, I decided I must make a change in my hair. Guessing I might not end up looking exactly how I wished, I imagined the hair would be an important start.

"Mom," I said after the movie, "can I go to a beauty parlor and get my hair curled?"

She smiled. "You want to look like Shirley Temple, don't you?"

"Yes. Yes. But my hair is so straight."

"It's also brown," she said. She looked me over thoughtfully, in no hurry. Finally, taking in my pleading expression, she shrugged. "Honey, you already have some curl in your hair. But I guess we could get you a permanent."

"We can? We can? Oh, thank you. Thank you, Mom."

Which is how I ended up in the local beauty parlor, sitting in a chair under long, electrified strands that hung from the ceiling, with each of two dozen hot curlers attached to a hank of my brown, partly curly hair. In 1938 getting a permanent meant you were hooked up to a kind of elevated octopus.

The hair sizzled and gave off the odor of something burning. Maybe a cat. On another level it was like being attached to an electric fence. For half an hour I couldn't move, and could barely see, what with the wires pulling up my eyelids.

But the ordeal was worth it. I knew I'd soon be beautiful. Shirley Temple beautiful.

At last released from the wires, I watched the hair dresser take out all the papers and let me look at myself—a head with 24 big knobs front, sides and rear.

"So now we must comb you out," she said, and began the process.

As she worked, my hair did not fall into long, graceful ringlets adorning the sides of my face.

Instead, my locks became an enormous halo of brown stinky frizz, protruding outward in all directions, leaving a face-like dot in the center. You could hardly see my eyes for all that hair.

The lady stepped back, thinking she was finished.

"It's … it's ugly!" I cried. Instead of resembling Shirley Temple, I looked like a girl with her head caught in a tornado.

"Dear," the beautician said in her most soothing tones, "the permanent is still new. It needs to tame down."

"Tame down? Tame down? When will that be?"

She shrugged.

"Will I have ringlets when it tames down?"

"Only if your Mother stops to wind each strand around her finger."

That will never happen. "You can't wind it now?" I begged.

"That's not part of my job." She might as well have admitted, *I haven't the faintest notion how to do it.*

And so I walked out of her place a hundred times uglier than when I went in. When she came to pick me up, Mother stared at me momentarily and turned away. To her credit she didn't laugh, or if she did, I never heard it.

At home Allan's eyes grew wide before he said, "Hey Sis—oh gosh …" then began working very hard at something he was building.

Hans just shook his head.

After that, it was just me and my mirror, me trying to tame the wildness, with water, with spit, and the mirror telling me, "Not yet, Maralys. Not yet." The word "permanent" took on new meaning.

At school nobody said anything. I wasn't well-known, so nobody cared.

About three months later, with a lot of scissoring, I finally had my own hair back. Come to think of it, that slight bit of curl worked pretty well.

Anyway, now that it was clear I'd never be a twin to Shirley Temple, I was enormously grateful that I'd stopped looking like a brown-haired version of Harpo Marx.

So beauty and fame weren't going to touch me, after all. But perhaps the ranch would wrap us all in a special notoriety.

CHAPTER SEVEN

Mt. Shasta, Fall 1938

LONG BEFORE THE DAYS DARKENED INTO WINTER, HANS completed the upstairs bathroom and a half bath downstairs. Our mother finished ripping off wallpaper, then brought in our first hired-hand, Ross, a wiry man hired for odd jobs. I saw him one day, bent nearly double as he re-papered what bit of wall remained under a steeply slanted bedroom ceiling. He muttered half to himself, "What midget walks on this side of the room?"

Afterwards, Mom cried in delight, "See?" and pointed to bright jonquils creeping up the far walls. "Each of you kids will sleep in your own garden." She paused. "It's yours until next spring, when our guests arrive." Her voice was suddenly tremulous with excitement. "Next spring," she repeated. "In April this place will come alive. Important guests will sleep here—in these very bedrooms."

Her excitement made my heart beat faster. Mom could do that to me, to everyone around her. With little sparks of gaiety she'd ignite her friends in town, and even down the road, where her joy would spread, reflecting back from Alice Deetz's face.

Allan and I were allowed to choose one of the slant-ceilinged rooms nearest the bath, while Mother and Hans took the larger of the two rooms in the rear.

In each bedroom sat a black cast iron stove whose stovepipe went out through the roof—more decorative than useful, since none of us spent much time in our rooms, and nobody ever felt like firing up a stove just before bedtime.

More important, each room sported a kerosene lamp, which sat next to the bed and turned us into experts in how-not-to-burn-down the house.

In fact every room in the house had one or more lamps, adding

46

to the pretext that we didn't, after all, need electricity. It became my job on Saturdays to wash the smoked-up chimneys. But that wasn't my only job.

From time to time, Mom said, "Honey, please scrub the upstairs bathroom. You're so good at this. You know how to do it better than any of us." Handing me a can of Dutch Cleanser, she gave me one of her dazzling smiles, intended to make me relish the job.

Except we both knew I didn't.

I liked the job about as much as I liked math, meaning a book was the obvious remedy. With the cleanser sitting nearby to ease my conscience, I sat on the potty and read.

Eventually I heard her call up the stairs, "What are you doing, Maralys? I don't hear a sound coming out of the bathroom."

"Oh, I'm ... well, I'll soon be through, Mom." Quick to turn an outright lie into half a lie, I jumped to my feet, grabbed the cleanser, and leaned into the tub, where I began scrubbing off all my family's dirt rings. Part of me knew we were lucky to have a bathroom at all.

"LET'S PLAY MONOPOLY," ALLAN SAID ONE SATURDAY SOON after we moved into the house. "Come on, Sis, I'll show you how," and he led me to Mom's den. As I watched, he laid out the board on a coffee table, and then waited anxiously for me to join him on the couch, not quite sure whether I would, or whether I'd leave him to go read a book.

We sat side-by-side on the den's small tufted sofa, the one that faced the nearly floor-to-ceiling windows, where we could look out across the meadow and see Mount Shasta gleaming in the distance.

"The windows, darling," Mother had said in the first week. "Hans, we must have windows in the den. Do please arrange this. We need tall windows that look out over the meadow. Why the Metcalfs never chose to gaze at the mountain, I can't imagine."

And so Hans, or someone, installed the great upper and lower windows that opened East to our meadow and, beyond the expanse of lush green, straight to the mountain.

Now Allan and I sat together, hunched over our game, but sometimes drawn to look out and see what the mountain was doing—whether, like a shapely maiden, it was flaunting its twin peaks, or hiding demurely under a cloud bank.

At first I thought Monopoly was fun. Under Allan's prodding, "Hurry, Sis, roll the dice," I began each game buoyed by my natural optimism. I was older, so of course I would win.

All too soon, reality set in. I saw it was possible to rabbit hop around the board several times, flitting from "Chance" to "Community Chest" to "Luxury Tax,"—or worse, to jail—so you not only paid fines but landed on one property after another that would never be for sale.

Meanwhile, Allan kept a low profile as he moved his piece from the Monopoly equivalents of a beach home in La Jolla to an acre in Bel Air … and, like a young Leland Stanford, he quietly bought up all the prime properties.

Of course by the third cycle I began stopping at buyable real estate … except Allan already owned it. I never understood why the dice seemed to favor his travels over mine.

"Sorry, Sis." He held out his hand, an earnest businessmen. "You owe me thirty dollars rent."

"Again, Allan? Again? You bought that one, too?" Like some kind of Wall Street tycoon, he spent half his time bent over the cardboard box, sorting through deeds and making change.

"Thirty dollars," he said. Then, seeing my expression, "Keep rolling, Maralys. You'll land on something good pretty soon."

That's what he said, anyway.

With Allan mysteriously controlling both our destinies, he grew ever richer while I slid into poverty … at last becoming so poor I could no longer pay his stupid rents. Frustrated, because losing felt important, as though the game was real life, I said, "I can't pay you anything, Allan. I have to quit. I have no money. You never land on my properties."

With that he drew back and stared at me. He was honestly surprised. "Wait, Sis," he said. "Wait! Let's keep playing. I'll loan you five hundred dollars!" He handed over a wad of money. "I'll give it to you," he added. "Here. Take this hotel, too. Come on. Please, Maralys, we have to finish the game."

"Finish? You've already beat me. What have I got? Just two

dumb things … Mediterranean and Baltic."

"I haven't won. You've got money now. And a hotel." The look he gave me was pure encouragement. "You can still do it, Sis."

I looked back at him. Generous Allan. Sympathetic Allan. Nasty, winning Allan. With even the slightest hint of meanness, I would have hated him, but he was so infuriatingly kind he made hating impossible.

Monopoly became our Saturday routine—which we could indulge in endlessly because we were only eight and nine and a half, and we lived on a ranch, and if we wanted to play outside with our only friends, the Deetzes, we had to walk a mile.

Most of the time it wasn't worth walking. The Deetz boys were always working. Milking cows, compacting hay by jumping on it, weeding gardens. Their Dad, Jim, was a loving man, but he needed his sons' free labor.

When it came to playing Monopoly versus doing hard work, Allan and I were lucky. Oblivious as kids generally are, we lived our privileged lives without stopping to compare ourselves to our neighbors.

Only the Deetz's unpainted house … their crippled car … the school bus… gave us a clue that Allan and I lived in one world. And the Deetz boys and the kids at Four Corners lived in another.

Chapter Eight

Mt. Shasta, 1938

On the days when Allan couldn't wheedle me into endless Monopoly, I slipped away like a puppy with a coveted bone and found a corner in which to hunker down and read.

First my own books. Then, as I ran out of childhood tales, the volumes owned by my mother. Around the edges of our Monopoly den were bookcases, all crammed with an intellectual's range of topics, everything from Kahlil Gibran's *The Prophet*, to *They Came to a River* … from the Gilbreth's *Cheaper by the Dozen* to Longfellow's *Song of Hiawatha*.

"I knew the oldest Gilbreth girl," Mother revealed to me one day. "She was in my class at Smith College." More frequently than most conversations would warrant, the name of her school seemed to come up with Mom, as though she'd gone to Smith and never gotten over it.

Yet privately, Mother admitted she'd spent only two years there and then gravitated to Radcliffe—which was closely associated with the all-male college, Harvard. "There were no men at Smith," she said. "And I lost interest in a college that left out half the world's population." She added with a grin, "The half that I adore."

Oddly, she rarely mentioned that she'd graduated from Radcliffe cum laude.

Mother never seemed to notice that I was consuming her books even more than mine. She and Hans were mostly out of the house, busy directing our hired hands, who had proliferated until they seemed to be everywhere on our property, pouring cement, carrying lumber, pounding nails.

Unlike me, Allan spent his non-Monopoly hours following the

carpenters around, absorbing the sheer masculine energy of sawing and pounding, then the wonder of structures rising from nothing.

Left alone to read, I quickly discovered that the emotional content of adult books was heavier and more compelling than in such youngish volumes as Heidi. Mom's books sometimes made me cry … with the result that I often sat in my upstairs bedroom and wallowed in the truly poignant scenes, reading them over and over. To deepen my feelings I added background music, the spicy strains of "Nola," which somehow made the scenes even more touching—though my anguish tended to dissipate when I had to keep jumping up to rewind the victrola.

There must have been a need in me to experience the full gamut of adult emotions, as though until then I'd been skimming over the surface of life. Yet as a small girl I'd suffered in ways that later seemed unthinkable. And until this ranch we'd lived like gypsies, often without a mother.

At last imagining that I might become a writer—and with no paper at hand—one day I systematically went through Mom's expensive volumes shelf by shelf and ripped out a dozen blank pages. On each of these I scribbled a few sentences, tied the pages together with string, and presented them to my mother. "Look, Mom, I've written a book." Pride rushed outward from my hands, enveloped me head to toe; I knew I'd done something great.

She glanced at my offering and said absently, "That's nice, dear." After a few turned pages she handed it back. Clearly, I hadn't brought her to tears.

As unsuspicious as Mom was in those days, she failed to notice the vellum quality and expensive ragged edges that would have revealed the source of all those blank pages … perhaps made aware only in later years when the opposing pages fell out.

BESIDES UNKNOWINGLY PROVIDING ME WITH BOOKS, MOTHER subscribed to *The Reader's Digest*, leaving copies scattered around the house. One day I absently picked one up, and soon I was grabbing them the minute I saw a new one. Written even then in the world's most digestible prose, the magazine had an almost magical ability to pull readers into its aura. *I love this*, I thought. *Some day I want my name in this magazine. Surely, later on …*

How avidly I devoured those little monthlies, and how thoroughly I absorbed their messages, by turns both inspiring and terrifying.

Skillfully using language to create a drumbeat that echoed through its pages, the *Digest* made me and its other readers believe that if we cared enough we could overcome all obstacles, even disasters: A fall into a storm-swollen river, or three days trapped in a malfunctioning elevator, or the sudden realization that your pilot has died and you must land the plane. No calamity was too great for any of us—if only we were quick-witted and gathered enough will power.

Why couldn't I make this work with Monopoly?

On the other hand, their articles on diseases turned me into a budding hypochondriac.

On alternate days I saw myself as the strongest, most determined victor over earthly impediments. Or conversely, as a once-healthy girl teetering on the verge of a deadly disease.

Without knowing it, I was slowly being transformed, raised less by my mother than a magazine. In my head I'd taken on a Reader's Digest Mother.

ONE MONTH THE READER'S DIGEST CARRIED AN ARTICLE about tetanus, and how the disease was often acquired by a hapless farmer stepping on a rusty nail. The final paragraphs were a vivid description of the horrors of lockjaw.

Since our ranch was a virtual garden of rusty nails trod on frequently by everyone, I became instantly fearful that I would succumb to lockjaw. To test my jaw against this awful possibility, on a daily basis I began using one of the joints in my finger to measure the opening of my mouth, reassured when the space never got any narrower.

From tetanus I moved on to other medical maladies, like severe allergic reactions and polio … the latter being, in fact, real enough. After swimming in nearby Abrahms Lake that summer, a few kids did come down with polio. Nothing on earth could have persuaded me to go near those waters.

Occasionally a strange sensation in my throat suggested an allergic reaction so severe that my throat would swell shut and I'd be unable to breathe—at which I panicked and turned cold, then burning hot all over. I was vaguely surprised, a few minutes later, to find that I was, indeed, still breathing.

THUS, AT THE BEGINNING OF FIFTH GRADE I WAS BOTH SOCIALLY inept and too often fearful.

After a few months with the magazine, I began to imagine life was so precarious that dying prematurely was highly likely, could happen without warning, and was therefore a constant, dreadful worry.

Clearly I was a child with too much spare time.

Guessing I'd be laughed at, I never shared my fears with anyone. I simply lived with a head full of rotating ailments, narrowly escaping each of them one by one.

HAPPILY, MY MOTHER'S PREPARATIONS FOR GUESTS WERE DIStracting and frequent enough to interrupt thoughts of death. Pulled away from my usual dire musings, I eagerly followed her trail of excitement.

With the additional hired hands, she and Hans built for themselves a rustic Swiss cottage, secluded from the rest of us but opening to the meadow. For obscure reasons, probably tradition, the cottage sported a kitchen—the one room it didn't seem to need, since my Mother never did any cooking. For as long as I could remember, whatever our circumstances, mother had always managed to hire a cook.

Finished with the cottage, those same intent builders transformed one end of our great, ancient barn. Some ten feet up and reached by a flight of steep stairs, our carpenters created a special, closed-off section that included two knotty pine-paneled bedrooms separated by a bathroom.

At first Allan and I were merely curious. Then we realized we would soon bequeath our brightly-papered bedrooms in the old house to incoming guests, and now we'd be the barn's first two-legged inhabitants.

Our two new bedrooms, fairly large and smelling of fresh pine, did not initially seem objectionable. Our single beds, tucked under a slanting roof, looked cozy and comfortable. The wood was new, the musty barn smells distant. But soon all that changed.

One night I happened to throw back my covers before climbing into bed—and there sat a huge barn spider.

I screamed. Even as a non-screamer, my revulsion could not be contained in fewer than several terrified shrieks.

The thing was horrible … enormous, black, and furry, a terrifying object against my white sheets. And to think I'd nearly climbed into bed with it!

What to do with this monstrous creature? I couldn't possibly come close enough to kill it.

Before I could summon help, the spider geared up its eight legs and ran off, doubtless even less attracted to me than I was to him.

But the creature had forever defiled my new bedroom. Never again would I climb into bed without looking first. Even so, barn spiders often appeared elsewhere in the room. I'd be absently gazing at a pine knot, only to see it turn into a spider that slowly crawled away.

Once, in the downstairs area, a large furry spider unexpectedly landed on my bare arm. Horrified, I screamed and violently shook my arm, sending the thing into space.

My spider-obsession had actually begun years earlier. Out back in Mom's La Cañada cottage were two deserted rabbit hutches. One day, as an inquisitive six-year-old, I decided to peek into one of them. My head was nearly inside when I realized I was looking straight into the belly of an outsized black widow. I'd never heard of them, but it didn't matter. The creature needed no introduction.

The spider seemed to stretch across the entire interior of the hutch, while its thin, arched legs clung to an enormous, irregular web. Suddenly repulsed by its ominous appearance, I slowly backed out, shaken that I'd come so close to sharing its small space.

With those spider experiences came an unspoken vow: I would never marry a man unless he promised to save me from all future spiders.

The nights grew colder, but up in our barn bedrooms we had no heaters. Hans said, "Kids, we can't have you burning down the barn, or yourselves," and Mother added, "We'll give you extra blankets."

At night, from inside the old house, we'd heard the wind outside our bedroom windows, moaning through the pines. Out here in the barn, the wind hurled itself against the outer timbers and shrieked in fury, as if it hated the ancient structure, enough to blow it down.

"It's kind of spooky," Allan said one night as we climbed the stairs, "but I kinda like the sound. We never had weather in La Cañada."

"They thought they had weather, but they didn't. It was boring." We reached the upper hall. "The barn must be used to this wind," I added, "or it would have given up and fallen over. In the mountains things happen. I can't wait for snow. We'll love it, don't you think? If it gets deep?"

"If it gets really deep," Allan said, "we might not love it that much."

You're wrong, I thought. But that was before I learned you can have too much of an exciting thing. Even snow.

Chapter Nine

Mt. Shasta, Winter 1938

Before our first winter storm, Mother turned Allan and me loose on the Montgomery Ward catalogue, and soon snow boots and sweaters and jackets arrived in our Mt. Shasta post office.

Always thrilled by new clothes and especially excited by the first snow I could remember, I set out with Allan in November to trudge down our newly powdered road to the Deetzes.

"Hey, it's like Lux flakes, isn't it?" I said. "Slippery but not soapy."

"Yeah. Boxes of them." He walked faster. "I'd like to get a sled. Hans says he'll buy me one. Come on, Sis, I'll race you." In tandem, we ran down our road as though outpacing the weather.

The snow landed in soft sprinkles across our noses, cool and beautiful. We stopped running to look. I loved the transformation, my beloved forest painted white, our footprints left behind on a smooth white surface, as though we were artists creating our own distinctive marks.

"If we had time, we could write messages," Allan observed.

"Let's run again," I said. For both of us, sprinting in a light snowstorm brought an explosion of feelings, an exaltation that came from a sense of the world's beauty combined with unexpected adventure.

Three weeks before Christmas, the road changed. The snow deepened and those few inches became nearly a foot. At a foot-and-a-half, we could hardly walk. Each step meant lifting your boot entirely out of the thick, glutinous stuff to place it someplace new. Snow crept over the leather tops, but we had to ignore it and plod on. The mile downhill to Deetzes now felt like ten miles. We were so slow we weren't sure we'd get there … on time or ever.

"I'm freezing," said Allan. "I need another jacket."

"I'm not that cold," I said. "Except for my feet." I didn't say it, but

I'd never before had feet frozen solid. "I can't feel my toes. I'm tired, too. I wish we could stop."

"We can't stop," he said with a sharp look. "If we do, we'll die." He tugged my arm. "You can't stop, Maralys. I know about snow."

Did he? He sounded so serious. What had he been reading?

"Come on, Sis. Walk faster. We can't freeze to death here."

He scared me, made me pick up the pace. Yet each step took intense effort and incredible will, more than I had. I stopped to breathe. *I can't do this. I can't go on.* Which is when my Reader's Digest Mother said, *Keep Going. You can make it, Maralys. A few more feet. One at a time.*

I lifted my foot again, took a step. Then another. Yet each lifting of my boot felt like the last time. I tried to stop thinking and go numb, but couldn't. A litany rang in my head: *Once more ... lift your boot.*

Time stretched and narrowed simultaneously.

Panting, we came to the top of a hill. And down below, there was Deetz's. To our surprise, the four-corners bus had done something different. There it sat, the big yellow bus parked outside their house. Here the snow wasn't so deep.

We climbed aboard, still out of breath, grateful to be sitting inside where warm air blew across our faces. With five of us aboard, the bus started off.

Sitting in back, I pulled off one of my boots. Snow came pouring out, so I left it on the floor and yanked off the other. More snow. Before we were part way to town, the pain began. My frozen feet were thawing, a return of blood and sensation that became nearly unbearable. I was startled, then as the pain grew worse, shocked.

I glanced at Allan, saw his face was contorted like mine. "Your feet hurt too?" I asked.

He nodded. But neither of us said more than that.

We seemed to know we wouldn't die from the pain, that it would disappear in time. And so it did. A half hour later the intense stinging was gone. But for the rest of the day we walked around school in wet boots.

Trudging home from Deetzes that afternoon was the same situation in reverse, except this time Alice Deetz brought us into her kitchen, stood us before her wood stove, and gave each of us a cup of warm milk and a cookie. "Before you start home," she said.

Better yet, one of our cars had left the ranch and forged tracks we could walk in, indentations that kept the snow out of our boots and made walking easier.

For as long as we lived on the ranch, winters for Allan and me came in two phases: the exciting, early fall dashes through light flakes, and later those grim mornings when the snow was so much deeper that our treks down to Deetz's were both painful and yes ... dangerous.

One evening in mid-December, Hans looked up from the dinner table and with a free hand signaled that Allan and I should turn in his direction. "Kids, zis is important," he said. "I want that you stay out of the den."

"Why?" asked Allan.

"Never mind why. Just don't go in." Beneath his serious expression lurked something else, a hint of conspiracy, a twinkle in his eyes. But his mouth remained strict and stern.

"Please pay attention," Mom added.

"Zis is my last word. You do not go in zere."

Allan and I looked at Hans and nodded. He'd said enough. We understood perfectly the den was off limits.

We imagined many things, all having to do with Christmas. But judging from Hans' mysterious insistence, we weren't quite sure.

For weeks we alternated between anxiety, excitement, and hope. Neither of us had the imagination to conjure up what was really happening in that room.

CHAPTER TEN

Mt. Shasta, 1938-1939

WITH THE PASSING OF EACH DECEMBER DAY, THE DEN BECAME more mysterious. Allan and I noticed every opening and closing of the den door, saw Hans and Mother scurry into the forbidden room and quickly close the door behind them, leaving us to stare at their retreating backs and fantasize about what might be going on in there.

"I hope it's something good," Allan said.

"Maybe they're building something, like a ..." I broke off, unable to guess what that something might be. "It's gotta be big, must take the whole room."

We were seated near each other in the dining room, finishing supper. "Anyway," I said, "I hope it's over soon. Mom's books are in there. Now I can't get them."

He sighed. "All you do is read."

"What's wrong with that? All you want to do is play Monopoly."

He looked at me. "Tomorrow's our last day of school. The carpenters all went home. Now it'll *really* be boring."

"I can give you a book."

He waved me off. "Maybe the Deetz boys have a sled."

But they didn't. For us the days dragged on.

EVEN ON CHRISTMAS EVE, MOM DIDN'T COOK. SHE HAD OUR maid fix an early dinner before her husband picked her up to go home and cook once more. Lucky for her, the snow was only inches deep.

For no reason that night, Hans and Mom seemed agitated and nervous. First one disappeared into the den, then the other. At last they both came out, exchanged glances and said, "Kids, come here."

Hans flung open the den door. Allan and I went to the entrance and stood there, gaping. Inside was a fully decorated Christmas tree, a Spruce almost as tall as the room. Every bough held lit candles, ornaments, bulbs, green and red paper chains, snowflakes, little cutouts that sparkled and glimmered. The tree was brilliant.

"Wow!" cried Allan.

Dazzled by color and light, by the wonder of it all, I echoed my brother. "Wow!" I said. "It's beautiful!"

"Don't just stand zere," Hans said, grinning. "Come in, kids." He waved an arm. "Zis is for you! Come in!" He ushered us into the room.

The tree was only the beginning. Underneath was a shiny red "flyer" wagon, a sled, piles of wrapped presents, a Shirley Temple doll, gifts spilling out from under the lowest boughs and cascading into a halo around the base.

My eyes kept returning to the doll. She was beautiful, a vision of sweet smile and perfect ringlets.

The whole scene, in fact, was unlike any I'd ever seen. If I'd once in my life stood before a richly-decorated tree, I had no memory of it. This was my first, until then my only experience of the vivid colors of Christmas. There wouldn't be another like it until I had children of my own.

"You like zis?" Hans asked, grinning.

Mother turned. "You know they do, Honey. Look at their faces."

"Shall we open presents?" he asked. "Or wait until tomorrow?"

"I don't think they can wait, dear," Mom said. "They've waited long enough already."

And so that night we feasted on Christmas. The presents. The colors. The joy on our parents' faces. "Just see how they love it!" I heard Mom whisper to Hans. The thrill of being ambushed, because that's what it felt like. An ambush on an elevated plane, a surprise that was more than worth the wait.

Hans and Mother had done this for us. All of it. We knew it perfectly and also understood that our joy enhanced theirs.

This was surely the best Christmas I'd ever had. In my heart I knew it was Allan's too.

THE JOY, THE EXCITEMENT LASTED FOR DAYS. WE NEVER

thanked Hans or Mom. We didn't have to.

I wanted to leave the tree up forever.

SPRING CAME EARLY THAT YEAR, WITH MELTING SNOW AND A sense that everything was new, or at the very least must be made to appear new. One Friday Alice Deetz decided to clean her house. "If you children will help tomorrow," she said to Allan and me as we got off the bus, "I'll make us all some ice cream."

Allan grinned. "I'll be there. How about you, Sis?"

I said I'd be there too, but I was thinking about the ice cream, imagining a bowl full of it, cold and sweet, while dismissing the cleaning: *how hard can it be?*

Alice was still talking, words I only half heard because my thoughts had drifted to "Emory Wheels," the pinwheel-shaped, chocolate-covered ice cream bars carried at Emory Windsor's drug store in Mount Shasta, and how, this minute, I could almost taste them.

She turned to me. "Maralys, you two please come down around ten. The boys and I will be waiting."

"We'll be here even earlier," I said, eager to get to what mattered. *I'll bet her ice cream is really good.*

On Saturday Allan and I appeared as requested, and with the Deetz boys we stood just inside the front door, surveying the kitchen/living room. The place was a mess.

"Gotta do it sometime," said Jimmie, his voice flat; I could hardly hear him. He threw us each a despairing look. "Guess we should start." Laddie stood by, nodding.

At first glance, the house appeared hopeless. Piles of clothes were strewn across the floors, cobwebs hung from the ceiling, dirt had accumulated in the corners of every room. We didn't know where to begin.

"Start in the boys' room," Alice said.

As well as we could, we began sorting clothes, though it was impossible to know which items belonged to which boy.

"Throw the dirty ones in the living room," Alice prompted. "Charlie and I will do the wash. The clean ones you can fold."

To my eyes, all the clothes looked dirty. Certain shirts had obviously occupied space under overalls, or under shoes, or under the bunk bed for God knew how long. Sorting farm-boy garments for cleanliness was impossible. We tossed everything into the living room.

"Now you may sweep the floors," Alice said.

We did. While the two younger boys wiped down the unpainted walls and pulled cobwebs off the ceiling, Allan and I swept. And swept again. The dirt from the wood floors just kept coming up endlessly, as though the floor itself was nothing but wood-grained dirt. Only after half a dozen sweepings did we get down to bare pine slats. Brown as it was, the wood swept clean seemed nicer than I would have guessed. With Allan I stood back and gazed at the floor, feeling a sense of pride.

"Looks good in here," Allan said.

"Aren't you glad we helped?" I pivoted left and right, admiring our work.

"Better than us doing it all," said Jimmie. Laddie grinned and nodded.

Alice and Charlie had disappeared into the barn, and now they returned, each carrying a wicker basket piled high with wet clothes. "Help us hang these on the line," Alice said. "And we'll all have ice cream."

With kid power ratcheted up to maximum, the five of us gathered under the clothes line, taking turns as we grabbed handfuls of wet shirts and overalls and threw them over the long jute line, anchoring the pieces with wooden clothes pins.

"It's done!" Alice cried at last, beaming. Proudly, she looked us all over. "You're good workers, all of you. You deserve what's coming."

For me, the new look of her house was suddenly all I needed.

"Charlie, run and get bowls," said Alice. "And spoons."

Early that morning, with her husband's help, she'd cranked the handle on the ice cream churn, which I knew from watching Hans was an endless job. Now Jim Deetz Senior was off working, leaving the rest of us to dip into the wooden container.

Whatever else Alice knew how to do, she excelled at making ice cream. Allan and I agreed that we'd never tasted anything more delicious.

As the six of us sat outside the house, dangling our legs off the small porch and eating bowls of her sweet, cold vanilla, Allan and I felt we belonged as much to the Deetz family as the Luginbuhls.

Our honorary membership in their family would last as long as we kids remained in Mt. Shasta.

NOW THAT THEIR SUMMER AND FALL CHORES WERE DONE, THE three Deetz boys were sometimes free to play. With the advent of spring, Allan and I often went down to their house on weekends. The first time we re-entered the place after that day of work, we saw to our dismay that the tiny living room was once again messy. And the kids' room looked almost as bad as it had before our massive spring cleaning.

I felt let down, as though here was a hopeless scenario nobody could change, akin to the old plows and engines forever rusting in the yard. Clearly we'd all spent our energy for nothing. It made me sad. *Some people are buried in work*, I thought. *When you've got too much to do, you can never escape. I hope I'm never like that.* Allan and I looked at each other, but neither of us said anything. Later I wondered if he'd been thinking the same as me.

In an unspoken agreement, we kids formed into two groups. Out on the dirt road, Allan played rough boy games with Jimmie and Laddie, while I was left to play house with Charlie.

Up the road a ways, Charlie and I found a tree and under its protective branches we imagined ourselves in a home, and for awhile we sat together on a log, trying to invent new lives. From the gleeful shouts drifting up to us, we could tell the other three were having a rollicking good time.

None of that held for us. Unlike Charlie, I wasn't exactly interested in games that focused on housekeeping. But we soon divided up our responsibilities. "Why don't I be the father?" I offered. "I'll go off and hunt for Indian arrowheads." We kids could never get enough of these relics, scattered across our two properties. But more than that, the idea of just sitting around didn't appeal to me.

To my surprise, Charlie nodded his agreement. "I'll stay home," he said, "and keep house."

Whatever that meant, I thought as I drifted away.

He stayed home, all right, and … well, I guess he cooked. Who knew?

Soon I came back and showed him what I'd found.

"An arrowhead!" he cried, "a perfect one. I'll put it on the kitchen table," and he laid it on a stone, and for a time we imagined ourselves talking like an old married couple … though even then I sensed we were somehow "off." If I was supposed to be the father, what did that make him?

Whatever our roles, neither of us found them entirely satisfactory. Charlie was tall and timid, and I was tall and energetic. We simply never blended. I was quickly bored. But then so was he.

Eventually we gave up pretending and waited to join the others.

From then on, what I remember best about playing with the Deetz boys were the times we all got off the bus at the Four Corners and with a few other kids our four boys took turns peeing in the road, seeing who could send his spray the farthest.

With the first budding hints of masculinity and endless curiosity, the boys cried, "Hey, Maralys! You do it too. Come on!" Two of them stared at me and kept begging.

But I refused. I wasn't into letting them take a peek.

Anyway, I couldn't enter the contest. All too well I understood the implications of having an inconvenient anatomy.

While it was still spring, perhaps late March, a stranger appeared on our ranch. Curious, I peered through the window and saw a man who, from a distance, seemed lean and well-dressed.

He was still outside when Mother called to us, "Come out here, children! Maralys and Allan! Come out!" She waved us on.

As the two of us edged closer, I could see the stranger was dark-haired and city-man handsome. Like Hans, he had a great face, but in a different way. He resembled one of the distinguished older males in the Montgomery Ward catalog, the ones who modeled suits and sports jackets.

"Allan and Maralys," Mom said, smiling. "You'll never believe who this is."

Allan whispered, "Do you know him, Sis?"

I shook my head. Like Allan, I'd never seen him before—at least not that I remembered.

Mother looked us over to make sure we were paying attention. Speaking slowly, her voice trembling with all the drama she could muster, she said, "Children, this is your father."

Our jaws dropped and we simply stared at the man.

Once again Mom was trying to give us shivers, and once again her intentions went right over our heads.

Thus did we kids help create an awkward start to a week that would begin in splendor but end in quite another way.

Chapter Eleven

Mt. Shasta, 1939

Even as we stood gawking, I knew I was supposed to feel something I didn't feel. I didn't know this man, or even very much about him. Mother had once told us briefly that he was an important person, that his parents had run a bakery shop in the Bronx and that they'd managed, somehow, to send their son to Princeton and their daughter to Cornell. Drawing on her gift for drama, she'd added, "And you know what, kiddies? They both became doctors!" With that bit of theater, she'd dropped the subject. For years she'd focused on her current life and rarely said anything about our father.

I came out of my reverie. Mom had just created an awkward moment, but it didn't last long. Like Allan, I'd thrown questioning looks at this well-dressed stranger, and felt the uncomfortable silence after our mother announced we were looking at our father.

Neither my brother nor I knew what to say. Or whether we should do something besides stand there, maybe move a step closer. It would have been easier meeting the Queen of England. Somebody would have coached us in advance, advising us to bow and murmur, *How do you do, Your Majesty?*

But nothing we could think of fit this situation, so we stood rooted.

Our father, Ted, quickly filled the silence. "It's about time, isn't it? Getting to know my two oldest children." He held out a hand to each of us and smiled. "Let's shake on finally getting acquainted."

Well at least that gave us something to do.

By the end of the day, the awkwardness had disappeared and Theodore Klumpp became something of a real father.

OF COURSE WE DIDN'T KNOW WHAT TO CALL HIM, SO WE DIDN'T call him anything—that is, until Mom found a private moment to explain. "He has three more children at home," she said. "I'm not sure why, but they all call him Ted." She smiled. "Maybe for the same reason your grandfather wants to be called Russell."

Thus began a week that was better than simply strange. Quickly it became magical—especially for me. Allan had bonded with Hans in a way I never did, so suddenly I had my own father, and he felt like he'd been mine all along.

WHEN OUR AMAZING WEEK BEGAN, I REALIZED I KNEW FEW details about Ted Klumpp's background. For now he was merely the handsome man whose attention was entirely focused on Allan and me. Neither of us could remember ever being the subject of such single-minded interest.

"Where shall I take you?" Ted asked on the first morning. "Where would you like to go?"

Allan and I looked at each other. Our father was asking a question for which we had no ready answer. Until then our months on the ranch had been narrowly focused … long hours of reading and Monopoly, plus school and fragments of time spent down at the Deetz house. We seldom went to town simply to shop; when we did, only one store seemed to beckon—Windsor's Drug Store with its Emory Wheels.

"How about we explore the towns north and south of Mt. Shasta?" he asked. "South to Dunsmuir, the quaint railroad town, and North to Weed. Or we—"

"You don't want to go to Weed," I broke in. "Mother took us there a couple of times and it's ugly and it … uh, smells. The houses aren't painted, either. They're all old, just muddy brown wood. And no one ever comes out." I added a thought. "Unless you want to go there and see a stinky town."

He waited me out, smiling. "We can skip that stop. But we might visit McCloud, which I hear is a famous old logging town. The lumber company runs a small private railroad train that takes people like us sight-seeing through the woods."

"We can go look at Abrams Lake," I offered, because polio season hadn't started yet.

"Or perhaps we can drive up Mt. Shasta," he said. "I bet we'll find some great views. Maybe we can have a picnic on the mountain."

Forty minutes later we were in our own town, at the Piggly Wiggly, buying local apples and bread and Oreo cookies and cheese and a bottle of milk, probably from the Deetz cows. In Ted's rented car we explored until we found a road that headed up the mountain. For awhile we just climbed, until we nearly reached the snow. "I think this is far enough," he said, and pulled over in a wide spot.

I'd never been there before, and Ted was right—the views were expansive and never-ending, stretching both south and north, but mainly looking west across the valley to the Mount Eddy range just behind our ranch, whose rugged shoulders still wore shawls of white.

In the cold air at four thousand feet, we spread out a blanket and laid down our parcels of food. Ted sat with his legs crossed at the ankles. His pants were not the overalls I'd seen on Jim Deetz, nor the sturdy blue jeans worn by Hans. Instead, Ted wore city pants, but on him they seemed perfect.

"Tell me about yourselves," he said. "You first, Allan. What do you like best about school?"

"Arithmetic," Allan said. "I know my multiplication tables through twelve. And I like long-division."

Ted saw the distaste that flickered across my face, but ignored it. "What do you like second best?"

Allan thought a minute. "Graham crackers. When Mom puts them in our lunch."

He laughed. "What else does she put in your lunch?"

"Nothing," said Allan. "All the other stuff I put there myself. I make a sandwich—peanut butter and jelly. Or sometimes the maid gives us sliced meat, and we take that."

"And you, Maralys?"

My answer was easy. "I like reading. Or trying to write stories. And I hate arithmetic."

Ted nodded. "Someday you might like it. But one thing, Maralys—you should learn your multiplication tables."

"I can do all the tens," I offered.

He laughed again. "So can I."

Ted wanted to know everything. He asked about our friends, and whether we played any sports, which we didn't except at recess, and whether we were getting enough sleep, and what Mother sometimes made us for dinner.

"She doesn't make anything," I said. "Our maid cooks dinner."

"What does your mother do all day?"

"Sometimes she buys a cow," said Allan, and Ted broke out laughing.

Allan thought a little deeper. "She brings home lumber so the hired hands can build rooms in the barn. She says they'll build us another house soon." He thought about it more. "I don't think she does very much. Except read."

Ted smiled, then murmured to himself, "A child's-eye view of adults."

Suddenly I thought of something he should know. "I can milk a cow," I said, and Allan quickly added, "So can I. And I can aim the milk into our cat's mouth. Straight in. He waits for me to hit him."

With that, Ted looked us over and he seemed happy. "You've developed important lifelong skills," he said. "I can stop worrying about you two."

The air grew chilly and Ted stood, then leaned over and pulled me to my feet. "We'll have dinner in Dunsmuir," he said. "I drove through there on the way up. It's a charming town. You'll like it."

And we did.

For the whole week Ted was ours. He spoke little about himself, but seemed fascinated by everything Allan and I told him. One day on the way to visit the town of McCloud, he called out to Allan in the back seat, "You've got the mind of an engineer, Allan. I can see you're logical about everything. You like to fix things, I expect. Don't you?"

I turned around and saw a modest smile break out on my brother's face. "I guess I do."

"And you, Maralys?"

I shrugged. Except for the day I'd created that one small book out of Mother's ripped pages and thought I could write books, I hadn't given a career much thought. "I don't know. Maybe I could be a writer. If I can ever think of an exciting story. I've tried to think up stories." I let the conversation lapse, knowing that my few skinny little tales hadn't been much of anything. Yet other writers managed to fill their pages with danger and terror and excitement and accidents and arguments and mystery, things I knew nothing about, and I couldn't figure out how they did it. Maybe Ted would know. "How do authors think up all those stories that go in books?"

My dad glanced over at me and smiled. "Life gives you stories," he said. "More material than you'll ever need. When you're ready to write them, Maralys, I'll help."

When you're ready to write them, I'll help. I tucked the thought away to use later.

Helping me was a promise my father eventually kept.

SUDDENLY THE WEEK WAS OVER. MOTHER AND HANS CAME outside to shake Ted's hand and together they returned to the house, leaving the three of us to say our good-byes.

Ted leaned over and put his arm around Allan's shoulder, patting him gently. He gave me a warm hug and kissed the top of my head. "I'll write to you," he said in his rich voice. "You'll hear from me often." With that he opened the car door.

Alone once more, Allan and I stood by the little fence, the tiny rails that were no longer falling down, and watched our father drive away. For years, probably.

As long as we could see him, or even see the dust, Allan and I waved and kept waving.

A terrible lump came to my throat and I turned away from Allan, knowing I was going to cry. They weren't momentary tears, they were a waterfall, a flow of tears that nothing could staunch. *He's gone,* I thought. *Ted is gone. My father is gone forever.*

What good were letters? … if they even came.

Dinner tasted like cardboard. When I went to sleep that night I lived with my father again, saw him listening as we talked, re-visited the warm and varied experiences we'd just shared, a night of dreams, all about the man who'd come to love us for a short while … but not long enough.

Waking up the next morning was agony. My loss came crashing into my memory with an impact even stronger than the night before. *Ted is gone*, I thought. *My father will never be back*, and the realization was unbearable and upset my stomach. *I won't see him again. How will I go to school?*

It was as though, for a short while, I'd stood in a special place, surrounded by love, by deep caring, and now the spot was empty and there was nothing under my shoes. I was empty. The world was empty. There was no reason to go on living.

Yet I had to eat. I had to get up in the morning. I had to go to school.

But there was no joy anywhere. The hollowness in my stomach, the place where sadness settles, seemed to envelop me entirely, robbing me of even momentary happiness. For weeks I didn't care about anything … about Emory wheels, or reading, or school, or my brother, or anything else. I just felt deserted and forlorn.

Ted was the first man I ever loved. I wouldn't feel that devastated again until I lost the first boyfriend I ever loved … though young as he was, Chuck seemed as mature as my father.

Odd as it now seems, both of them were doctors.

RECOVERY WAS SLOW, BUT IT CAME IN TIME. AT NIGHT, IN BED, I thought about Ted, how I wished he hadn't come at all because I had to work so hard to get over him.

Sometimes I thought back to my earliest memories and tried to recall when I'd last seen my father. I wasn't sure whether my images were real, but I think they were.

And gradually a picture emerged from somewhere, buried deep … and yes, it was a happy time. But it was only a brief moment of happiness, a few years at most, a deep baby-years contentment that ended then—and now once more—in acute pain.

Ted with President Kennedy—nominated to lead President's Council on Fitness.

To Dr. Ted Klumpp
With best wishes,
Ronald Reagan

Ted receiving an award from President Reagan.

*Ted's Curriculum Vitae as it appears in his article as President of the
American Pharmaceutical Manufacturers Association. (below)*

"THE ROLE OF THE PHARMACEUTICAL INDUSTRY IN RESEARCH"
Theodore George Klumpp, B.S., M.D., D. Sc., LL.D.
President, Winthrop Laboratories

Chapter Twelve

Boston area, 1929

THE MEMORIES DRIFTED BACK IN FRAGMENTS.

In the middle of the night, my mother gently lifted me out of bed. Through sleepy, half-closed eyes I saw the edges of the crib, and then I was up and beyond the slats and deep in my mother's arms. She took me through a doorway, and from a distance I was aware of laughter and bright lights.

I was six months old.

Mother carried me downstairs. The laughter and lights grew louder and brighter. People leaned over me, somebody patted my head, and then a man, probably my father, took me in his arms and showed me around.

The room was full of people, some looking at me and smiling in a way that told me this was my moment, a special time.

The memory fades; before long I am lowered down between the slats. Once more I am back in my crib.

THE NEXT SCENE IS NOT A MEMORY, BUT A PHOTOGRAPH. I AM standing in a play pen, holding the top rail, and nearby my German grandmother, Marie Klumpp, sits in a chair and watches over me. Her dark blue stockings gather in bunches at the ankles and her face is wrinkled but kind. Other family members appear in the background. As before, it's a happy time. Then somehow, these happy moments end.

AT AGE THREE I AM OUTSIDE, CLINGING TO A FENCE. My mother has left. All the relatives who loved me are now gone. Only the fence is there, which is where I stand and cry. It's been days since I've seen my mother, likely months since I've last seen my father.

Perhaps I would no longer recognize him. In any case, he's gone ... my mother is gone ... For hours I cling to the fence and cry.

Feelings of insecurity well up inside, a vast emptiness that overtakes me. I am no longer me. I am a deserted child. An empty child. The child who once had a family but now doesn't.

A maid comes outside and leads me back in the house. It's a bad time. I know I must stop crying. But somehow I can't.

THE SCENE CHANGES. MOTHER HAS RETURNED, AND NOW SHE is driving a car, and I'm sitting beside her. Allan is in the back seat, at the moment not speaking.

"We're going to spell your name, Maralys," Mother says lightly. "I will teach you how." Carefully she recites the letters of my first name and I repeat them after her. Before long I know how to do it, I've memorized the letters I'll use the rest of my life. But that moment of learning feels less important to me than the fact that I'm once again sitting beside my mother.

UNAWARE OF HOW, EXACTLY, WE GOT THERE, ALLAN AND I ARE playing in our mother's new house in La Cañada, near Los Angeles. It is bright and light and has only two bedrooms. For awhile it's just the three of us—Allan and I and Mother.

But one day I see her there with a man ... a man with dark hair, augmented by a mustache that makes him look sinister. But even worse, he's someone who doesn't seem to like us. "This is Walter Ellsberg," mother says gaily, "we've just gotten married."

Walter Ellsberg pretends he is glad to have us there, but Allan and I know he isn't.

One day, unaware that it is off limits, I wander into mother's bedroom, only to find her in bed with her new, swarthy husband. As he shouts at me to leave, he makes it clear that I am the intruder, not he. His anger scares my mother, makes her cringe.

But not as much as he scares me. I feel his venom like a physical blow, and quickly I retreat.

Before long, mother is driving me to another part of town. "You're going to continue third grade here,"* she says, trying to add

76

expectation and excitement to her voice as we get out of the car. "I just found it for you."

As we approach the school, a sudden fear jolts me. What I see are stark white buildings. A lawn that extends away in both directions, but without many trees. A plain cement path that leads to the two-door entrance.

I sense that I am about to begin a different phase of my life … though my fears are vague and based on a stunning lack of knowledge. Mother has shared only her emotions, which somehow ring false. She hasn't actually told me anything.

As though a barrier has lifted, I am now fully conscious, acutely aware of everything around me. I have entered a period where memory is stark and clear.

MOTHER TOOK MY HAND, CARRIED A SMALL SACK IN THE OTH-er hand, and led me up the path. "I think you'll like it here, dear. See, there's the name."

I looked up, could make out only the easiest of the words above the door: "Sacred Heart Academy."

Mother rang the bell and a strange woman pulled open the door. Her head was covered in a long black scarf with white cardboard around her face, and she wore a flowing black dress. I'd never seen anyone dressed like that, didn't know I was looking at a nun. But then I'd never heard anyone say the word "nun."

The woman smiled down at me. "I'm Sister Ruth," she said. "What is your name?"

I stared at her, hardly hearing the question.

"Tell me your name, Child," she said again and Mother gave me a nudge.

I fumbled out my name.

"I'm not sure I understood that," said Sister Ruth, and Mother said it again, slowly.

"Maralys," the sister repeated. "I've never heard it before."

"I made it up," said Mother. "I didn't like the name on her birth certificate."

"Oh." The woman seemed startled, as though suddenly faced

with an unexpected decision. "Well. Then we won't be using her given name, I presume."

"She wouldn't recognize it if you did."

The woman collected herself, reached for Mom's little sack. "I'm glad you didn't bring any outer clothes," she said. "She will wear the school uniform."

"Oh … yes." Mother seemed uncharacteristically vague. "The uniform. That's what I've been told." It was clear she'd forgotten. She looked back toward her car, caught in a moment of indecision. "She's tall. I hope you have something that fits."

"We have everything she'll need."

I could sense Mother was stalling for time. "Well, dear …" she hesitated further, glanced down at me. Suddenly she stooped low and gave me a kiss. "You will like this school, Maralys. Inside are lots of children."

I looked through the door and saw nobody.

"I will visit you on Sunday," Mother said, and with that she turned away and walked down the path to our car.

Thus began the second most miserable period of my life.

Mother with her first baby. Me.

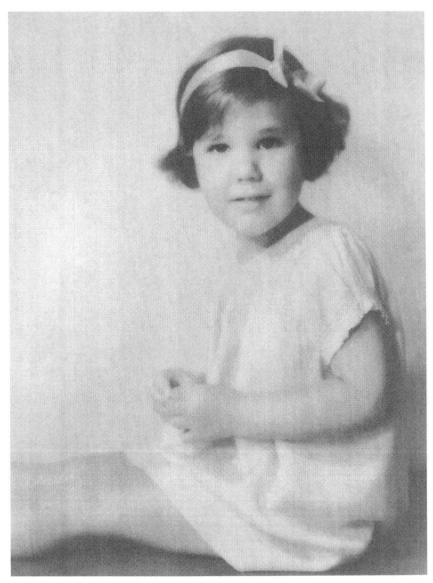

My bows-and-ribbons days.

Allan and me. Our core family still intact.

Chapter Thirteen

Catholic School, 1937

Before I could see the last of my mother, Sister Ruth took my hand and led me farther into the building. We passed a classroom filled with girls my age seated at small desks. They were all dressed alike. I didn't see any boys.

Deeper inside she guided me to a room with a series of closets. "You are seven," she said. "As your mother said ... tall. You will need a size eight uniform." With that she sat me on a chair while she rummaged through closets, finally extracting a two-piece dress which she looked over carefully. "This should fit," she said, "Please put it on."

The uniform was a green jumper with a white blouse. I put it on as best I could, leaving some strings hanging loose.

"Let me tie your sash, dear." Reaching behind me, she pulled the sash tight.

With that I officially began my stay at a Catholic boarding school.

No freedom. Minute-by-minute regimentation. Endless memorizing. Prayers before and after meals. Longer prayers before and after each class session. A school with no boys. I couldn't get used to any of it.

"They don't believe in boys," I said to my mother the next Sunday, and she surprised me by laughing. "They do, dear. But not here." She'd arrived late, so her visit was short. By the end it seemed I'd hardly seen her. Woof! A few minutes together, then she was gone.

With each passing day I became more frightened, felt more acutely the pain of being left, of being utterly deserted. For me the place was not a home, it was just a school ... with constant mumbled incantations and a few books, plus girls who couldn't become friends because they dared not speak during most hours lest they be reprimanded.

But the nights—those were the worst. The hours after supper when we sat stiffly in our chairs while the nuns read us religious stories. As in the daytime, we never ran, we never played.

In early evening they ushered us into a large room full of cots, and there we slept.

Except I didn't sleep—I cried. Night after night I sobbed into my pillow, and one night I leaned over the edge of my cot and threw up.

I WOULD ONE DAY LEARN THAT MY MOTHER, TOO, WAS SUFFER-ing her own agonies. As miserable as I was, so was she.

Her father came to town and took Mother to the most expensive restaurant in Los Angeles, the posh dining room at the Biltmore hotel. There Russell ordered two steaks and sat down across from her, absently fingering the white tablecloth as he talked. "Ginny, you've married the wrong man," he began, "someone beneath you. He's not one of us."

"You're not married to him, Dad. I am."

"But I'm involved." He took a deep breath. "Do you think I paid for your husband's education only to have you leave him for … for this?"

"I didn't ask you to pay for Ted's education."

"But I did. I did it for you. And because Ted will go far. Head of the FDA, for God's sake. He was worth it."

"Well … he wasn't worth it to me. He …" She broke off. "He lacked something I needed."

Russell grunted. "So instead you married a Communist," with a curl of the lip, "a Communist Jew. You left a distinguished doctor for this … this loose-living bum from Greenwich Village." His agitation grew. "You think you can disgrace our family with this man? Am I to stand by and let you throw away your life?"

"I'm not throwing away my life. I … I love Walter Ellsberg." She hesitated. "I didn't marry him to defy you."

"As far as I'm concerned, you did. He doesn't stand for anything we stand for. In Greenwich Village they live like cockroaches. You ... you, my favorite child, you've done this to me! You've done it to me personally. I will not allow—"

"I don't care what you allow!" She jumped up, left her untouched dinner behind. "I'll do what I please."

"Not with my money, you won't."

She was walking away from him.

"If you ever want to see another dime of my money," he shouted after her.

But she was gone. Outside the door she hailed a taxi, then dropped into it, trying unsuccessfully to hold back her tears.

RUSSELL DID NOT GIVE UP. HE TRIED TO SEE HER ONCE MORE before he took the train back to New York, but she refused. He called from New York. He wrote scathing letters.

Throughout his bombardment, Mother lost weight, found herself unable to eat. Walter Ellsberg began to find her unattractive. They quarreled.

Between phone calls from her father, she and Ellsberg quarreled more intensely. At last Mother, out of sheer desperation, told him to leave.

She imagined Walter Ellsberg would leave and soon come back. He didn't.

With his final exit she understood that she hadn't really loved him much, after all.

For mother, Walter Ellsberg was merely a symbol of emancipation from the Allan family's rich-father lifestyle, and a rejection of her father's anti Semitism ... a fling with a man who briefly bridged a gap. He didn't care for her children. She wondered then if he'd ever really cared for her.

One thing began to stand out starkly: he'd cared a great deal for her money.*

FOR ME, THE NIGHTS AT SACRED HEART BECAME INCREASINGLY desperate. On a particular night, soon after I'd gotten sick, I crept out of bed and went down the hall searching for a nun. I finally found one sitting in her small, spare bedroom. Her veil was off, her hair cut very short, but she quickly reached for the veil and clapped it back on.

"Why are you here, dear?" she asked. "You should be asleep," and with that I burst into tears.

She beckoned me into her room and for a few moments held me tight. "Why are you crying?"

"I want my mother."

She rocked me back and forth. "Your mother will come again on Sunday."

"My mother doesn't come on Sunday. She comes late. I'm always the last one." I pictured the tiny bare room where we sat primly on chairs, waiting for our parents. Over a period of an hour, one by one the other girls disappeared. A bell rang, a girl's name was announced, and the child walked out the door and another chair was left vacant. Soon all the chairs were empty and I sat there by myself, waiting. Waiting for what seemed like an eternity, waiting ... and knowing my mother was using up the precious few hours I had with her. The minutes in that room had never felt so long, or so painful.

By the time she came, apologizing profusely, I was disconsolate, bordering on angry. "I'm so sorry, dear," she always said, but her apologies didn't matter.

And now I was hearing it again. "I'm sorry, dear," the nun offered. "We will speak to your mother."

"I don't like it here," I said. "I want to go home."

"But you must stay, Child. Your mother has arranged for you to be here."

"I'm sick," I said, coughing.

"Well, we will have to see about that."

Eventually I went back to the dorm, back to my bed.

But the next night I again crept to her room. And this time I did not leave so quickly. I stayed as long as I dared, until Sister Marie tired of rocking and cajoling me and led me back to bed. "We must do something about that cough," she said.

For the next few days I coughed whenever a nun was nearby—and I gave it extra effort. The added noisy elements were gathering attention, even drawing concern. "Does she have whooping cough?"

I heard a nun ask.

"We can't keep her if she does."

I coughed harder, hoping to create a sound like a whoop, whatever that was.

Before long I was coughing loud and furiously, making it up as I went, trying desperately to cough my way out of Sacred Heart.

That did it. Within a few days my mother was summoned to come and get me. I left the school joyfully, left my tiny imprisoned soul behind, entered my mother's world of freedom and gaiety, and tried never to think about it again.

When we arrived back at our little house, Walter Ellsberg was gone. And my coughing days were over.

FOR AWHILE, PERHAPS A FEW MONTHS, ALLAN AND I HAD OUR mother to ourselves. But life with our restless mother was not meant to last. Once again she packed us up in her car and took us away. But this time it was both of us. And as always we had no idea where we were going.

---

*The Catholic school still has mother's application, in her distinctive handwriting, showing that she was entering me, at age seven, in grade 3B.

*In 1950 Walter Ellsberg called Allan, trying to reconnect with our mother. Allan never responded.

Chapter Fourteen

Barton School, 1937

Before I turned eight, I learned that sometimes Mother understood us better than we thought. Though once again she abandoned Allan and me, this time she chose a place that suited us rather well.

Barton School in Topanga Canyon couldn't have been an accident.

As Mother navigated the curves to a hilltop building surrounded by oaks, by wild grass bent to a light breeze, by unpruned shrubs, Allan stared out the window and remarked, "I think I'll like it here."

Mother laughed. "Allan, sometimes you're like a horse before a race. You see a little wild country and you're ready to get out and start running." She pulled up near the woodsy building and parked.

I'd had enough of homes that weren't home. I stared but said nothing.

Mom noticed. "I think you'll like it, too, Maralys," she said. "It's nothing like the Catholic school." She opened her car door. "Here you'll have freedom to explore the hills, to dash around where you want." Yet her tone suggested more hope than certainty.

Moments later, she was in earnest conversation with a young, smiling woman, who turned to us and held out her hands. "Welcome, children. Please come with me." Even as she led us inside, Mother spun on her heels and quickly drove away.

Within a day I felt the difference between the Catholic school and Barton school, that they were as dissimilar as a fenced corral and the endless Serengeti.

This time Mother had found an easy-breathing boarding school where, even beyond my brother's presence, the place became a refuge.

Now that the two of us were here, a feeling of comfort settled over us, for this was an environment we understood. Somehow she'd managed to locate a community of good-natured free-spirits. Like her, the faculty was fun-loving, loose, and charmingly disorganized.

THE BUILDINGS WERE PERCHED HIGH ON A HILL, AND ALL around, especially in back, a steep, wild, typically Southern California slope descended into a canyon, spotted by random brush and Eucalyptus trees.

Once outside at recess, Allan and I were allowed to romp down the hill, at the bottom of which meandered a stream bordered by oak trees. The largest oak stood uphill from the stream, extending a limb to support a long, sturdy rope swing with a big knot at the end ... for some reason called a bag swing. We kids wrapped our legs around the knot and waited for someone to give us a push, out over the incline as though headed for the stream.

Every day we ran down the hill, laughing, chasing other children, taking turns at the swing. Or running back up again, because going up seemed as easy then as running down.

During the morning hours we sat in classes where sunshine poured in and our teacher taught us according to her best whims. All of it was casual and pleasant.

As always, I was aware of the meals. Three times a day we ate food that looked good and tasted better. Mornings it was oatmeal with chunky brown sugar and, sometimes, berries and apples. At night we saw bowls of cooked carrots, beets, and squash. Salads. Often a piece of turkey or a chicken drumstick.

As I wandered by their table after lunch, I noticed that the adults were eating something odd, a white, blubberish mess that looked, moved, and smelled like spoiled milk. One or another teacher would sprinkle it with brown sugar and cinnamon.

"What is that?" I asked once.

"Clabber," said my teacher, and looked up, smiling. "It's a grown-up taste. You children wouldn't like it."

I was sure we wouldn't.

ALLAN WROTE HIS OWN MEMORIES OF OUR NEW SCHOOL. "THE first thing I liked at Barton School was the food. I always ate much more than others, and often would eat anything that classmates sitting around me didn't want. Were seconds and thirds not allowed? I never went hungry, but classmates often called me 'garbage pail' a term I understood but didn't dislike.

"I very quickly bonded with my housemother and told her I loved her more than my own mother, having in mind that my mother was always getting rid of Maralys and me ... My housemother responded with alarm, telling me I must never say or think such things. But as was my practice in such situations, and believing I was right and she was wrong, and it would be impossible to convince anyone her age, I said nothing. I loved her anyway."

ONE DAY, DOWN AT THE BOTTOM OF THE HILL, ALLAN AND I took turns swinging in the bag swing, way out over the gulley. It was a joyous ride, fast and long and high. On my last turn, at the height of the swing's arc, something unexpected happened. To my horror, I was suddenly detached and flying through space.

Down below, Allan yelled, "The rope broke!"

For a moment I continued to sail onward, clinging to the swing but with a horrible expectation of agony to come.

Abruptly the forward motion stopped. Then down I went, hard, on my left wrist.

Chagrined and in pain, I somehow found my feet. Followed by my brother, who kept saying, "Oh ... oh," I slowly made my way back up the hill. Allan ran ahead of me and opened the door.

Once inside, I searched for a teacher. "The rope broke," I said, clinging to the injury. "My wrist hurts a lot." I was holding back tears. "Do you think it's broken?"

"No," she said. "Of course it's not broken." I could feel her thinking, *Really now, the children of Bohemians don't get hurt, they are all too healthy ... though some may be hypochondriacs.*

I, for one, thought my wrist deserved to be taken seriously. In some subliminal part of my being where the drive for recognition takes root, I imagined I should be noticed for my injury, clucked over and comforted. I ought to be wearing a sling.

But since nobody at the school seemed inclined to check on me further, I endured a few weeks of slowly declining pain, waiting until a visit from Grandma Alice, who stopped by regularly, before I mentioned it again.

Once she appeared, driving her elegant car, I clung to my injury.

Grandma Alice immediately noticed. "Why are you holding your wrist, dear? Is something wrong?"

"I was swinging on a long swing," I said, "when the rope busted. I think I broke a bone. But my teacher said I didn't."

"Oh, dear," said Grandma. "We'll certainly have to check on this. I'll take you to a doctor right now."

Within the hour I was getting an x-ray. Afterward, the doctor came out and gently took my wrist in his hand. He turned it over, studying it carefully.

"Yes," he said at last, "the wrist is broken all right."

I knew it. I just knew it. "Shouldn't I wear a sling?" I asked.

He smiled. "The wrist seems to be healing. But if you'd like a sling, of course you should wear one," and with that he arranged a taffy-colored cloth across my shoulder and down around my forearm, leaving only my fingers poking out of the cradle.

How proudly I re-entered school with my newly-diagnosed broken wrist, wearing an expression that must have said, "So there!" ... and how triumphantly I displayed my medical appliance.

And how quickly the sling got to be a nuisance.

For a few mornings I put it on carefully, proud to be among the notably-injured. Surely the other children were impressed.

Whether they were or they weren't, the novelty quickly wore off, and the sling was getting in the way.

My sling days could not have amounted to a full week. Before I'd acquired my fair share of sling-driven attention, it became such a wicked impediment I conveniently misplaced it.

Thus my glory days at Barton School faded away.

Just as my need for attention dwindled into complacency and Allan settled in with his surrogate mother, our days there came to an abrupt end.

CHAPTER FIFTEEN

Los Angeles, 1937-1938

ONE DAY MOTHER APPEARED AT BARTON SCHOOL AND, AS USU-al giving us no reason, she took us away. And so Allan and I found ourselves back home in La Cañada, once again living with her.

I returned to my former elementary school with its aromatic hamburgers and a magical maypole. With what excitement I redis-covered the best playground toy a school could have. An amazing contraption, the maypole required only determined running through a large circle and a strong grip on one of the rings to send you flying straight out from the pole, for all the world like a blowing ribbon. Every inch of me loved it. Effortlessly I pumped my legs, felt the wind in my face, held on tight and soared ... and now I was more than a ribbon, I'd transformed into an eagle!

I ran and ran. And flew and flew. The rings were my little round ticket to windy space. Each recess I returned to grab my silver ring and take off for the heavens. I could have kept flying forever.

MEANWHILE, ALLAN ENTERED FIRST GRADE. HE SOON LEARNED that our school was more than books. It was also great lunches and an exhilarating playground. Once more our lives took on a comforting harmony.

Often at night our mother read to us, curled up on one of our beds with A.A. Milne's book, *When We Were Very Young*. Like a stage actress she intoned dramatically, "The king asked The Queen, and The Queen asked The Dairymaid, 'Could we have some butter for The Royal slice of bread?'"

Here she hesitated and smiled at us, a short pause that invited us to fall in behind her with additional words. "The Queen asked The Dairymaid, The Dairymaid Said, 'Certainly, I'll go and tell The cow, now, Before she goes to bed.'"

As one, our three voices blended into a rich tonal mix, a kind of music folded around words. Invariably we ended by smiling at each other, then dissolving into laughter.

Soon the author's entire collection of poems, with Mother's drama attached, rollicked through my head, creating between me and A. A. Milne a warm, if unrequited, friendship.

I could feel his lovely rhythms, sense that he played with his characters in his own jaunty style, exposing their foibles and flaws, until you had an intimate view of them all ... neatly wrapped in unforgettable cadence.

Thanks to Mother's love of AA Milne, I would one day emulate her drama as I read those poems to my children.

And much later, when I wrote my own poetry, I never gave up until I'd achieved a perfect, AA Milne rhythm.

As for Allan, he had his own epiphany ... the day Mother took him into her brightly-colored bedroom, and in a moment of ebullience said, "Before I die, Allan, I will be married seven times."

Allan stared at her in disbelief.

"Seven times," she exclaimed, "and the last one will be an Indian Prince—from the country of India!" She laughed gaily. "Won't that be fun? Won't you love meeting my Indian Prince?" She waited, expecting him to laugh with her, even applaud her choice of an exotic seventh marriage.

She must have been disappointed. Allan did not for a moment think her destiny would be fun—or even slightly admirable. He was simply not that kind of child. On a list of what would today be called hippyish-tendencies, scaled one to ten, Allan was a minus five. He continued to stare at our mother, not answering, but making his own private vows.

As he explained many years later, "I thought nobody would marry anyone who had had more than two husbands, and that one day Mother would be a lonely old woman without anyone. I also thought, I'm not going to live my life that way."

He was then still new to first grade. "The next day," he said, "I went to school and began looking for a wife. I studied the first grade girls, made myself learn all their names and thought about each girl separately, especially Marilyn Thore. I thought about her a lot, but I doubt I ever spoke to her."

Allan did not find his wife, of course, until years later. But neither did Mother ever turn him into anything resembling a Bohemian. Nor did she basically alter me. Between the pair of us, Mother found herself outnumbered by two dead-serious children, as stubbornly German, as dully conventional, as our father, the husband she'd discarded years earlier.

With the disappearance of second husband Walter Ellsberg, Mother was at last freed from the worst of her father's tyranny. But between our grandfather Russell and our Mother the cord was never completely severed. For the rest of her life she would need his money. And never more so than when she fell in love with a Swiss skier and decided to buy a ranch in Mount Shasta.

From then on, in subtle ways, Russell could still manipulate her, but unlike his Wall Street investments, he could never quite own her.

CHAPTER SIXTEEN

Mt. Shasta, Spring 1939

IN THE SAME WAY THAT MOTHER LIVED HER LIFE ON WHIM and caprice, she thought nothing of arbitrarily re-labeling her children ... meaning as her circumstances changed, Mom gave us new last names. Sometimes I wasn't quite sure how I was listed anywhere: at school, on official documents, or even in my own head. In Mom's mind, I suppose, life was anything but fixed, and instead we were all part of an unfolding drama, a troupe of actors on a great evolving stage. Somehow she made this seem normal.

Thus, in some years I was Maralys Allan, in others Maralys Luginbuhl, in still others, Maralys Klumpp. By the time I went to college I'd had enough of explaining to bewildered records keepers that yes, this buffet of last names did lead to only one person. "And now," I said, "my permanent name will be Maralys Klumpp." *And never mind that you'd have to live in Stuttgart to love a name like Klumpp.*

But back in the early spring of our first year on the ranch—now formally dubbed the Luginbuhl Guest Ranch—both Allan and I had been re-named Luginbuhl. At the time, neither of us minded ... in fact, we rather liked it.

Once I'd recovered from my father's visit, I began to revel in Mother's magical vision, a family resort peopled by sophisticated guests from the city. The elite, she told us, would search out our guest ranch, looking for Eastern snobbery set in a Western pine forest. "You'll see!" she cried, "we will have the most important people here, eating our food and gazing across the meadow at our magnificent mountain! Right here in the den they'll see it, the best view anywhere of Mount Shasta." She threw us a radiant smile. "In winter, Hans will take them skiing."

As a natural part of her zest, she wove an atmosphere of

94

anticipation that snared us all, made us feel involved in something larger than our bucolic little town. It was impossible not to share her optimism. Mom made me believe that being part of the Luginbuhl Guest Ranch was a lofty aim, right up there with being Shirley Temple.

At times her dreams of grandeur for us, her children, were made explicit, but in a different way ... those moments when she declared, as though viewing us through supernatural eyes, "You and Allan will be educated. You'll rise above this town! I know it, I've known this for years. You'll both be somebody."

I thought, *We will?* And for a brief period both of us reveled in her fantasy.

But then I forgot she'd ever said it, which came of knowing that Mom, on occasion, had a mystic's proclivity for seeing things no one else saw.

We were so busy now, so drawn into Mother's breathless plans for our ranch, daily participating in her mad whirl of catalogue shopping and painting, wall-papering and out loud dreaming, that my insecurities faded, and I stopped worrying about being left in strange places, or that I might die any minute of polio or lockjaw.

As a family we began branching out, going to more movies in town, but often sitting with our school friends instead of our parents. Still, we always knew when one of them was in the audience. "Isn't that your mother I hear?" whispered my best friend, Jean Adelle Sheldon, giving me a nudge. "She laughs louder than the men!" I could almost feel Jean Adelle smirking.

Oh, God, I thought, not again. *Why does it have to be MY mother who laughs too hard? My mom whose voice rises above all the others?*

Now that Allan and I were living in the barn and Mother and Hans in their own cabin (and a new, even larger house going up nearby), Mother had created four beautiful guest bedrooms in the old Metcalf home. The wallpapers were all different—lively, multi-colored gardens of roses, jonquils, Iris and wandering ivy ... antique beds and bureaus polished to a high shine ... a clean kerosene lamp sitting on each bureau. "We even provide a box of matches,"

Mother said with a smile. "And just outside the windows, music whistles through the pines."

Soon after dropping off literature with resort booking agencies in Los Angeles and San Francisco, Mother began receiving a trickle of letters, then visitors. "We have two people coming from San Francisco," she exclaimed one day. "He's a college professor and she's a pediatrician. They're looking for peace and natural, woodsy beauty, just what we've got!"

Her voice was vibrant with expectation. "Maralys, go pick me two bunches of wildflowers." And so I ran into the nearby woods and found tiger lilies, wild pansies and daisies, far more than we needed. The assignment couldn't have thrilled me more.

By late April, the guest ranch was finally, officially opening, the first sweet notes in what would soon be a full cantata, and now it was time to celebrate. One Saturday night in early May, Mother and Hans organized a great barn party, inviting all their new-found friends from town. Our three hired hands were conscripted to wash down the old, split and cobwebbed barn walls, to decorate the open spaces with hay bales, to scatter corn meal across what would be the dance floor.

Ross, our earliest hand, used red paper streamers and small nails to draw on the vast wall a mocking picture of me—a young girl's face with two hanging pigtails. As I stood and watched, he tapped away with his tiny hammer, throwing me little looks, actually smirking over his artistry.

I was indignant. "I don't look like that," I said. "And I've never had pigtails." I asked him to take it down, but he just grinned, leaving my face to decorate the barn wall for the future entertainment of hired hands and cows.

Drawing on his ingenuity, Hans found a Western combo with a guitar, two fiddles, a harmonica, and a banjo. "Zay are from Weed," he said. "Imagine, a guitar and two fiddles living in Weed ... but zay play nicely." And so the group came out in late afternoon and inside the barn they set up a makeshift stage.

By early evening it appeared that Hans and Mother had managed to reel in most of the town of Mount Shasta. Allan rushed over to the barn with a report. "The cars and pickups have filled the turnaround," he said, "and now people are parking halfway to Deetz's."

With a few guests I stood near the cookie plate. "You want a ginger snap, Allan?" I asked.

"No. I'm going out to count the cars." And he was gone.

The music started, rocking the barn. I looked around at all the people, some sitting on hay bales, most tapping their feet, a few clapping in time to the beat, others too busy dancing to stop for punch or cookies.

Mother's bursts of laughter punctuated the evening, sometimes floating above the fiddles. Her dances with Hans were full of exuberance, and yes, love. In her gathered, frilly white blouse and full, multi-colored skirt, she was once more an energetic young college girl, just reaching her full-blooming maturity. She twirled and smiled at Hans. In front of us all, Hans stared down at her in a way that told us he was smitten. As though he'd just met her, he smiled and held her tight and courted her gallantly.

Allan and I stayed up until the last guests departed: our bedrooms were, after all, at one end of the barn. Not yet dancers, we were the mouse children that peeked out between dancer's legs, that crept from the punch bowl to the cookie platter, that swayed unobtrusively to the music in our own solo rhythms.

"Kind of like Christmas, isn't it?" Allan murmured that night as we climbed the stairs to our rooms, "I'll never forget this," and I echoed, "Me neither."

That must have been the night Mother and Hans wrought a permanent change in our family.

Allan, about 8, on our ranch.

CHAPTER SEVENTEEN

Mt. Shasta, Early Summer, 1939

THAT EARLY SUMMER OF 1939 OUR PLACE HUMMED WITH A kind of electrical charge and great promise ... of guests soon to arrive in ever larger numbers, of our unsung ranch becoming a preferred destination for elite travelers. All we Luginbuhls felt the drama, and though outwardly we seemed calm enough, inside, our bodies were a-quiver.

Yet some of us still had mundane chores. To supply guests with fresh milk and cream, Larry, the newest hired hand, regularly milked our three cows and was happy enough that Allan and I had learned how ... hoping, I suppose, that we'd take turns helping out.

But at ages eight and nearly ten we were unreliable, and worse, we grasped our family's dynamics. Unlike the Deetz boys, who understood their labor was essential, we knew ours wasn't. Mother could always hire another man to deal with cows.

On those few occasions when Allan took over the milking, his focus was less on the milk bucket than the cats. "I hit him right in the teeth," he crowed, watching a white stream arc into a cat's open mouth.

Just then Larry showed up. "You're spoiling them," he said, "we don't need all these critters hanging around. If you keep doing that, I'll have to take over. Do all the milking myself."

One day, as Allan was milking and I was watching, the cow stopped cooperating and threw out an impatient leg and kicked over the bucket.

"Oh, shoot," said Allan.

We looked down in dismay. All that spilled milk! We felt like kicking her back.

"Guess I'd better do it," said Larry, thus ending our participation in the more interesting part of cow-dom.

Which left the less attractive part. Now that we had Holsteins parading through the meadow, the grass had become a mine field of cow pies, no longer an endless lawn where we could run without thinking. Our least-favorite moment became an inadvertent step into one of those nasty, squishy mounds. "eeeoow!" we'd cry. "*Ugggh!*" And there went a perfectly good shoe.

"How do the Deetz boys stand this?" I mumbled one day, pulling off my shoe, and Allan said, "I guess they don't do much running. For them, cows are work, and even the manure is work." He paused. "Their shoes are always in this stuff."

We looked at each other. He shrugged, but I was thinking, *Not my shoes. Never again.*

With our guests paramount in everyone's minds, even Mother and Hans sometimes took on old-fashioned chores. On a few occasions Mother poured sour milk into our wooden churn and paused long enough to turn the handle and create little flecks of butter. Or Hans turned it even longer as he combined sweet cream, vanilla and sugar to produce ice cream. Of course the mere mention of ice cream was magical. Allan and I flew to him and hung around watching, waiting to see what was down in the bucket; at the right moment we were allowed to slurp the sweet stuff off the paddles.

"Zis is work," Hans said one day, and we could see him sweating. "I think next time I buy zis ice cream from ze store."

In early June school was over, and Allan and I moved again, now into the half-finished new house. Our quarters were roofed, with rough siding between the rooms and sub-flooring under our beds and bureaus pushed against unfinished walls.

The new house became an exciting change. I was happy to see the last of barn spiders, to stop climbing steep wooden stairs to my bedroom. Each of us had a closet of sorts, and we shared a bath between our two rooms.

The house was so large it felt like an unfinished mansion. For now we were the early campers, the pioneers in what would soon be a grand new home. Already the chimneys reached for the sky, promising open fireplaces in four of the main rooms.

It was clear we would eventually dine by firelight, entertain friends in cozy rooms enlivened and warmed by brightly-sparking pinewood flames. Mom and Hans often spoke of the new house. "We will rent out our cottage as a small guest house," Mother declared.

"Zis will be our family home," Hans agreed. "Children. A dog." He grinned. "Maybe a new child. Zay will all love it."

Allan and I listened to them talk and I, for one, took pleasure in what we heard. I suppose Allan did, too. We never actually said it to each other.

ONE HOT DAY IN MID JULY, WHILE ALLAN WAS AWAY AT SUMmer camp, I was walking across our dirt turnaround when Hans rushed out to join me. He was hardly aware of me, though. Instead his head was craned toward a distant point in the sky, his gaze fixed and staring.

"Up zere," he said, pointing. "Look, Maralys—top of the mountain."

Following his finger, I finally saw it—a few wisps of whitish stuff high in the sky, so vague and distant they could hardly be taken seriously.

Yet Hans was very serious. "Smoke," he said, now in an ominous tone that surprised me. Usually a calm man, Hans was not given to histrionics. "Your mother thinks it might be a fire on Mount Eddy. I must go to town and let zem know."

I felt his tension, saw the frown that furrowed his forehead. But he was overreacting, I thought. What we'd seen was nothing. Or almost nothing. Why was he all excited?

"Leaving now," he said. "Want to come?"

"Sure," I said, and jumped into his pickup, surprised at how fast he roared away.

He stopped at Deetz's, honked his horn.

Alice Deetz came to his window, and he said, "Smoke up there, Alice, on top of Mount Eddy. You should watch it. Somebody in town needs to know." As he talked and pointed, she frowned, almost as worried as he.

"I'll get out here," I said, because his driving scared me. Anyway, Deetz's was my second home.

I jumped out, and with that Hans careened on down the road.

It was there, standing with the Deetzes for something over two hours, that I learned more than a child should ever know about a forest fire.

Gathered on the dirt road in front of their house, the five of us, Alice Deetz and I and her three boys, discovered what happens when a fast-moving forest fire roars down a distant mountain and soon envelops a nearby hill. And then part of it, a few burning twigs, disengage and wing by and land at your feet.

Literally at your feet.

That was the day I became convinced that if we spent another hour on their unprotected road, all of us would die.

Young Charlie Deetz and I, alone among the group, could not endure the terror—the small flames that erupted in the weeds around us, threatening to make us part of them.

And so, as one of the hired hand's pickup trucks barreled down from the Luginbuhl Ranch, the two of us darted into its path. "Take us to town!" we cried and, feeling no shame, the two of us escaped into the town of Mt. Shasta.

I, for one, did not recognize that moment as a turning point in my life.

Only later did I know—that for all of us, that day in July marked the end of a unique and special era.

CHAPTER EIGHTEEN

Mt. Shasta, 1939

A DAY LATER I WAS STANDING NEAR THE OLD HOUSE, FEELING terrible, when I saw a dust cloud boiling up our road—our ranch's version of an air-raid alert system. Especially now, after the fire, you couldn't just sneak in or out of our place, you left a kind of contrail that flowed between the charred branches and added to the smoke, a signal that anyone could read and keep reading.

I moved toward the turnaround and watched Allan get out of Mom's pickup. I hadn't slept anywhere yet except in town, and I was only there because that morning Alice Deetz brought me. *I hate it here,* I thought. *I hate the way it looks … I hate the smell.*

Now here was Allan. He'd arrived on the same horrible road I had, he'd seen everything, the burnt trees and now this skeleton of a house and two chimneys, where a week ago we'd both been sleeping.

Mom left him by the car and walked slowly toward the old house, as though she didn't really care whether she ever got there. But Allan just stood by the car. I could see the shock on his face, the bewilderment.

I feel just like you do. Maybe worse.

He said more to himself than me, "Our stuff's all gone, isn't it?"

"Yeah, it is. It looks pretty all gone to me."

His shoulders slumped in resignation. "I had some science books. And a train set-up." He paused to look around. "Hans moved the train to my room, said it belonged there. Mom was going to buy me some new stores. And a bridge."

I turned to see her enter the old house and the door slowly close behind her.

Allan fell silent. We both knew there'd be no stores or bridge, now that the train had melted. We looked at each other. What would happen now? What would our mom do with this blacked-up ranch? Where would we sleep?

"I had a bracelet," I said after awhile. "A stone bracelet. Maybe it didn't burn. Maybe I can still find it." I started toward what was left of the new house and Allan followed. But the closer we got the more we could feel heat. At the edge of the cement we stopped. You could look into the middle and see embers, and some of them still looked red and dangerous.

"I'm coming back," said Allan. "When it's cool. I've got some special rocks. And rocks don't burn." He stared at the mess with cold anger. "The fire didn't get everything." There was certainty in his eight-year-old voice, a determination I knew well, because I'd seen it all the times he beat me at Monopoly.

Allan didn't brag. But he had this will. You could feel it and you had to watch out for it.

MOM AND HANS MOVED US INTO THE OLD HOUSE, INTO THE empty rooms she'd kept for guests, except now there wouldn't be any. For a year she'd called our place a guest ranch, and it was hard to break the habit—you had to call it something, even when Allan and I and the cook and two hired hands were the only guests.

So we did have places to sleep. It's just that we didn't have any clothes.

"Here's a catalog," Mom said, handing me the fat Montgomery Wards book. She added without enthusiasm, "You can pick out what you need for school. Whatever you want."

I was growing, so maybe my old dresses wouldn't fit anyway.

She went to town and bought Allan some new pants and shirts, which she had to do, because Allan ignored the catalog and never cared what he wore.

FOR A COUPLE OF DAYS, ALLAN AND I HOVERED NEAR THE burned-up house, testing it like you'd test a hot oven to see if it was getting cool.

One day Hans loomed over us. "Stay away from zat house," he said. "It's dangerous. It's still hot. Ze ashes will burn you."

We backed away. We knew we could return when Hans wasn't there, or when he'd let down his guard.

One day we found the burned house had cooled. Stepping carefully across nails and black chunks and ashes, Allan and I made our way across the charred foundation. We studied the layout, trying to figure out where we were. "I think this is my room," I said finally. "This must be where it was."

"So this has gotta be mine," said Allan. He was carrying a charred branch, long and sturdy. "Get a stick, Sis. Here, I'll get you one." He ran off and came back with a piece of new board with a nail in it. "You can poke with this."

Together, like scavengers at a dump, we stirred and prodded the spots where we imagined we'd once had a closet, a bureau, or a bed. All those embers and lumps and strange black pieces. Some were wood and some weren't. I pushed them around, while Allan poked others. It was hard to tell what was anything. You knew which things were metal because they were hard and shiny and melted together.

But we kept on, like crows. And then I found something. "My bracelet!" I yelled. "I found my bracelet!" Slowly I pulled it out of the mess. The stones were still there, and the metal chain, and if you didn't mind that every bit of it was grimy and dark and not beautiful, you knew you still had a bracelet. Maybe I could scrub it off, make it look okay.

Allan moved closer to peer into my hand. He was holding a couple of nubby rocks and a twisted piece of train track. "Your bracelet might clean up." He held up the piece of track, stared at it a moment, and tossed it back into what had been his room. "You got a bracelet. I got two rocks. Nothing else." His observation was matter-of-fact. He dropped his stick and brushed off his hands.

We never poked around in the mess again. We were through with that place. We'd found where we'd once lived and the one precious thing—the only thing—worth saving. "They can have that burned-up house," said Allan.

A few weeks later school started. One of the days while we were gone, somebody removed the pieces of house that were left, even the chimneys.

We hardly noticed.

THE HOUSE THAT DISAPPEARED WAS ONLY ONE CHANGED PART of our lives. As we'd always done, Allan and I walked together down the road to Deetz's.

Those first days after the fire I began to understand something that made boys different from girls. We kept seeing smoky trees that were still burning deep down, around the roots, and Allan kept stopping to pee on the flames.

I don't know what he thought he'd accomplish. The flames would sizzle and start right back up again, and he'd soon run out of pee.

It wasn't something I cared to watch. He just slowed us down. "Hurry up," I said, "we'll miss the bus."

"I just have to put out this flame."

"It'll never go out. Come on."

Anyway, by then he was out of flame killer, so we'd start running and barely make it to Deetz's on time.

The blackened forest. The thick, stifling smell. The heaviness in the air. And a kind of heaviness in our hearts, too, as we trudged or ran down the dirt road. How different this trek had once been. And how I yearned to see it again as it was before.

Sad ruin of our new house.

CHAPTER NINETEEN

Mt. Shasta, 1939–1940

FOR WEEKS AFTER THE FIRE, I FELT PERSONALLY STRICKEN BY the bleak, ugly look of my beloved forest; I hadn't known how much I loved what we had. Or that all along I'd basked, however subliminally, in those rich and varied shades of green, from lemon-green to blue green to dark forest green. I was young and I'd taken it all for granted: beauty, beauty everywhere.

And now it was gone.

I wondered, at first, what Mom would find to do. It felt like everything we cared about had melted in a few awful moments.

If Mother cried over the sudden loss of her bountiful guest ranch, Allan and I never heard her. If Hans ever cursed the fire and all its devastation, that was never apparent to us, either.

There must have been discussions, mental re-tooling, arguments—now that everything they'd planned for and counted on had been jerked to a sudden stop.

What would they do with those desecrated 320 acres? How would they make a profit out of a burned-out ranch?

Was my mother now wholly dependent on the largesse of Russell?

Self-centered child that I was, when I returned to school that fall it wasn't with a heart full of empathy for my mother or worries over Hans, or concerns about how they'd make a living. Instead I was focused on my own little anguishes—that I wasn't one of the "in" kids, never as popular as some of the others.

And yet I was growing so tall! Which wasn't a good thing, not then, because tall means you always stick out. And what young girl wants to be a head taller than most of the boys?

One Friday afternoon, late in the semester, our teacher decided it was time we children learned to dance. Of course as one of the more serious, non-frivolous kids, I suspected I wouldn't be rushed off my feet. What little male squirt would choose me as a partner?

To my great relief, our teacher took the decision out of our hands. Nobody would be obliged to choose anyone. Instead, the boys were lined up on one side of the room and the girls on the other, and each of us would be paired off as we reached the heads of our respective lines.

And here he came! Across the room I saw him—the shortest, sharpest-talking male person in the room.

Stuck with each other, we took our places in dance mode, my arm on his shoulder, my hand in his. My eyes gazing across the top of his brown hair. With the music coaxing us, we started off.

Absolutely nothing worked. I hadn't a clue about dancing, except the vague notion that I shouldn't be stomping on his feet. He knew about as much as I—except he considered it his manly duty to somehow propel the two of us from one spot to another.

Within seconds my face felt flaming hot.

We must have looked awful … that is, if we appeared as awkward and clumsy as I imagined.

After a few inharmonious, body-bumping moments, he stopped short, abruptly dropped my hand, and stared into my face. "Who's leading this dance," he demanded. "You or me?"

Oh god, if only I'd had a fast tongue … if only I'd been able to come up with a quip like, "I don't know—I thought we'd both give it a try." Anything but what I said.

Purple with embarrassment, I felt pushed into the response of an idiot child. "You are," I mumbled.

The minute I said those words, I could have killed him. How dare he blame me for this entire mess? How dare he make me say those demeaning words?

I remember him now as a smart-ass young boy … a kid who should have been shy but wasn't, not even slightly. He probably became a lawyer.

ABOUT THEN, IN THOSE YEARS OF SLOWLY DAWNING SEXUALITY, I began dreaming of a hero-rescuer suddenly appearing out of the woods, blackened as they were, to take me away. After school, on my walks home through the spooky forest, I just knew one of those days the handsome man would be there, not riding a horse, exactly, but somehow … just there! And he would instantly recognize me as the person he'd been seeking, and together we'd float off to another land.

As I walked, I gazed from side to side … hoping. Waiting. With fantasies making anything seem possible, I fantasized away.

Whatever my future with the opposite sex might hold, anything was better than any further moments on the dance floor, my feet brought to a sudden halt by a smallish, impertinent male. Never again, I vowed, would I be called on to answer the demeaning question: "Who's leading this dance—you or me?"

My Reader's Digest Mother spoke in my head: *You can learn to dance!*

IT WASN'T UNTIL A FEW MONTHS AFTER THE FIRE THAT ALLAN and I understood why Mother's devastation over the disaster might have been tempered in an important way.

She was going to have a baby!

For her, for the four of us, her pregnancy seemed a gift, as though something profound had risen from the ashes, our loss softened by a benediction.

With childish awe Allan and I observed our mother's expanding girth until on January 28, 1940, she and Hans brought home our new baby brother, Hilary. With our first glimpse, we saw Hans leaning over his tiny son, nuzzling the infant with his nose.

From that moment it was rather like our home was enlivened by a new puppy. Even the fire's aftermath somehow retreated.

Allan and I were delighted with this fetching creature and used our every wile to engage him. "He's smart," Allan said, "look, Maralys, he's trying to speak. Say 'Allan,' he said. "Listen, he's trying."

Once Hilary was able to spend time in a play pen, Allan and I became his entertainment committee. Noting that Hilary seemed to enjoy tearing up loose paper, we filled his play pen with so many newspapers and catalogues that he looked like a baby buried in a dumpster.

Hilary liked to make spitting noises, so we made them back at him, entertained by his giggles.

Of course my brother and I overdid everything. And eventually, not only did we tire of our antics, so did Hilary.

But by then the little boy had learned to walk, and now Mother really did need us to run through the house, forever chasing him down.

For all of us, that year, the baby made up for everything. Well, almost everything.

Even a baby can only take you so far.

Hans and infant son, Hilary.

Chapter Twenty

Mt. Shasta, 1940–1941

It seemed to happen overnight. With a ranch no longer suited to guests, Hans and Mother turned their attention to cows.

"We'll sell the milk," Mother declared, "we'll make this ranch self-sufficient," and gradually the meadow was dotted with an increasing number of black and white Holsteins mooing and grazing. Our barn became a real milking barn, and our lunch hours were filled with men eager to wolf down steak, corn, and potatoes.

Usually we had a cook, someone able to cope with our enormous, black, wood-burning stove. But when we didn't, Mother increasingly turned to me. Whatever made her think I could cook had to be the careless imaginings of a desperate mind. I was female, she reasoned, so of course I had The Gift.

She was always gentle about it, running me down wherever I happened to be reading. "Dear," she said sweetly, "Isn't it time for you to stir around in the kitchen?"

And so I did ... though her "stir around" made it clear she thought there was nothing to it, that any idiot could, by simply moving a bit, turn out a meal.

Surely the hired hands had to be leery that, from time to time, a twelve-year-old was at the helm.

One day, once again without a cook, Mother determined she would give the job a try. From somewhere she found a recipe for one of her favorites—the beet soup, Russian Borscht.

I was sitting in our formal dining room with the five hired hands when Mother appeared with a tray of red soup, each bowl with a blob of sour cream floating on top. As she paused before Ross, the nearest man, he stared at the tray and asked, "What is it?"

"Borscht," she replied cheerily. "Russian Borscht."

Thinking fast, Ross shook his head. "I never did care for Borscht," he said … and even I knew he'd never seen it before.

Mother moved to the next man, who held up a hand. "I never cared for Borscht, either."

Somehow the men managed to keep straight faces. For the remaining few it got easier. One by one, each of them declared his lifetime aversion to Borscht … whereupon Mother silently returned to the kitchen, her loaded tray untouched. Around the table, the men were quietly laughing … which she probably heard.

I doubt she ever again made anything resembling beet soup.

While Mother seldom cooked, she seemed willing enough to wash the dinner dishes, usually with me commandeered to help. As we stood together at the sink, she washing and me drying, Mother often began to sing, leading us both from "I've Been Working on the Railroad," to "Red River Valley," to "You Are My Sunshine."

"Maralys, here's how you do the harmony," she said, handing me a plate, and with me repeating the notes after her, I learned, by rote, the harmonies to half a dozen popular songs.

Even better, I developed an ear for harmonic thirds, a talent I was able to use for a lifetime of sing-alongs. Those wash-up sessions in the kitchen became one of Mother's lasting gifts. As few of today's children will ever learn, there are real compensations for having no dishwasher.

SUDDENLY MOTHER AND HANS WERE NOT DOING WELL. Mother was no longer nursing her baby, so the intimacy between her and Hilary had diminished. But worse, she no longer seemed harmonious with Hans. Allan and I felt the tension. Cold silences. Quiet arguments at night.

Neither of us understood why.

More and more, Hilary's entertainment came from Allan and me.

When Mt. Shasta Elementary school let out in June, Mother took me aside. "How would you like to go East to visit your father? Maybe for a few weeks."

By then I'd nearly forgotten him. "Well, uh …"

"He's eager for you to come, Maralys. To visit him and his wife and their four children."

"Oh … yes, they do have four now," I remembered.

Before I could absorb this, she added, "Ted says they might even want you to live with them and go to school there."

School? Away from here? Living with my father?

I had no opinion yet, but of course my mother had already made up her mind. "We'll make arrangements, honey. I've talked to your father by phone. He's eager to see you. You can go East this summer, just for a visit at first, and see how you like it."

Whether I agreed or didn't agree, it was soon clear that I'd be going.

What I didn't know until almost time to leave was that I'd be traveling by myself—for five days alone on a train. But the train was only the first traumatic event.

As it turns out, it was a miracle that I lived through the summer.

CHAPTER TWENTY-ONE

En Route to Long Island, 1941

As the train prepared to leave Los Angeles, I stared out the window of my small Pullman compartment, trying to catch a last glimpse of my mother. Perhaps I was on the wrong side, or maybe she'd already left, but I couldn't find her. The platform outside teemed with people gazing up at the Los Angeles Flyer—but not her. In vain I searched until I felt a slight bump, then a sense of motion, and knew the train was pulling away.

I turned back and looked into my small bleak compartment, at my few things scattered on the floor. So there I was once more—deserted. But this time with nobody, anywhere, to talk to.

If ever a child can revisit old insecurities, fill her stomach with acid and a sense of being lost, within a few hours the train managed to accomplish it all.

As I crossed the country, my fears magnified. Though I had enough money to eat in the dining car, the heavy doors between sections were hard to navigate, and once in the diner I sat alone. But all that hardly mattered; the food became impossible to swallow. My stomach felt strange, sickish. A sour taste rose in my mouth, and I began to fear I was seriously ill.

But who could I tell? How would I find someone to help?

A kindly porter guided me through the change of trains in Denver, and for a while, perhaps an hour, the rush to switch Pullmans became a distracting factor, and I felt a little better.

Then once again I was by myself.

Instead of finding comfort, for the rest of those five days I sat in my small quarters staring blindly out the window, once more worried about my fragile health. Would I even live to get there?

The bumping, rocking train should have been soothing, but

wasn't. And my quarters were too small, too confining. Now that I had my sickness to fret about, that demon eclipsed the feelings of desertion, and thus I rocked and belched my way to New York City.

My mother should have known: an insecure child of twelve does not do well crossing the country by herself.

At grand central station in New York City, there stood Ted! His hair was still dark and wavy, his face unlined, almost the look of a mature student, and even more handsome than I remembered.

"Maralys!" he cried, and my father smiled and lifted me off my feet, then grabbed my small suitcase. His smile was contagious. Together, we trotted off to his car. "How was your trip?" he asked as we turned toward Long Island.

"Uhhm ... " I began, then stopped.

"Not so good?"

"Not so good," I said. *Should I tell him I felt sick?*

"We'll soon be home," he offered, not waiting for further comments, and anyway, the sickness was rapidly vanishing, so I let it go.

By lunchtime, I once more felt like eating. And then we pulled into his modest home (not the House Beautiful I would visit later), the front door opening into a shiny hardwood floor with a throw rug in rich blues and greens. His wife, a second Virginia, met us in the living room, and tagging behind her were three girls. In the distance, I could hear the crying of a baby.

"How ahh you, Dear?" she asked perfunctorily, with a lilting Southern accent. She held out a slim hand. "These are our daughters." As she introduced them, I noticed her patrician aura: blonde hair secured in an elegant bun, a cool smile that didn't involve her entire face.

In bored tones, the two oldest girls said hello, while the youngest grinned and said nothing.

Walking briskly, Virginia led me to a small bedroom, which I would share with her oldest daughter, V-Ann. "We moved one of the girls out ... temporarily," she said, and for me the word "temporarily" hung in the air like a cloud.

Thus I began sharing the home life of my father.

Though she was distantly polite, Virginia Morgan Klumpp didn't consider me one of her children—that much was clear. Especially after the accident.

Oh yes—the accident.

Not sure how to play with those young girls, I brought forth a game that Allan and I had played with Hilary. I would lie on my back and, with a small girl sitting on my shoes, give a sudden push, hard enough to boost her into the air. At first the girls loved flying into space. But sadly, after one of those flights, the middle daughter, Kathy, landed hard on her head. I was horrified.

A thump, a shriek of pain, and Virginia Klumpp came running. "My god!" she screamed, scooping her injured child off the floor, "Good god!" while I sat in place, utterly chagrined.

"I didn't mean to!" I cried, "I'm sorry. I'm sorry."

"I'm sure you didn't mean to injure her," Mrs. Klumpp said acidly, "but that was a dangerous game. We must take her to the doctor."

Though sporting a sizable lump on her head, Kathy soon recovered. But I didn't. After that incident, my presence, with Madam Klumpp at least, seemed to be merely endured.

On a weekend soon after my arrival, the Klumpps took me to their small beach home and threw a party. Invited was a puffy old medical school friend of Ted's, Dr. Harlin Baker, and Ted's sister Margaret, a dermatologist, plus her husband, Art.

"Maralys!" cried my aunt Margaret immediately, eyeing me up and down. "So I see you again! Lovely! Lovely!" While the others sat in the living room, she grabbed my hand, pulled me away to another room, then whispered, "Let's go get some ice cream! But don't tell anyone." She hunkered low, like a creeping cat, and led me to the freezer. Nearby she scrounged some dishes, then scooped up generous portions of chocolate ice cream.

"Shh!" she said, with a grin that made us co-conspirators, "tell no one … let's sneak off," and she, the large-boned, generous-spirited doctor, led me to a quiet spot in the house where together we devoured our treat. Somehow she seemed about my age. Twelve—maybe thirteen. Though only one of us remembered the other, I loved her instantly. Her nose may have been a tad large, but her laugh was far bigger.

But then, I learned later, everyone loved Margaret.

Out on the patio, Virginia served a salad lunch. My seat was next to the fat doctor, a spot I wouldn't have chosen. As I prepared to sit, he reached out for me, inadvertently brushing my chest. He gave me the creeps. I moved my chair, widening the distance between us. Still, for the next hour his hands kept brushing me accidentally. Or so I thought. But the strange, lascivious look in his eyes—that was no accident.

AS THE SUN GREW HOTTER, WE SCROUNGED BATHING SUITS AND headed for Jones Beach. Years earlier, Allan and I had spent most of a summer with Helen Healey, one of mother's friends who lived near a beach in San Clemente … dropped off for a long period, as always. In those days, seemingly for weeks on end, Healey's three children and Allan and I stayed in the water nearly the entire day, utterly disrespected by the Pacific. Large waves picked us up and flung us back down, but knowing we'd eventually bubble to the surface, I, for one, was never scared. Nor did I ever tire of the ocean.

But this was Jones Beach, bordering an unfamiliar Atlantic, albeit with smaller waves. I assumed I had nothing to fear.

The water was cold, so I edged in slowly, paddled about for a few moments, then surfaced to contemplate my next move. With my back to the ocean, I stood by myself in waist-deep water, ready to return to my towel.

Suddenly I felt something odd. The sand under my feet was sliding beneath my toes. The water was getting deeper. Alarmed, I bent forward, dug in my toes, and headed for shore, struggling to shorten the distance.

But the sand kept sliding, and it was clear I was making no headway. The sliding stopped, and I pawed the water, trying to touch solid ground.

There was no solid ground.

Abruptly I realized the truth. Though I was still upright, still pawing the water, I was no longer able to reach anything solid.

Instead, I was floating—or swimming—in deep water. And inexplicably, the water was getting still deeper and the beach was now farther away.

The full horror hit me all at once. Without warning, the ocean had sucked me out. Frightened, no terrified, I turned onto my stomach and tried to swim back to shore. But it was useless. The more I swam, the farther away the beach became.

With no clue about what had happened, I looked around, trying to find some other human being. And then I saw him. Nearby, Dr. Baker was swimming as I was, flopping helplessly, trying to make it back to shore. And not succeeding. If I was stuck, so was he.

A further horror hit me, the ocean issuing a kind of decree: *You will swim or you will die.*

Already tired, I yelled over at the doctor. "Can I hold on to you for a moment? Just a few seconds?"

"Don't touch me!" he shouted back. "Don't touch me!"

"Just to rest?" I pleaded.

"No! Don't touch me!"

The selfish puffball imagined I would drown him. Of all the people to get stuck with, I thought, it had to be him.

At that moment a sound … a deep, heavily drawn out man's voice floated past us across the water. "Heeelp! Heeelllp!" Astonished, I realized someone else was in trouble, just as we were. Whoever he was, I couldn't see him. He must have been waves and waves away.

He yelled again, and I considered adding my own cry for help to his. And then realized my small voice would never carry more than a few yards, that any yelling I might do would be futile, so why even try?

Cries for help sounded again. It was obvious the ocean had betrayed us all—the doctor and I and whoever else was out there.

Desperate, I rolled over on my back, trying to rest. And found I could do it. With minimal effort, I floated … up, down, up, down, as waves lifted me, then dropped me down again into a trough. With limited vision, I could still see the water pile up, as though to dump its load over my head, then feel myself lifted again out of the way. Then back into the watery valley. Once down, I saw only brief glimpses of the sky because my vision was riveted on the mountainous oncoming waves.

Now, more than ever, I was aware that the sea was endless. In some crazy part of my mind I wondered how long it would take to reach the opposite shore. How far away was it, anyway? Would I turn up in China?

But I'll never see any shore. Before then, I'll die. Part of me knew it was inevitable. I would soon drown. To my surprise, the thought became less terrifying. My mind had dulled; I actually became used to the idea.

Suddenly my Reader's Digest Mother appeared in my head: *Keep swimming, Maralys. You can make it.*

I turned over again, once more trying to find the beach—and discovered I was still capable of white-hot fear; one look, and a new wave of terror washed over me. The shore was now so distant I could scarcely see any people. They'd become nothing but specks. Even the doctor was no longer visible. The truth was beyond imagining. I'd been carried out into deep ocean, so deep I was no longer related to dry land.

With a sight so terrible, I turned over again on my back. I had to rest.

From afar came those cries again … distant male shouts for help. *Oh God … somebody please hear him.*

Then abruptly, from nowhere, a lifeguard swam up beside me. In the turbulent sea, he was bobbing up and down just as I was. But at least he was pushing ahead of him a rubber lifeguard's tube. *Why don't you give that to me?*

"Are you all right?" he asked, and I tried to nod. *Well, I'm still alive.* What I wanted to say was, Give me that tube!

"Hold on," he said, "someone will come," and I thought, *You already came. But you're doing nothing.* As suddenly as he appeared, he was gone—a kind of sea-borne mirage. *So it's decided, I thought. He won't help; I have to save myself.*

By now the time seemed endless. I'd been out at sea for what felt like hours. Days. An eternity. Vaguely I wondered when swimming would no longer be possible.

Time slipped away. My sense of the minutes, the hours, became blurred. I was existing, nothing more.

Suddenly I saw something else. A boat!

I should have been thrilled. Somehow I wasn't.

Nearly flying past out of control, the boat swept up beside me and hands reached out. With supreme effort, a collection of male fingers gripped my arms and pulled me up and over the edge, slid me down past their legs, then let go. With a thump I dropped into a new environment—the wet, bumpy floor of a boat!

It was the Coast Guard—one of their very large rowboats, full of oars and men. About eight rowers. Moments later they also hauled in the doctor. The groper. I pulled in my legs, putting as much space between us as I could.

So we would live after all. For reasons I'll never understand, I wasn't elated. Just numb. Numb and tired. Idly I wondered what had become of the man who'd been yelling.

And then the atmosphere changed, became electric. Within moments a new crisis loomed and our lives were threatened once again.

For the second time that afternoon I, and everyone in the boat, thought we might die.

CHAPTER TWENTY-TWO

Long Island, 1941

OUR RELIEF HAD ONLY BEEN GOOD FOR SECONDS. WHILE THE doctor and I crouched low in the boat, a man in the bow served as a lookout and called out orders. Everyone else pulled hard on the oars.

Suddenly that front man leaped to his feet. "Goddammit!" he roared. "When I say row to port, you row to port! NOW ROW! TO PORT!" He was agitated, his eyes wide with alarm. For seconds he remained standing.

I craned my neck and saw why. Ahead of us, looming ever closer, was a massive rock jetty, extending endlessly into the ocean. Our boat was flying toward it, full speed. In moments the boat would crash against the rocks and break up. We'd all be thrown back into the sea.

"ROW TO PORT!" the leader thundered again, powering them with his voice. "ROW TO PORT!"

His fury filled the boat. The rowers pulled. And pulled harder. The jetty loomed closer.

We were headed straight for the rocks. Fast. And Faster. I could hardly breathe.

At the last second, literally, the men pulled so hard their faces reddened, arm muscles bulged. The rocks were right in front of us. The boat veered, swept around the rocks, skimmed by within inches. The open sea lay ahead.

We'd missed the jetty.

Nobody cheered, nobody said anything. But once again, we were all breathing.

Propelled by forces we couldn't see, our boat took an unexpected shoreward turn, flying faster even than men could row.

The sea had a mind of its own.

With our course determined by nature, a few men laid down

their oars. The boat still hurtled onward, but now propelled by the ocean. We were aimed for the beach.

Ahead of us stood a crowd of people. Dozens. Maybe a hundred. As a unified mob, they'd all left the water and walked a mile down the sand, following our seaward progress. Now they waited for our arrival.

We sped toward shore. Fast. Narrowed the gap. With a jarring thump, our boat crunched into the sand.

Instantly we were surrounded by well-wishers, or the simply curious. People rushed over to us, reached into the boat, tried to pull us out. They shouted questions, expressed concern.

To my surprise, and then anger, the doctor was suddenly at my side, grabbing my arm in his fat fingers. Shouting, "No publicity! No publicity!" he propelled me through the crowd.

I could have kicked him. The nerve! The utter, rotten nerve. After our harrowing ordeal, *I wanted* some publicity. I'd earned publicity. I deserved to be a heroine, if only for a moment. I wanted to tell people how scared I'd been, how awful it felt to be caught in the ocean's clutches, how horrifying to spend hours thinking you might die.

Only vaguely did I grasp my reasons—that recounting the ordeal would be like a blotter sopping up a spill, absorbing some of the anguish. Oh yes, I needed to say it.

What was the doctor afraid of, anyway?

He gave me no choice. With the strength of a bulldog and still shouting, "No publicity!" he jerked me through the crowd, away from the shoreline and far up onto the beach—away from anyone who might ask questions, or even speak to us.

In a day of terror, he was the final ugly straw. Twice that day he'd proven himself rotten, starting with the pawing at lunch. And now this!

With a passion, I despised that doctor.

We soon caught up with Ted and, to our amazement, learned it was he who'd been shouting for help—he and his brother-in-law, Art Searing.

Ted was still panting, bent over in recovery mode next to his sister, Margaret. Nearby, Art was panting too. On the beach lay a yellow, blow-up raft.

Unknown to us, the three had been using the rubber raft to ride smaller waves into the beach. But then they, too, had been caught in the inexorable tide.

"It's called a Sea Puss," Ted said. "And it damn near got us." He was breathing hard, making an effort to towel off. "It's a violent body of water … sweeps out to sea, moves down the shoreline. Later sweeps back into shore."

He took a deep breath, tossed aside his towel. "The three of us were in the water, but fairly near the beach." A shrug toward the ocean. "Then suddenly we found ourselves out. Way out, in very deep water." He looked at Margaret, and she nodded and came over to give me a hug.

"There was nothing we could do. We put Margaret on the raft. Art and I held onto the sides. We took turns yelling for help."

"I could hear you," I said. "A spooky voice coming over the waves. I didn't know it was you." I shivered. "The waves kept bouncing me around. Then I'd hear that big Heellllp again, and I prayed, *Dear God, please let people on the beach hear it.* I kept wishing they'd come find us … before I couldn't swim anymore."

Margaret hugged me tighter.

"We were out there a long time," Ted offered. "You, too, it seems. Long enough for everyone on shore to catch sight of us."

"Hours," said Margaret. She smiled down at me. "Felt like years, didn't it?"

I nodded. *I didn't think I'd live.*

"We finally saw the Coast Guard boat," said Art. "But by then we didn't need it. The Sea Puss was sweeping us back toward shore." With a noticeable shudder, he glanced toward the sea. "Anyway, that ocean was moving so fast, we'd never have gotten aboard. Even the boat was helpless and couldn't do much."

Dr. Baker started to speak, but I cut him off. "It finally did do much," I said, loud enough to drown him out. "But only because the captain cussed everyone out. He howled like a banshee. "When I say row to port, goddammit, you row to port!'"

That broke them up. Before they'd finished laughing, I added,

"And that's how we missed the jetty."

The doctor nodded and tried to say something. But I broke in again. "And that's why we lived through it. Those guys were rowing like maniacs, so we barely swept around the end of the rocks." I paused, looked Ted in the eye. "I think we should call the newspapers."

My chubby swimmer shook his head, No, No, No, but nobody noticed.

Ted smiled. "Good idea," he said, and Margaret broke in with her usual enthusiasm, "Our little heroine, here, has her own version. She should tell it. She's one gutsy girl."

Buoyed by her support, I began collecting my thoughts, searching for words to define the ordeal, re-living it on two levels—the original distress and now the re-telling—all to make me feel better.

An hour later, while Dr. Baker backed away looking shocked, as though his face was on a billboard in the post office, a reporter sat on Ted's patio, scribbling. I'd hardly started my story when the disgruntled man broke in. "Don't use my name!"

All of us looked up except the reporter. "Go on," he said to me. "This is fascinating," and he wrote as fast as I could talk. At the end he grinned. "Okay if I name the beach?"

THAT NIGHT AT DINNER THERE WAS ONLY ONE TOPIC.

Dr. Groper had suddenly packed up and gone home, but the rest of us could speak of nothing except the event: how terrible our ordeal had been, how powerful the ocean, how helpless we all felt. As the night progressed, our stories grew detailed, more dramatic. Yet all our tales were somehow alike. We all knew in our various ways that we'd cheated death.

It was one of those nights where you had to let loose, had to get the fear out of your system. None of us wanted to go to bed. We were all trying to talk away the trauma.

Mid discussion Art Searing momentarily broke the tension. "Dr. Baker must have his own Sea Puss story—more to do with bedrooms than oceans."

Ted glanced at Art and smiled.

Eventually, of course, we did have to sleep.

In the middle of the night, I suddenly awoke, my heart pounding. In a dream so vivid it was terrifying, I was once again standing in the ocean, felt the sand slide out from between my toes. With increasing horror, I felt myself lose the security of a firm footing, knew I was being sucked into endless water.

I lay there panting. It was hours before I once more drifted off.

I would have that same dream, on and off, for the next fifteen years.

THE NEXT MORNING, THE NEWSPAPERS CARRIED OUR STORY, plus the Coast Guard's harrowing tale of intense rowing. The men had saved our lives. But they'd also saved their own.

DAYS LATER, WITH THE THOUGHT OF DROWNING STILL FRESH in my mind, Ted took me aside and brought up the topic of school. I imagined he'd talk about the neighborhood Junior High. Instead he said matter-of-factly, "We're enrolling you in a boarding school."

"What?" I thought I hadn't heard him right.

"The Sands Point Academy," he said. "I've already filled out some papers."

"A boarding school?" I was bewildered, then shaken. "I'm not going to live here?" I stared at him. "Why not?"

"Virginia and I think you'll love this school!" he said, ignoring my question. "You'll visit us on holidays."

"But I thought ... but I thought ..." I was speechless, facing another sort of drowning. "Why can't I live here? At your house?"

"It's all arranged," he said, his voice as smooth as he knew how to make it.

But I didn't hear *smooth*. I heard *Boarding School*. I heard *no home*. Once again, *no home*.

"Why can't I? ..."

Ted had already begun to move away, in effect cutting me off. He made it obvious there'd be no argument, no further discussion. If I spoke at all, I'd be speaking to myself.

Eventually I would learn this was how my father always handled conflict—by ducking any hint of unpleasantness. He simply didn't engage.

I stared after him, feeling new resolve. *I didn't give in to the ocean. Now I won't give in to you.*

Within an hour I'd found a phone and complained to my mother in Mount Shasta. "Ted is putting me into a boarding school," I wailed. "Another boarding school. I won't even live here, I won't be in his house, I won't have a home."

"Really?" Mom said. "Did you discuss it fully?"

"Ted doesn't discuss," I said. "Especially when he doesn't want to."

"How well I remember," she murmured.

"He wouldn't even argue, Mom. He just said I'd be living at that school."

"Well, we can't have that, Honey. You don't need another boarding school. You just come on home. I'll fix it. I'll wire you the money. You come home."

"Oh, good, Mom. Oh thank you." Her love, her support, her genuine concern, flowed over me. I'd never been so grateful to my mother—that this time, of all times, she'd fully understood.

THAT FALL I STARTED EIGHTH GRADE, STILL AT MOUNT SHASTA elementary school, while Allan entered fifth. It was 1941. Hilary was getting ever cuter, walking freely, beginning to talk. He certainly knew both our names.

But between our mother and Hans the tension grew. They snapped at each other, argued frequently. Once in awhile they mentioned money.

Allan and I seldom heard their big arguments. But once again, since we were all living in the same house, sometimes at night we heard her crying.

IT HAPPENED IN THE MIDDLE OF THE NIGHT.

Sometime in the fall of 1941. Distant harsh words. A slammed door. Then our Mother appearing in each of our bedrooms in a frantic state, waking us, saying in distress, "We're leaving."

"Leaving?" Allan and I asked together. "Leaving for where?"

"You'll see," Mother said. "Now get up. Pack a suitcase with clothes."

A suitcase? In the middle of a Monday night? *But tomorrow is school.*

Bewildered, Allan and I staggered from our beds, and still half asleep, we threw clothes into suitcases provided by our mother. Neither of us had any idea what to take—how much, and of what? Jackets? Tooth brushes?

Hans was nowhere around.

By dawn, fortified only with quick bowls of cereal, we were in the car, suitcases in the trunk, three children and our mother headed south.

Hilary, about 18 months, with Mother

CHAPTER TWENTY-THREE

Berkeley, California, 1941

WE ARRIVED IN A PLACE WE'D NEVER BEEN BEFORE, TO BEGIN a strange new era.

Quickly Mother enrolled Allan and me in a big-city school. But we were living like tenants in a boarding house, an old place near the University of California, in Berkeley.

Our new town was bewildering.

Yet our home was odder still. As often as Allan and I had been fobbed off on strangers or sent to boarding schools, we'd never experienced an out-and-out boarding house, a place where no one in particular was in charge. This time our mother and baby brother were there, along with everyone else.

Like most of the homes in Berkeley it was no longer young—a dignified old Victorian that boasted a tiny cupola and a wide front porch, and nearly filled its city lot. The four stories offered six bedrooms, a stuffy sitting room, and meals. So of course Mother wasn't cooking. But she was eating three meals there, like all the others.

Almost accustomed, now, to strange uprootings, Allan and I seldom asked questions. We just did as we were told, though like sailors on a heaving deck, we struggled to maintain our footing.

On the second day, Mother took us aside. "Whatever else you're up to, you must be here every night at six," she explained, "because that's dinner—and nobody will feed you later."

The residents were expected to assemble in the dining room, where we all sat at the same table, strangers thrown together as though we were a family.

Except we weren't.

"I don't know any of them," said Allan one evening. "I guess I never will. Nobody speaks to me."

"We aren't exactly talking to them either. I thought Mom would be gabbing with everyone. I've never seen her just sit there and eat—and that's it."

"She doesn't like it here," he said. "Do you like it, Maralys?"

"No."

"Me neither. I wish we'd stayed in Mount Shasta."

Soon I had a peculiar problem. Nobody knew this because I didn't tell, but at dinner and on weekends one of the boarders kept staring at me, making me blush. To me he was old, maybe twenty, and except for the staring, he might have seemed okay.

One Saturday when nobody was in the sitting room, he stood in a doorway and asked me to walk through it with my arms up.

"Why?" I asked, squirming inside because I sensed he was breathing too hard, watching me too intently.

"Just do it," he said. His eyes had that look—the same expression I'd seen on the face of Ted's friend, the puffy doctor in Sands Point.

"Come on—do it," he urged again, "lift up your arms." Stepping closer, he reached toward me.

For an instant I stared at him, scared but curious about his intentions. He was an adult, and usually I obeyed adults.

Somehow this was different.

Suddenly overwhelmed by the sinister vibes pouring into the doorway, I ducked through the opening and ran. Glancing back, I saw him still standing there, pretending innocence, as though thinking, *Oh well ... so that one got away.*

I dashed up the stairs to my bedroom. Soon after that he must have moved on because I never saw him again.

OUR SCHOOL DAYS FELL INTO A ROUTINE. EACH MORNING Allan and I rushed downstairs, quickly consumed a bowl of dry cereal with milk, and trudged down the streets of Berkeley to John Muir Elementary school. Instead of making friends, we listened hard and tried to remain unnoticed, as though creating waves might swamp our fragile boat.

For Allan the new school wasn't all bad. "I've got a good teacher," he announced one day. "Better than Miss Hayward in Mount Shasta."

Mother hardly looked up. Only I seemed to be listening.

"Is she pretty?" I asked.

"No," said Allan, "she's old."

As to my male teacher, I had no opinion. Some of the students seemed smarter than my Mount Shasta friends, better at math, anyway, and a few were keenly interested in science. For me, they were all figures on a stage, actors to be catalogued and observed. I belonged in Mount Shasta, where I supposed we'd some day return, since most of our stuff was still there.

Once Allan wondered aloud, "What does Mother do all day? With no cows and no meadow. No Alice Dietz to visit. No Hans to talk to?"

"I don't know," I said. "But she's got Hilary," and, like Allan, I wondered how she spent her days.

Neither of us knew.

Each day after school when I returned to the boarding house, Mother seemed too listless to ask what I'd been doing in class. Less and less did she reach out like an interested parent. Without giving it much thought, I began to see her as just another boarder in a nearby room.

PEARL HARBOR WOKE HER UP. SUDDENLY, ON DECEMBER 7TH, Mom became Rip Van Winkle emerging from a long sleep. "We've been attacked!" she cried that day, shaking a newspaper in Allan's and my faces. "The Japanese have bombed Pearl Harbor."

Pearl Harbor? "Where is that?" we asked in unison.

"Hawaii!" she burst out. "The Japanese have destroyed our ships in Honolulu. The President will speak to us tonight. I predict we will soon be at war!"

"We will?" Allan asked. He seemed to be thinking, *So what will happen next?*

"Read this headline!" she cried. "Read the story."

We did. The two of us knew nothing about war—nor had we ever spoken to anyone who seemed interested in the subject. War was sometimes referred to in our history books, but it was always an abstraction, a concept without reality.

But now Mother was involved—and suddenly so were we.

At school, our teachers began talking about World War Two. Daily the topic grew, until even Allan and I saw it on a larger scale, grasped that it was bigger than we at first imagined, and included numerous other countries.

My teacher said, "This is a war that isn't just for grownups. You kids probably won't see our enemies, but you'll know people who will. Some of your fathers may be sent away to fight."

Once again, our Mother was alive. She had a topic she cared about. All day long, now, she read newspapers or listened to the radio. The very air around her crackled with excitement. By herself, Mother supercharged the boarding house. People began talking to each other, and they all talked to her, as though she was the popular new dorm mother.

The war almost took over Christmas. But for us, not entirely. One Saturday Hans showed up at our house. He looked thin and downtrodden, like a beautiful but neglected German Shepherd. He stared at Mother hungrily. "Please—may I take ze children out Christmas shopping?"

Mother gave him a cold look. Without answering, she surveyed the room, ignoring him. For long seconds she let him wait. Then she glanced at him again. "Why not?" she finally said. "Go with him, kids. What can it hurt?" Under her breath she added, "What do I care?"

Hans' face sagged further. Clearly, he'd heard her.

In a quick aside, Allan said, "She's being so mean!"

As though afraid she might change her mind, Hans urged us, "Gather your coats, kids. Quickly. Ve must go."

Within minutes he was ushering us out the door—a fast escape from a truculent witch.

Our stepfather had just taken the first step toward pulling us into his aura.

HANS TOOK US EVERYWHERE. IN DOWNTOWN BERKELEY, WE went from store to store—from fine women's wear to specialty jewelry stores. In some he studied the aquamarine bracelet, the diamond-speckled necklace, staring at each of them as though it was the magic key. "Will your mother like zis?" he asked.

We nodded or shrugged.

"What about zis lovely silk nightie? Does zis look like her?" Fondly, he fingered the nightgown as though her slim body was already in it.

Allan and I could only agree that Yes, our mother might like that. Obviously we weren't shopping for anyone else. But Hans did seem to care about our opinions, as though we had special knowledge he didn't, as though he were tapping into two conduits that led to the same sweet place: Mother's affection. "Tell me, kids ... what can I do? How can I make your mother take me back?"

We stared at him helplessly.

"I love her so much. I've missed her with ... with all my soul. I need your mother back in my life. Without her I am ... how you say ... empty." He was fighting back tears.

Near tears ourselves, we could only listen, small pulsing hearts without solutions. We could only feel Hans's broken spirit. He was dumping buckets of emotion over our heads, more than we could absorb. We weren't psychologists, we were just young kids.

Our shopping trip consumed a whole afternoon and most of an evening, with Allan and I like two dense chocolate bars, slowly melting into liquid.

But also, thanks to our stepfather's pain, we'd unexpectedly become determined warriors, now infused with our private mission, bent on repairing our splintered family. "We'll talk to Mother," Allan said with his ten-year-old chin jutting out. "We'll tell her not to be so mean."

LATER, TALK WE DID. THE NEXT DAY, BECAUSE SHE WAS THE only one there, both of us cornered our mother in the sitting room. "He loves you so much," I said, and Allan added, "We think he was crying."

Mother turned her face away.

"Why are you so mean?" Allan went on, "making him so sad and everything?"

I said, "You should talk to him, Mom. He'll tell you the stuff he told us."

Mother tried not to listen.

"We miss Hans," said Allan. "Because of you …" he broke off. "Well now I've got no father."

Though I soon gave up, unable to fight on, Allan couldn't stop. For as long as she remained in the room, her son berated her meanness, told her everything he felt she should know, argued Hans' case like a young lawyer giving his summation in court.

Hans would have been proud.

OUR MOTHER WAS A GYPSY, WITH A HEART THAT WANDERED and sometimes broke. And we were the gypsy's children—who managed somehow to heal the gypsy's heart.

Soon Mom found the will to talk to her lover again. Near the Christmas holiday, Hans moved into Mother's room.

Though I can't recall how our family spent Christmas, I do remember that this was the year it rained typewriters.

Two typewriters certainly exceeded my wishes. But they helped cement my vision of myself as an author. Driven by the Klumpp stubborn streak, I used an instruction booklet and learned conventional finger placement, so before long I could type without looking at the keys.

One day I studied the two machines side by side, and decided they personified my relatives—a practical father and an extravagant grandfather. I told Mother, "Ted's typewriter is for everyday work, like book reports. I'm saving the fancy one for letters—or important stories I want to keep." *Someday*, I thought, *people will read my stories. Maybe they'll read everything I write.*

SOON AFTER CHRISTMAS, THE DRAFT BOARD FOUND HANS, long since an American citizen, and he went for a physical and reported ruefully to Mother, "I've been rated 1-A."

Mother smiled. "Oh you are, Darling. You definitely are."

He gave her a strange smile, as though he wasn't sure whether to be glad or sorry. But soon his smile was gone. Within weeks he was called up.

Early the following year, while Hans reported to the Army, Mother brought the rest of us back to the ranch, and now Allan and I returned to our old, familiar grammar school.

Our lives on the ranch took a new twist.

On the surface, everything seemed the same … yet nothing was the same. How could we return to normalcy without the man who'd been the reason for Mother's lofty aspirations? The man who'd fueled her dreams?

Even as she cared for her baby, her light spirit plummeted, as though she was existing, not living. Only occasionally did we see the gaiety that had once been a daily part of her persona.

How would she survive here without Hans?

Only years later did I learn Mother's reason for leaving him in the first place. Allan told me somberly, "Hans had an affair with one of our guests, you know. And she didn't learn about it for months."

For Mother, the blows were piling up. If she hadn't initiated the separation herself, the Army would have done it for her.

As it was, the war intervened and made her life worse.

But for Allan and me, the ranch meant a return to some kind of normalcy.

We thought it would last indefinitely. But of course it didn't.

Chapter Twenty-Four

Mt. Shasta, 1942

"Your photo album is kind of empty," Allan said one Saturday as we sat side by side in the den. He never took pictures, but once in awhile he paused to look at mine, all taken with a little box Kodak.

In the distance, as always, the mountain peered at us across the meadow, enduring and frosted white—the one thing in our lives that didn't change.

Paging through the album, Allan said, "You'd think nobody lived here but you and Mom and Hilary. I don't see Hans anywhere. And only one picture of me." He snapped the album closed.

"You're always down at Deetz's," I said. "And Hans—"

"I know. Don't say it, Sis, I know. But he's here once in awhile."

"Yes. But nobody's taking pictures. And you know how Mom is half the time."

"Always crying," he began, and stopped. "Or laughing too hard," he finished. And that ended our conversation about the photos.

Ours was once again a matriarchal family—Allan and I and Hilary sailing an isolated craft on a lonely sea, with only our mother guiding the ship.

Occasionally, when Hans came back on leave, the atmosphere became electric. "My God, he's here!" Mother screamed, and dashed out the door and flung herself in his direction.

Smiling broadly, Hans waited, then clasped her to him, pulled her against his khaki uniform. We could hear him murmuring, "Ginny … Ginny …" into her hair.

Somewhere in the distance, nearly forgotten, were the three of us, a knot of gawking children.

Those home leaves were short, too short, and afterwards they

136

left Mother bereft.

For Allan and me, there was always school, a unifying thread that wove through our lives. Only Hilary was anchorless, left to undulate as his mother did—back and forth with the tide.

I WAS ABOUT TO GRADUATE FROM EIGHTH GRADE. TO MY SUR-prise, during my hours in school, Mother made me a Swiss dirndl dress, bright and light with wide straps over the shoulders, a fluffy blouse, and a full, gathered skirt—a costume right out of Johanna Spyri's *Heidi*.

Disappointed only for a moment, because it wasn't the kind of outfit I would have chosen—too innocent, too girlish—my mother's having made it changed everything. I saw myself in the Heidi dress and knew I was too tall for a dirndl skirt, about a head too tall, but I pretended it was exactly what I wanted.

"You are a young girl," Mom cooed, tying the sash in back, "still twelve years old. This is the kind of dress a young lady your age should wear. Oh my, Maralys, you do look nice."

I never told her that no one else in our graduation would look like she'd just arrived from an Alpine village. On the other hand, how many girls would be modeling something their own mother had made?

With the dress finished, Mother and I had to find appropriate shoes. In Mt. Shasta's only shoe store, nobody could locate a girl's size nine. With averted face a clerk pretended such an item actually existed. "I'm sure they have a nine in the big city—just not here. Still, Mrs. Luginbuhl, we do have this ladies' eight. The heel is a bit high. If she pulls in her toes a little …"

Thus Mom was forced to buy a women's eight, into which I crammed my oversize extremities. "Oh, Mom," I said, "they don't fit. They hurt."

"It's only for one night," she said. "I'm sorry, dear." She stared down at my generous feet. "I haven't thought of this in ages. Your father also has your … well, your build."

For me, that was the start of a shoe problem that would go on for years.

Less important to our family, Allan also had big feet, but he seemed to love them—even later, when they grew and kept growing to a size fifteen. While he seldom had trouble finding shoes, he also acquired more than his share of laughs. "Hey, Klumpp," people asked, "how big ARE your feet?"

For the graduation ceremony, I was chosen to deliver *the Gettysburg Address*, which I suppose was an honor. The event would be held at Mount Shasta High School, where, like other bewildered students, I would deliver my bit from on high, or so it felt, because I'd be up there on the school's large, elevated stage.

Memorizing the speech was no problem. Within a few days I'd said it aloud so many times at recess that a crib sheet was no longer necessary; the words had affixed themselves to my brain. Yet one night I dreamt I was standing in front of the crowd turning red and stammering, "oh ... uh," because I'd forgotten my lines and was making a fool of myself.

That was just a dream; by day I wasn't aware of being nervous.

Then why, suddenly, did I feel ill, with an upset stomach and a sour taste in my mouth? Why was food no longer appealing? And why, at recess, did I sit on a bench by myself, wishing I could find an adult to talk to, somebody who would listen to my symptoms and not laugh?

What are my symptoms, anyway?

That was the problem—they were so vague, so inclined to come and go, that I vacillated between finding comfort in their vagueness and worrying that I might, somehow, be fatally ill. Though I didn't recognize it, this was the train trip all over again ... a secret disease that left no room to fret about the speech.

On graduation night in early June, the speech loomed large. In my cute dirndl dress, I walked out and stood behind the spotlights. At a signal from my teacher, I began.

Nobody had thought to coach me.

In one long sentence I poured out the entire *Gettysburg Address*, all without effort, pauses, or taking a breath. It never occurred to me that I was actually delivering a historic bit of oratory, that somebody out there might wish to savor a few of those famous phrases. I just opened my mouth and without conscious thought let the speech find its way out.

I doubt that anyone in the audience grasped a word.

Later, I couldn't recall even doing it. But one thing I did notice. The moment I finished, the strange sickness disappeared.

Only years later did I realize that all of life's stresses went to my stomach—for me, the one spot where an otherwise healthy body broke down.

At age thirteen I entered Mount Shasta High school, where tallness was no longer important, but being a good student was. On the first day my mother's long-ago words drifted back. "You will rise above this town. You will be a scholar, and someday people will know you." It was a nice thought while it lasted.

Of course Allan received a similar anointing; Mother declared he was one of Mt. Shasta's outstanding minds. But then, because he'd proved so mechanically adept around the ranch, she embroidered the thought by adding dramatically, "Allan, you are the reincarnation of Thomas Edison."

"I am?" Allan shook his head, confused. "I don't know what that means. But I think I'm just me."

Years later, Allan smiled as he refuted this honor, noting that Mother's pronouncement had a slight hitch. "When I was born, Thomas Edison wasn't dead yet."

Despite our mother's assurances, the gravity of being a student, and a high school student at that, began to loom large.

More than ever, my classes seemed important. Chemistry was fascinating, especially as presented by our youthful, curly-haired male teacher, Edward Graves, who laid out the chemical nomenclature in a way that made sense. Spanish provided not only new words, but glimpses into a unique culture. History took me back into centuries I'd never thought about and introduced me to people who influenced their worlds. English, especially writing essays, was just plain fun. I worked hard and reveled in being one of the top students.

Only weeks into high school, Mother and Hilary disappeared,

following Hans to his newest assignment in Oklahoma. From then on, whenever Mother faded out of our lives, we lost Hilary as well.

Alice Deetz's parents, the calm and comfortable "Mammy" plus her husband, came out to the ranch to watch over us, even drive me the seven miles to school.

It was Mammy who shook her head one day at dinner and said, "I don't know how you kids have survived—always the tail on your mother's kite." To make up for her perception of us as mother-deprived, Mammy cooked scrumptious meals, and after awhile my clothes grew tight.

Allan simply grew and grew.

Mammy was as "there" as our mother wasn't. "Tell me about school," she said as she picked us up in her modest Chevy, "what great new thing happened today?" To her, great things were always happening.

"You won't believe it," I began one day, "a girl in English wrote an essay about her job as an assistant fire spotter. She spent the summer up on Mt. Eddy, searching for smoke."

Mammy was driving, now near our house. For a few seconds she simply stared straight ahead and when she spoke, it was more to herself than Allan and me. "I wonder if anyone was there back in 1939."

"Our fire," I said, and we all fell silent.

That night at dinner I told her more. "Every twenty minutes the girl and her boss, a woman ranger, had to circle the catwalk, searching the forest through binoculars."

Mamie said, "Two women? Weren't they lonely?"

I shook my head. "She says it was the best summer she's ever spent. Summer after next, she'll do it alone."

"This I can't imagine."

"You don't know Laverne Richardson. She's the smartest girl in our class. She must love her own company."

"I've heard of her," said Mammy. "She wrote an article in the *Mount Shasta Herald.*"

Some day that'll be me writing. A little thrill went through me. *I'll be famous, like Laverne.*

Under Mammy's care Allan and I did more talking, and yes,

more eating, than at any time in our lives. She gave us some of our best, our most predictable months, a stability we craved. With Mammy we had the day-after-day sameness we'd wanted desperately but never known.

As always, that interval ended abruptly. One day Mother was back at the ranch again with Hilary, who was now cuter than ever and talking fluently. But no Hans.

"Mammy, dear," Mother said as we all converged in the kitchen, "will you watch Hilary for a little while?"

"Of course. Let's go out on the porch, honey." She leaned over to extract a chocolate cake from the ancient cast iron oven, then took our brother's hand. "We'll have a glass of milk and a slice of cake."

Allan and I could see our Mother was up to something. She was breathless and excited, the way she got when life was about to change. She took us into the living room, where we so seldom sat, I sometimes wondered why we needed that room. "Allan," she began, "for awhile now, you will live with the Deetz's."

"I will?" He looked surprised. After a long pause he said, "Oh."

Watching him, Mother waited. Allan had always been a slow talker, especially at times like this, when he required a long stretch of thinking before he spoke.

He said "Oh," again and frowned, looking off in the distance. Finally he asked, "Where at the Deetz's?" and stared at our mother. "Out in the barn—with the cows?"

She burst out laughing. "No, Silly. Your barn days are over. I've ordered an extra bunk bed, so now they'll have two in that second room. Enough beds for all four of you boys. You'll be stacked up, of course, one above the other. A regular boys' dormitory. Won't that be fun?"

"Oh," Allan said again. But I couldn't tell how he felt. Whether by temperament or a reaction to our volatile mother, Allan's emotions were often buried so deep I couldn't read them.

Allan was still lost in thought when Mom turned to me. "Honey, my sister wants you to come visit. She lives in Rochester."

"Rochester? Where's that?"

"New York," she said. "Her husband, Horace, is now a Major in the army, and Katherine—we call her Kotsie—says she's lonely, even with three little girls. She said she'd love to have you come stay with her. You can go to the Rochester High School."

With that, Allan stood and went outside, where I could see him through the window, leaning against a pine tree.

"But I like Mount Shasta High," I said.

"You'll like Rochester, too. Academically, it's one of the nation's finest schools."

"You mean it's hard."

"Well … perhaps. But you'll catch on, Maralys. I'm sure you'll do fine."

"I'm doing fine now."

"Then you'll do finer," she said, and laughed her big laugh. "Come on, honey, don't you want to be a Big City girl?" She gave me an affectionate up and down look.

"No." And that was the truth.

But I knew I was going anyway, because that's how it always turned out. With mother, her latest impulsive idea was inevitably master of our fates (even other people's fates), except now I had a term to describe it: *The tail on my mother's kite.*

A FEW DAYS LATER I STOOD IN ALLAN'S DOORWAY, WATCHING him shove a few clothes into a brown paper bag.

"Aren't you going to use a suitcase?"

He threw me a quick look. "Why should I have more clothes than the Deetzes?"

I couldn't answer that. As it was, he'd probably have to store his crumpled paper bag on the floor.

"I wish Jimmy's father was home more," Allan said. "I like him."

"I like him too." *We both need a man around—you especially.* I never prayed, but now I summoned a quick one. *Dear God, please give him a father.*

Allan tied a couple of his big shoes together by their laces, threw the shoes over his shoulder and picked up the bag. "I've gotta walk down there. Mom's too busy to take me."

"You want me to go with you?"

"Naw. Then you'd have to walk both ways." He gave me a look. "See ya, Sis."

I followed him to the porch, saw him plodding along, stirring up particles of dust. The oversize shoes flopped against his chest and the brown paper bag hung limp in his hand. Even without those shoes it was obvious he'd be taking up too much space at Deetz's.

Mom found a woman friend to drive me across the country, and suddenly, or so it seemed, I was standing at my Aunt Kotsie's door, suitcase at my feet and once more feeling lost, and not, as Mother promised, "getting used to the idea."

Just as the lost feeling reached its peak, Kotsie opened the door. "Oh, you darling girl," she cried, and swept me into her arms.

"Mammie" who took care of us on the ranch.

Mother made me this Heidi dress for my 8th grade graduation.

Chapter Twenty-Five

Rochester, New York 1943

WHO COULD HAVE PREDICTED THIS WOULD BE A YEAR TO CHER-ish?

"I'm so glad you decided to come East," my Aunt Kotsie offered after she released me. She stepped back on the flagstone porch, threw me a quick smile and picked up the small suitcase that held all my worldly possessions.

I thought, *I didn't decide anything.*

"Come on in, dear. You'll like it here, just as your mother predicted. You'll be part of our family—the Horace Ford family." She made the words sound important.

As we entered the house, I felt more than saw her facial expression, sensed deep down that her welcome was genuine. Besides, out there in front was the word that mattered most. *Family.*

Then I noticed she was limping, yet she said nothing about it. *Should I ask?*

The moment passed, my question lost in a burst of voices.

From the back of the house, others joined us in the front hall. Kotsie pointed to the oldest girl, a solemn-looking child with exuberant, curly brown hair. "Carol is nine," Kotsie said, "and Margot, here, is seven." Margot looked up and grinned through missing teeth. Her short, sleek pageboy matched her impish, guileless smile.

Behind them stood a round-cheeked woman who smiled broadly and jiggled the tiny girl riding on her ample hip. "This is Pauline," said Kotsie, "my helper and friend. And my baby, Linda, taking a free ride. Linda is only 14 months and hasn't yet decided which of us is her mother."

"Oh, go on," said Pauline good-naturedly. "The minute we're out of the kitchen, she knows." She smiled at me. "Welcome, honey.

145

Kotsie's been looking forward to this day, wishing you'd come a whole lot sooner. But now I've got cookies in the oven." She and the girls retreated.

Gesturing toward a large, formal parlor, my aunt said, "We seldom use this room, but let's get acquainted in here. We could have built this house without a parlor." She limped farther into the room, dropped onto a soft blue sofa, and patted the empty spot next to her.

Sitting beside her, I took it all in. The room was large and airy, with another, smaller blue davenport, two easy chairs in pale yellow, and a white carpet. At one end, near the fireplace, sat a big leather chair, which I decided must be used mostly by her husband, Horace Ford.

Kotsie turned to me. "Maralys, I've sensed your life has been … well, chaotic. Now that you're part of our family, you can forget all that confusion, a new school every month." She looked down at her lap, collecting her thoughts. "I know more than your mother thinks. Once in a while Grandma Alice lets it slip—that you kids have been caught up in your mother's vortex."

I nodded. *Grandma is always letting things slip.* "Mom keeps changing her mind," I began. "She's—"I broke off, unwilling to criticize my mother behind her back.

"Don't worry, honey," Kotsie said, smiling. "There's nothing you can tell me about her I don't already know. Both the good and the bad." She searched my face. "Don't misunderstand, I love your mother. As a girl she was delightful, earned nothing but praise—and deserved it." She paused, thinking back. "When we were kids, Ginny created the family excitement. She was the one who rode the fastest horse or invented the funniest game … or even drove the latest car. She inspired all of us to do things we didn't think we could do, like swim farther into the lake than any of us had gone before."

"She still does stuff like that."

"Does she?" Her expression changed. "I have to admit, as a girl I was a bit jealous. Even our Dad was under her spell." She smiled ruefully. "He couldn't help it, I suppose. In my parents' eyes I never measured up. I had polio as a child, and I was frail and much too serious. Never as funny as your mother."

"I noticed you limping."

"Well, I can walk, and that's the good thing. As a youngster I wasn't particularly strong." She smiled. "Now I am. Maybe stronger than your mother."

And maybe not, I thought. I asked, "Has Mom always jumped from one thing to another?"

"Always," she said. "Like a hummingbird. Of course when you make life entertaining, nobody minds."

"We don't mind, either, especially when she's happy." I suddenly found it hard to describe our current lives. I kept thinking about my words, wanting to be fair to my mother. "When Hans left, she was only happy sometimes—when he came home. In between she tried to work up a smile or a laugh, but mostly she read books and looked sad ... except she seemed happy while she was making my eighth-grade graduation dress." I stopped. "Well, she's with Hans now in Oklahoma—I mean, if they're still there. Seems like the army doesn't know where to put its soldiers."

"That's true for most of them," Kotsie said. "The officers not so much. My Horace—"she pointed to a stern-looking picture, "has been stationed in New Jersey for quite some time. But then he has a specific job. Ordnance."

Whatever ordnance means, I thought.

Pauline entered and sat in one of the yellow chairs, followed by two of the girls, who plopped down on the floor. With them came the tantalizing aroma of chocolate chip cookies.

"What you don't realize about your mother ..." Kotsie let the thought trail off. "She's a good person, basically. She's always been decent, maybe a tad too altruistic for her own good. On the other hand, she's always craved stimulation. If drama isn't swirling around her, ready to scoop her up, she creates it. And that's where it gets hard on you kids."

"We never minded drama. We just minded that she left us places ... but never stayed there herself."

Kotsie gave me a long abstract look, pondering. "That's exactly what I didn't want to say. Selfishness. Her underlying trait. Self-centeredness. With her, the kids .." She stopped abruptly. "Let's go have our dinner. Are we ready, Pauline?"

The other nodded and stood.

Kotsie patted my knee. "Welcome to our family, honey. You'll be good for all of us."

I wasn't so sure of that. But within a month I could see that we six would be like a sorority, except on the rare occasions when Horace came home and altered the family mood. Yet among us, no two were alike.

Pauline was nothing like my aunt. Comfortable and cheery, she was an easy laugher, with a body as unrestrained and relaxed as her personality. I soon learned that as a young girl Pauline had come from Poland and was hired at once by Kotsie, then remained with the family ever since. Pauline did most of the cleaning and cooking, but she was also Kotsie's confidante and friend. Together, and in harmony, Pauline and "Kot" ran the household.

From the first, with my three cousins all younger, I was swept into Senior Position and remained there.

Once again, Mother had accidentally chosen well, though doubtless it was only a last-minute guess. Her sister was a Godsend, better for my spirit than Mother could have imagined.

On the other hand, Rochester High was not, as Mother predicted, a challenge I could easily conquer. To a girl from Mt. Shasta it was Everest.

But then my Mother was full of predictions that didn't work out.

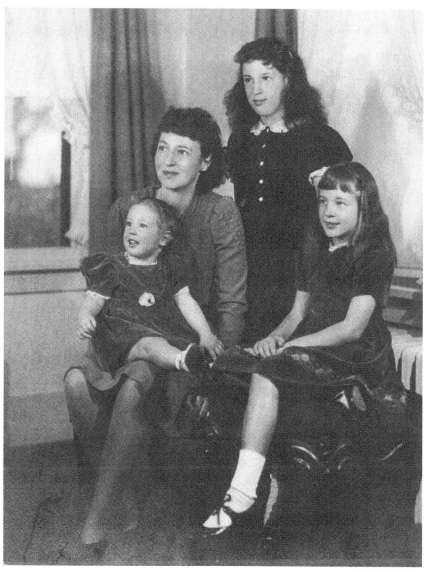

My Aunt Kotsie and daughters in Rochester.

Chapter Twenty-Six

Rochester, New York 1943

Never mind the war waging overseas, I was at war with my new high school. There I sat in the fifth row of my chemistry class, perplexed that the teacher seemed determined that I wouldn't understand a word.

I swear, the teachers at Rochester High deliberately kept their subjects dense, thicker than a Pittsburgh fog. Even as I squinted at the blackboard in Beginning Chemistry, I wondered if I'd strayed into the wrong place: *Is this high school or college?*

Whatever that chemistry teacher was trying to do, he'd left me flying blind.

Naturally, the parents revered my teacher, in fact they loved the whole school, mainly because they never had to go there.

Until then I'd thought Mount Shasta High was all the High anybody needed. Now I was fairly sure Rochester would have thought otherwise, that they would have sneered at bucolic Mount Shasta. In most of my current classes, not only could I not figure out what had gone before, the homework assignments kept piling up until they flowed over my desk like a tsunami.

After a few days I complained to my two sympathetic listeners, Kotsie and Pauline—because that's how the family was organized; whatever was to be discussed included both heads of state. For this, we all sat in the sunroom, while around us smaller children drifted in and out.

"It's unfair," I said, "so much homework. Two long chapters tonight for history, a five-page paper due in English, and seven worksheets to finish for chemistry. It's a wonder they don't want me to stand up in Spanish and deliver a twenty-minute speech."

Both Pauline and Kotsie laughed.

Encouraged, I went on. "It's a miracle the history teacher isn't demanding I give the *Gettysburg Address*."

Now they laughed harder and seemed to be hanging on my words.

"I could do it," I said. "I'm just waiting to be asked."

Still laughing, the women exchanged appreciative glances.

Suddenly my life had taken on a new dimension. From that day forward, my two-women audience was always right there in the sunroom after school, eager to be entertained, and more and more I found ways to keep them laughing. If the right events didn't land in my lap, crazy observations usually did. Or I dreamed something up.

Until then I'd never thought of myself as funny. But now that others thought so, here was a new element added to my personality—the knowledge that humor is knowing how to tell your story straight-faced ... that funny is essentially something gone wrong plus a few days. All at once my life had changed.

For hours each night a struggle took place in my upstairs bedroom: the will to conquer my courses, beset by doubts that this could ever happen. When had I ever been a failing student? How did the other kids handle all this homework?

For parts of those first weeks I ducked the homework and instead wrote in my diary. I poured out my frustrations with school, then jumped ahead and tried to imagine how I'd feel when I got really old, maybe sixty ... while only half believing time would ever move fast enough to get me there.

Alternatively I retreated into a few hours of reading, steeped in imaginary worlds that outranked the real one. When had books ever failed me?

At last I tackled an English assignment: *Describe your most frightening event.* That was easy. For a couple of hours I typed out my story of being swept out to sea ... my initial surprise, then terror. I relived every moment—the horror when I saw that land and people had become so far away I'd never get back. The despair of minutes escaping with no hope of rescue. Finally, a grim resignation that death was close and probably inevitable.

151

With that paper came an epiphany. The writing had relieved some of my pent-up anguish. Now there were two of me sharing those feelings—the real me and the me on the printed page. *If reading is an escape,* I thought, *maybe writing is another.*

I began to grasp a truth: in the midst of life's most depressing or threatening moments, it might help to retreat mentally and view the event from a distance, something soon to be described on paper. Instead of gathering emotional bruises I'd be gathering material.

I saw myself living life on two planes—the actual moment and the story version. As I began to convert real-life stress into words-on-a-page the pain would be diluted, shared equally between the real me and the anecdotal me. Since I never confided this to anyone, nobody ever whispered, "Oh, she's schizophrenic."

It was there in my Rochester bedroom that storytelling became more than a frivolity; it was a way to ease my way through life.

In my head I'd become a writer.

EVENTUALLY I TACKLED MY OTHER ASSIGNMENTS. IF HISTORY was now long and tedious, chemistry had turned impossible. Even knowing the nomenclature for all the elements helped only slightly. Someone had inserted carbon chains into our textbook and we were supposed to memorize them—or worse, understand what we were memorizing. Suddenly, in the middle of the chemistry text they'd popped in a new language—about as fathomable as Chinese.

I can't do this. I can't do this. Before my eyes the sentences and symbols all blurred, and even my Reader's Digest mother never reassured me that *yes, you can do it.*

I carried the text downstairs. "My Chemistry book was written in Shanghai," I told my aunt. "It's all symbols and no English."

"Really?" For a moment she was startled, then she smiled. "You got me, dear."

"Well, it might as well be Chinese. I've never gotten an "F" in my life, but now it's about to happen. I'm going to flunk Chemistry."

"I doubt that, honey."

"Please. Look at the book. Right here in the middle."

Kotsie glanced through a few pages. "This is rather dense. I don't comprehend a word of it."

"Why did they write something nobody can understand?"

"I'm not sure," she said. "Why did they?"

The next day she took me to see the school counselor, who ushered us into her office. Mrs. Henderson asked firmly, "What do we need to discuss?"

I explained the problem.

With a smile she leaned back in her chair. "You don't have to take chemistry as a freshman," she said. "You've transferred into one of our hardest courses ... which, in midyear, begins dipping into Organic Chemistry. I've had seniors who couldn't handle it." She glanced at my registration card. "You're new here, and a young freshman at that. Why don't we move you into something easier. Do you like to sing?"

"Oh, yes."

"Then chorus it is." She smiled, started scribbling on a paper. "You sound like an alto to me."

I didn't ask, *What's an alto?* Whatever she meant, that's what I would be. In my head I was already singing.

WITH CHEMISTRY EXCISED FROM MY COURSE LOAD, I SLOWLY emerged from Rochester High's stifling, dense atmosphere into clear air. I could fill my lungs, I could breathe again. After a month I once again became a reasonably good student. No longer straight "A"s, but good enough. Still, among the courses that remained lurked assignments so difficult I would never see their like again until college.

THROUGHOUT THAT YEAR THERE WAS NEW TALK OF RATIONING cards, then discussions about shortages: most American families would now be without enough butter, sugar, and meat.

But in our household Pauline worked some kind of magic, so we never felt deprived. As always, wonderful meals kept appearing on our table, and as a group we were anything but hungry. At a distance, the war raged on, as I would learn from occasional newspapers or the radio. But here in my Rochester home we enjoyed a great sense of peace.

From time to time I wondered about the rest of my family, and Allan especially. How was he doing at Deetz's? Had the war come to Mount Shasta?

By the end of the academic year, I felt secure and confident. Together, Kotsie and Pauline had made me feel valuable, certainly loved. Deep inside, some part of me was rescued, so the outside world no longer seemed a scary place.

As I'd been doing all along, I grew a little taller, but more than that, my inner spirit was nourished in ways that had never happened before.

When school ended in late June, Kotsie came to me with a suggestion. "How would you like to go to camp this summer? I've been reading about a wonderful place in Canada, Camp Wapomeo. Lots of lakes, forests, canoes, and games. It sounds like a spirited atmosphere." She smiled. "I'd go too, if I could."

Immediately I said, "Oh, yes," because traveling to Canada sounded like an adventure.

But the implications were greater than my simple Yes. You have to feel secure to welcome adventure.

Chapter Twenty-Seven

Canada, 1943

With a light spirit, Kotsie drove me to Camp Wapomeo in Ontario, Canada, part of the Algonquin Provincial Park. She squinted at the road ahead. "There are lots of lakes where you're going. I swear, Maralys, when I studied my Canadian map, your region especially, I was seeing more water than land."

"You told them I can swim?" Involuntarily I shuddered, tried not to let my mind drift back to the horror at Jones Beach, which I'd already described for her in harrowing detail—doubtless with more death-defying elements than the original event.

She nodded. "Swimming skills were on the application. I checked 'expert,' deciding you'd proved that nicely."

"Well at least a lake can't suck you out into a deeper lake."

Kotsie laughed. "I promise, Honey, lakes are eager to please—except when they're riled up by storms. Unlike the ocean, they're predictable. You can trust them."

We fell into silence. I'd helped her pack, and now I thought about our efforts. Deep in Kotsie's trunk was a new sleeping bag, sturdy hiking shoes (no one would know mine were sold only to boys), shorts, jeans, a few colorful shirts, bathing suits, and sweaters.

I didn't know I was missing an important piece of equipment.

When we arrived at camp, with its rustic, peak-roofed assembly buildings perched next to a sparkling lake, I watched in surprise as girls kept hopping out of their cars, only to reach back and pull out brightly decorated wooden paddles. *Do they all own canoes?* I began counting. Except for a couple of us, every girl seemed to have one, and I felt like a living cliché: Up the Creek Without a Paddle.

Kotsie regarded me with a twinkle. "I've never paddled a canoe myself, so it never occurred to me that might be part of your equipment list. Guess I didn't read it carefully enough." She looked around at the girls, all of them so fit that some were bouncing on their toes. "I think I'm turning you loose with a bunch of Amazons."

"Who all live next to a lake."

"They do seem a bit maniacal," she added in a worrisome tone. "Hope you can equal them with your swimming."

"They're probably good at that too." Around us were campers with short, no-fuss hair, perfect for water sports—but all now looking like icons on the prow of a boat. "I've never even been in a canoe."

"And I just once," she said. "The minute I stepped in, the thing tipped over. I managed to dunk three other people." She grinned. "By the time they yelled, 'Watch out!' it was too late. Need I tell you to be careful?"

"I may just skip the canoeing," I said, "and hang around camp and do whatever they do."

"Games," she said. "Contests. Just what you love. By the end of two months you'll be half Canadian."

We headed for the wooden lodge, where we studied the small metal plaque beside the door that declared, "Camp Wapomeo. Opened, 1924." This was now the summer of 1943, and I had just turned 14. I said, "This place was here way before I was born."

Kotsie winked at me. "I'll bet if you return in your sixties, it'll still be here. Canadians have a way of clinging to their traditions."

Within the hour, Kotsie and I had carried my few possessions to a small cabin with six beds, and Kotsie prepared to drive away. "I'll write," she said. "I promise. And who knows, Pauline may send cookies." With that, my alter-mother was gone—and with her one of the best years of my life.

CAMP WAPOMEO WAS MORE FUN THAN I WOULD HAVE IMAG-ined. We ate at long, unpolished tables in the wood-planked lodge, a large room with rough-beamed ceilings and a huge stone fireplace. The older girls, and I was one of them, took turns serving as waitresses, a job to be taken seriously. On the first night I learned that paper napkins were called "serviettes."

How vivid was that first night ... how I jumped when, for no apparent reason, the girls around me suddenly started pounding the table! And then they stopped and other tables took over, until the whole dining room erupted in rotating rounds of fists and thumps. And laughter. I never discovered the point, but it didn't matter, the pounding made me feel part of an elite group, a member of a strong and powerful team. Like the others I was thinking, *I love this!*

After dinner the girls sang, and I soon memorized the Canadian National Anthem.

Though discipline was loose, at times barely perceptible, the twenty-four of us caught on quickly to our leaders' expectations. Young college women, only four or five years older than we were, took us outside and led us into wild, active contests, tossing balls, running … games of deception and trickery that awarded points for excellence.

Suddenly my competitive spirit was aroused. I was determined to win one of the awards, desperate to repeat any game where I thought I might improve.

I became a whiz at dodge ball, figured out how to win at three-legged relay. Nobody could touch me in numbers of pine cones held in one hand … big hands being the consoling accompaniment to big feet. For the first week, once or twice a day we were taken down to the docked canoes, handed paddles and tip-over warnings, taught to keep the canoe within a few yards of shore.

Perhaps I would end up paddling a canoe after all.

On our first Saturday night, the boys from across Canoe Lake—male campers who attended mile-away Camp Ahmek—gathered in two 20-man canoes and paddled over for dinner and sing-alongs. Girls and boys, hesitant about mingling, were assigned to eat with one another. That night we gathered around a campfire, where we sat on logs and waited for musical cues from a guitar.

Which was when young Peter Bedford fell in love with me.

Chapter Twenty-Eight

Canada, 1943

Peter Bedford's love was not something I chose. Too short for my taste, he managed to sit next to me and didn't seem to mind that I had no trouble looking over the top of his head. Perched side-by-side on our log like birds on a wire, with the brightest stars in the world overhead, and staring into a monster fire, we sang together nicely. He was fifteen, with a voice only slightly deeper than mine. Actually, I liked hearing him sing.

But I didn't like what happened next.

Five nights later the boys came again, and one of them, not Peter, sidled up to me. "Peter has a thing about you," said Bill. "He's been stomping around our tent saying, 'Klumpp! Klumpp! Klumpp!'"

Oh, no. Immediately I felt my face burning, knew it was turning scarlet.

"He keeps us awake, pounding his feet and mumbling your name."

I could almost hear his tent-mates laughing. Embarrassment consumed me, slithered all the way to my toes. I felt like I might throw up. *Why, oh why, am I named Klumpp?*

"He probably won't talk to you. We've been giving him a hard time."

Oh, God.

The boy began to laugh. "He says he dreams about you."

It's getting worse.

The kid laughed harder. "He's a real case. You should change your name."

"I would if I could. Oh, would I ever!" I stole a look around. Peter was sitting many logs away, deliberately not looking at me.

"Well, I thought you'd ..." The boy broke off, took a long look at my face. "I guess you're not too happy hearing this."

"Happy?" I almost choked. *Happy?* "Tell him to stop. I'm not his girl friend. Now I'm not even a friend." *Besides, he's too small, practically a runt. A stamping-around runt.*

Klumpp. Klumpp. Klumpp. Indeed. The whole thing was so embarrassing I vowed never to tell anyone. And until this moment I never have.

THE RESONANT CLANGING OF A SHIP'S BELL WOKE US EACH morning. Perched high atop a tower, it began pealing at seven-thirty. We scrambled off our cots and into clothes. Breakfast in the Lodge— chunky oatmeal and fresh blueberries or strawberries—was at eight, and horseback riding, swimming, and sailing, began at 9:30.

After lunch we made woven belts, small leather purses, or lanyards for around our necks, useful for whistles or keys. We painted pictures, wrote stories (my specialty), or read books.

The schedule was so organized we were occupied every minute, leaving no time to be homesick.

Yet for the first few nights one of the girls in my cabin cried herself to sleep. The rest of us plugged our ears and tried to dream through it. Luckily, her crying soon stopped.

TWO MONTHS AT CAMP. IN RETROSPECT, IT FELT HALF THAT long.

Sometime during the second week, a package arrived from Pauline. Inside were cookies: four dozen of her wonderful, rich chocolate chips and oatmeal, plus brownies. With the other girls in my cabin I feasted, never wondering how Pauline gathered enough ration coupons for sugar and eggs, or who actually mailed the package. That day I became the go-to girl in my cabin, and felt a long-distance transmittal of the love I'd experienced in Kotsie's home.

Cookies from home; they defined the word "family." Since Mother wrote only once, I realized I didn't miss her. I missed Kotsie.

THOUGH I WOULDN'T HAVE ADMITTED THIS TO ANYONE, AFTER a few weeks I also missed Peter Bedford's presence on the singing log.

We sounded good together, me dipping into a lower third register to emulate Mom's harmonies, Peter with a nice tenor. Two or three times I glanced over at him, perched a couple of logs away, and twice I caught him eyeing me from a distance.

Once I smiled. For me, it was an invitation to come join me. He caught the smile and shook his head. He must have figured he'd already taken enough razzing from his cabin mates.

It's sad, Peter, I thought. *Except for the stomping, we might have been singing friends.*

Only later did I realize that Peter Bedford was the first male my age who ever loved me. Flattering, I suppose ... except not the way he expressed it.

WE WERE WELL INTO OUR FOURTH WEEK WHEN SOME OF US were deemed ready for a week of canoe-tripping, a journey into the wilderness that would test our survival skills.

Abruptly the day's schedule changed as preparations took over: we girls pulled out sleeping bags, jackets, our toughest jeans, an extra shirt, and rolled them into the smallest possible bundle. The counselors gathered sacks of food, emergency medical supplies, and canoe paddles, one for each girl.

Excitement vibrated the very air. The four counselors leading us—two men, two women—were animated as they worked, hurrying us up so we could leave that same day. Before noon, one of the women called the eight of us into the lodge. As she waited for us to quiet down I saw she was all dark curly hair, trim legs, and cinched-in waist.

"These are the rules," she began. "You will not, under any circumstances, leave the group." She paused to make sure we were all listening. "You will do your share of paddling and not take breaks just because you're tired. On land, you'll move ... you'll hug the trail, walk in formation, and keep up with the others." She paused again. "We'll quit each night long before dark ..." Here she finally smiled, "and we won't worry about lights out."

We girls grasped this was big, without knowing exactly How Big.

An hour later, with two campers and a counselor in each of our four canoes, we set out across our own lake. By now we'd learned how to step into a boat (carefully, and right in the middle); we knew how to paddle middle or front; we understood that the rear person had to guide the craft's direction with a half-forward, half-backward stroke, manipulating the oar according to the boat's heading.

After awhile, any one of us could have done it.

That first day we paddled across three huge lakes, and in between, we "portaged," carrying the canoes on our shoulders up and down hills. Or we lugged food, paddles, and equipment.

I soon discovered that this adventure was not for weaklings. The whole thing was exhausting. When we were in the canoes we—or at least I—soon wearied of the constant, unrelenting strokes of my paddle, of arms that felt ready to fall off. It never seemed to end. Stroke, stroke, stroke, with no time to rest.

The evergreens bordering each lake were thick and lush, and the lakes themselves seemed endless, bigger and extending into more fingers than any I'd ever seen. Beautiful, yes. Sparkling, yes. But so damn big.

As we kept stroking, I began thinking, *I don't like this. I'm tired. It's too hard.* I couldn't wait to get out of the canoe and do something else.

But then the something else turned into more work. The canoes may have been light balsa wood, but when you hoist ten feet of light, light becomes heavy. Besides the shell there were cross-bars, seats, inside slats, and they all added up.

Nobody promised we'd be on level ground, either, which we weren't. On skinny, winding paths we carried our big loads up, up, into deep woods, and then down again, and the footing was awkward and unstable and we were soon breathing noisily, like panting puppies.

Climbing a hill with half a canoe on my shoulders, I'd soon be thinking, *I can't wait to stop walking and get back in the boat.*

In every direction the scenery was postcard beautiful.

I only half noticed.

The lakes were crystalline, unspoiled.

I saw only enormous …

Some girls loved the whole experience. I loved only those moments when we stopped doing one kind of brutal exercise and just before we began another.

For a while evenings were the best part. All of us helped gather firewood, and the four counselors cooked, magically producing food that was aromatic and tasty.

Before darkness stole away our vision, each of us found a spot to lay out our sleeping bag. Every evening at dusk I searched diligently until I found a nice smooth space—only to discover during the night that I'd been jinxed. As with most other nights, my choice included an unseen rock. Or possibly several. But you couldn't re-do your nest in inky blackness, so for hours I shifted one leg or the other, or an arm, or my hips, and consequently only half-slept.

And waited anxiously for daylight.

On the rockiest nights, of course, morning took its sweet time in coming. Yet even during the day when voices and faces might have offered distraction, none of us did much talking; we were all too busy paddling or hiking or gathering wood.

The trip began to seem long.

For days we saw no other humans. Then, suddenly, out there deep in the woods, we'd find a tiny shack of a store—all crooked angles and shingles atilt. It happened twice.

Each time we abandoned our equipment and rushed into the small establishment, eager hands clutching a few dollars. We wanted to buy candy … any kind of candy, just something sweet.

Both times the store keeper—different versions of the same wrinkled, deep-woods hermit—shook his head sadly. "No candy," he said. "Haven't had any in months. There's a war on, you know."

In dismay we stared at his near-empty shelves. Around me, all the female shoulders sagged.

From under the counter he drew out a few small bags. "Got some tater chips. Bags of jerky." He pointed to a basket. "A few apples over there."

We already had apples. I, at least, felt no yearning for his old, salty chips, even less for shoe-leather jerky.

Those candy-less stores became our canoe trip's biggest disappointments. Until those two stops I hardly knew there was a conflict raging.

That was the week that World War II really hit home.

By late August it was time to leave. Kotsie came to get me, eager to hear whatever I hadn't said in my few letters.

"You liked the camp?" she asked.

"I loved it! And I've learned the Canadian National Anthem. Want to hear it?"

"Of course, dear."

So right there in the car I sang the entire song "Oh, Canada…" Nothing to it.

On a smooth stretch of road Kotsie threw me a quick smile and noted, "Honey, you really ARE half Canadian."

A little later she broached the subject I'd been expecting. Rather, dreading. "Ginny called last week. Hans is now teaching skiing to army troops in the Colorado mountains. Which explains why she found a home in South Denver. She asked if I could bring you there."

"Can you?"

"I expect you're eager to get back to your family."

I didn't have to ponder long. "I'd rather stay with you."

Kotsie shook her head sadly. "Horace will now be home oftener, more time on leave …" She let the thought trail off.

I understood. *Horace doesn't want strange kids living in his house.*

"Do I need to get on a train?"

"No, honey. I've just enough time now to drive you. That way I can visit with Ginny."

So that's how it would be. Once more I was about to trade Ford Family tranquility for Luginbuhl turmoil.

CHAPTER TWENTY-NINE

Denver, Summer 1943

KOTSIE AND I ARRIVED IN A CITY THAT SEEMED NOT TO KNOW a war was on. A high-altitude destination full of trees, Denver celebrated its verdant, late summer look. Silver maples, cottonwoods, and elms in full, bright green lined the streets and gave a pastoral flavor to residential neighborhoods. Automobiles moved slowly and so did pedestrians.

Here and there, street cars clanged in noisy abandon, but only down a few of the busiest boulevards.

I don't know what I expected; but certainly there were no signs of conflict here, any more than there'd been in Rochester.

With only slight difficulty we found Mother's home in South Denver: 2236 South Milwaukee.

Mother opened the door, stared at us, then in a tone of surprise cried, "Kotsie! Maralys!" as though she hadn't known we were coming.

"Good to see you, Maralys," she said, and gave me a warm hug and a little peck. Then she briefly clasped her sister. "Thanks, Kot, for all you've done. You stepped in at the right moment. One of my saviors." She searched her sister's face. "Was it a long trip?"

"Not for us," said Kotsie, throwing me a warm smile. "Maralys and I had lots to talk about."

And we'll always have lots to talk about, I thought.

After that, Mother led us to a generous, low-ceilinged living room and rushed off.

Our new home was modern and boxy, perhaps 2,500 square feet, but lacking mother's usual ambience: no high ceilings, no shoe-worn oak floors or polished banisters. Maybe she simply couldn't find "old" in a new part of town. She'd obviously chosen it in a hurry.

I didn't recognize the couches or chairs, and wondered where she'd found them. I would soon learn she'd rented the house furnished.

"I wonder what she's up to?" asked Kotsie.

"And Allan and Hilary—where are they?" We looked at each other and shook our heads. I suspect we were thinking alike. *The whirlwind has begun.*

And then Mother rushed in again. "Sorry," she said, breathless. "People are going to be living here. I'm making arrangements."

People? What people? I was bewildered.

"Where's Allan?" I asked. "And Hilary?"

"Oh …" she waved toward the front door. "Allan is walking Hilary home from pre-school. It's half a mile. They'll be here soon." She perched on the edge of a chair, crossed her legs and kept one leg bouncing up and down. "Maralys, tell me about your year with Kot."

My aunt and I exchanged glances. *It would take a year to tell it.*

"Well," I began, not knowing how to start. "Pauline is part of their family, and—"

"I know about Pauline," she broke in.

"And Horace was mostly not there, and—"

"I know about Horace, too. He was away in New Jersey."

Kotsie held up a hand. "Ginny, what would you like to hear?"

"Well, everything." She gave me a radiant smile, tried hard to listen. Yet her leg kept bouncing up and down. "How was Rochester High?"

"Hard," I said. "Like you predicted. Way harder than Mount Shasta. The chemistry course was a killer, full of Organic Chemistry, so hard I had to drop it. And then—"

"Really," she said distractedly. "And how are your cousins?"

"Cute," I said. "Darling girls."

"Oh, good." Suddenly the phone rang and she was up and away, darting toward the kitchen.

A long silence followed her departure.

Kotsie finally turned to me. "I think you've just told her the whole story," she said wryly.

She stood up, walked across the room and gave me a long hug. "I might as well go. Ginny has no time for us. Especially me." She paused and looked intently into my face. "I hate to leave you here. I honestly do. But Honey, I know you'll survive. You're a lot stronger now than you were."

"I guess," I mumbled. "Maybe I am." This was getting harder by the minute. "I can't ... well, I don't know how to thank you." I could sense tears coming. *Oh God, don't let me cry.* "You were ... you know how I feel, Kotsie. You and Pauline and the kids were terrific."

"It was my pleasure, Maralys. For us a wonderful year. You're like my own daughter." She hugged me again. "Write us, honey. Let us know how you are." She paused again. "We'll miss you, dear. While you were away at camp we already missed you." Turning, she quickly limped toward the door. "Tell your mother I said good-bye."

That said, Kotsie was gone. With a lump in my throat, I watched the door close.

THE DAYS THAT FOLLOWED WERE CHAOTIC.

By the time we arrived, Mother had assigned three of the five bedrooms of this latest house, leaving the fourth and fifth for me, Allan and Hilary.

One of the rooms went to Mother's newest friend, a beautiful woman named Mercedes Talliaferro. Mercedes was black. And though I wouldn't have known it because her skin was so light, she knew it. Right off, she made it clear. "I'm a Negro," she said.

I didn't know how to respond.

"Your mother is quite exceptional, giving me a place to live."

"I don't know about exceptional," I said. "She likes you, so I guess that's why you're here." I wanted to say, *You don't look like a negro,* but quickly realized the comment would come out sounding tinged with prejudice.

So why does your race matter? I wondered. Except I knew it did. We'd never had black friends before, and neither did any of Mother's acquaintances. The truth is, nobody ever spoke of this other race, as if it didn't exist.

But then I remembered an incident from long ago when we lived in Los Angeles, and I was three or four, a day I hadn't recalled in all this time. It was Mom driving me to a neighborhood I'd never seen before and taking my hand as she led me up a short walk to a shabby, unpainted house. When the front door opened I saw that the woman's face was dark. Very dark. And that she wasn't alone.

As Mother released me, I looked around in surprise; all the faces were dark.

People rushed up to clasp Mom's hand, to throw an arm across her shoulders—friends I'd never met.

Mother left, and after that these men and women took care of me. They smiled warmly and one of them said, "Come heah, Honey, come sit heah bah me," in a way I'd never heard before. Somebody even took me out driving, putt-putting down the street in an old Model-T Ford, with me beaming from behind, my upper half visible in the rumble seat. I had no opinion of where I was or how I ought to relate to any of them, except I knew they were kind … but oh, so different looking.

At the end of the day Mother picked me up again and thanked her friends, and I went back to my white-bread home. In our world of the 1930s, this was not an everyday event.

WITHIN A FEW WEEKS I BEGAN MY SECOND YEAR OF HIGH school at Denver's South High, traveling to and from school on the nearby streetcar. School left no impression, so it must have been easy. But for all the vividness lacking at school, my home life had aspects of Denver's famous amusement park—Elitch's Gardens, where something unexpected was always around the next corner.

What wasn't around the corner was Kotsie and Pauline. I missed their laughter, our afternoons on the sun porch, their avid listening. I wrote them often and Kotsie wrote back, but love in all its fullness doesn't tuck easily into an envelope.

What I had instead was a mother who listened on the fly—though more often I listened to her.

With Hans still in the Rockies teaching military skiing, we seldom saw him. Instead of a life with him, Mom became involved in politics. On numerous afternoons she drove me around to Denver's homes and businesses, lamenting the country's state of selfishness as we went. "For every person who has money to squander," she said, "a thousand don't have enough for food. I've seen it first hand. The rich don't care." She delivered her words like an actress, slowing the car because it was difficult to both pontificate and drive. *"They don't care at all!"*

The car picked up speed. "I've met someone who does care. Here, Maralys," she said as she finally parked on a business street. Handing me a flier, she gently nudged me out of the car. "Go tape this to the front door."

I could tell the sheet had something to do with a man of Mom's choosing running for office, but for me, at fourteen, it was little more than a picture followed by words without a lot of meaning. I was simply Mom's legs.

Eventually I gathered that Mother was campaigning for a Democrat named James Marsh, running for the Senate against a Republican, Eugene Miliken. In time I would learn that she'd joined a group called National Council for American-Soviet Friendship.

I doubt that she shared any of this with her father; Russell was so steeped in the opposing philosophy he would have harangued her without mercy. Even as she spoke up for the poor and voiceless and joined organizations she saw as carrying the underdog's torch, Mother recklessly flirted with a powerful man's revenge. Had he known, Russell would have done more than yell; he'd have cut off all her money.

Later, when the Council was relentlessly investigated by Joe McCarthy ... and its members, including famous movie stars, were called enemies of the United States, Mother protested to friends, "I was never a Communist."

OUR HOME BEGAN TO CHANGE IN ODD WAYS. ONE DAY AS I entered the kitchen I saw four wrinkled Oriental men and women sitting at a table in the far corner. Each had a bowl in front of him and, with heads bent over their food, they were using chopsticks to shovel grains of rice into their mouths. I was awestruck by their skill ... at how the rice flowed in a continuous stream from bowl to mouth, as though on an invisible conveyor belt. Nobody I'd ever seen ate like that.

"Where did they come from?" I asked Mother.

"They're Japanese," she said, "from California. They were being sent to special relocation camps. I've rescued a few of them—said they could live here instead."

From then on, the group ate in our kitchen and slept in one of the bedrooms. With impenetrable language barriers between us, I was never able to speak to them. They were just "there," the four of them ghosting around the house, scarcely speaking even to each other, but at meal times filling that one corner of the kitchen with their rice bowls and their gentle slurping.

As for Hilary and Allan and me, once we grew accustomed to the Asians' presence, our lives continued as before, as though these strangers were part of the furniture.

Like children who grow up with abusive parents, imagining that their traumas at home are duplicated elsewhere, Allan and I only dimly recognized that our mother and the home life she'd created did not fit any recognized norms.

When our friends came over, Mother was invariably cordial. "What is your name, dear?" she would ask, and with a polite nod add, "How nice that you could come over to play." Yet she was quickly gone again, and the moment was overlaid with an otherworldly aspect, as though she had just dropped by in her own living room, always on her way to someplace else.

During our visits with friends, Allan and I never felt compelled to explain why various people of other races occasionally wandered across our home landscape.

Wasn't this how everyone lived?

At these ages we were seldom together.

Hans, doing what he does best.

CHAPTER THIRTY

Denver, 1943-1944

THAT YEAR IN DENVER THE KISSING PARTIES BEGAN. A SMALL group of high school friends appeared early on Saturday evenings to sit on our back porch and play "Spin the Bottle." Mother either didn't notice or didn't care. During the height of those games she was not to be seen. But that spinning bottle ... and those quick, furtive kisses ...

To a girl who'd never kissed a boy, the game was so delicious it bordered on wicked. I gasped when the bottle pointed at me, felt a lovely shock rippling through me as a boy leaned in to touch his lips to mine. In bed later, I could hardly sleep ... and when I eventually dozed off, my dreams were full of tingling moments—and yes! my sense of them in places beyond my lips.

From one of those games came my first boyfriend, a bright and supremely confident young man named David, who walked me to the streetcar and actually held my hand. As though it belonged to someone else, my arm tingled all the way to my shoulder, and when I sat on the wooden seat beside him I was in a rare state, floating in hand-holding heaven. Surely everyone could see I was much older than fourteen.

David's manner was so bold, so take-charge, he made me weak. After school he often stopped by our house, the only boy I knew who could talk to a girl without becoming a blithering bundle of nerves.

One Saturday David said mysteriously, "Come to my house, Maralys, I've got something special to show you."

Once there, he seemed to emanate little sparks as he rushed me up the stairs to his Private Place, which turned out to be the attic. Down on the floor, partially blocking my view, he did a quick assembly, then, in a virtual Ta Da! he revealed a long and beautiful electric train. Together we sat on the floor and watched as the various cars slowly circled through a complex series of tracks.

I thought, *Oh ... this is it?*

I'd secretly imagined something better. Perhaps we'd read together from an exciting book. Or we'd sit close as we played Monopoly.

Or we'd kiss.

Nothing like that happened. Mesmerized by the little community he'd created with its tiny figures and one moving part, David was so absorbed by the wonder of it all that he abruptly ran out of conversation. Meanwhile, the train went in circles ... over ... and ... over.

Pretending an equal interest, I sat beside David for a while in bored silence.

After the engine's fifth cycle, I knew I'd seen its entire repertoire, which held no promise of future excitement. A crash would have been nice. Maybe the engine jumping the track and skittering across the wooden floor. Or one of his little people getting run over.

As it was, I felt the need to stretch, then fight back a yawn.

Finally I asked innocently and without thinking (beyond hoping to make his visits to my home more entertaining), "David, are you ever bored when you come to my house?" My exact words, I'm afraid.

"What!" he cried. He jumped to his feet and loomed over me, staring down ... and even his brown hair seemed to bristle.

I tried to backpedal. "I didn't mean that the way it sounded. I just meant ... I was just wondering ... " I stood and backed away. He was one boy-sized monument to fury.

His face turned red. "I know what you meant. I know *exactly* what you meant."

"But really, David, it wasn't what you think." *I guess it was what you think.*

"Get out!" he shouted.

"But ... But I didn't mean anything, David, I mean I'm not bored—"

He pointed with a resolute finger. "Leave!"

"Please let me explain …"

"Now! Get out!" Hands on hips, he stared me back toward the wall, then around a bend toward the stairs.

I scuttled down the stairway and sailed out of his house. I feared we were finished.

Well, we were. David never spoke to me again.

I've since wondered if David ever married—and if so, did he honeymoon on Amtrak?

THOUGH I WAS FOURTEEN AND PARTIALLY RAISED ON A RANCH where animals in the meadow leaped on each other immodestly in full view of everyone, there was much about human procreation I didn't know. Whatever salacious rumors might have been circulating out there among my friends, none ever reached me.

And then one day Mom's lovely friend, Mercedes Taliaferro, barely thirty, took me aside and sat me down in a corner of the living room and explained the mechanics of sex.

I stared at her, wide-eyed. "Really?" Her explanation was beyond belief. "How do you know? Is that what really happens? Oh, ugh."

"That's what happens, dear. It's really pretty nice."

"Nice? Oooh … how could that be nice?"

She smiled a secret smile. "Someday you'll know."

Not me. I'll never do that. I made a face.

"Don't be so quick to judge," she said.

But here was a topic that invited an instant opinion. How could you not judge? Besides, it was all so … well, nasty.

The knowledge simmered in my vast system of disbeliefs and for a long time remained mysterious and repugnant. How could people actually do *that?*

ALLAN AND I WERE TOGETHER AGAIN, YET MOSTLY WE WEREN'T. We kept different hours, played with different friends, went to different schools. He was at Grant Junior High, and I was a Sophomore at South High.

Now that I'd hit my teens the two years between us seemed wider and our differences sharper. He drifted in and out of my view, and these days we seldom played together.

As for Hilary, at only four, he occupied a whole different universe. But at least we all shared the same house.

COMPARED TO ROCHESTER HIGH, DENVER'S SOUTH HIGH WAS easy. But that excepts my class in French.

Our instructor was a French woman who guided us through her native language with a heavy accent and dramatic overtones. She cared about us and despaired when we couldn't hear the difference between "eiu" and "oui".

Yet whenever she lit on a certain topic, she became a woman possessed. With intense black eyes, gesticulating hands, and a theatrical voice, Mrs. Odette Combs made her classroom a stage as she tried to tell us, yet not tell us, a secret she knew about the war.

"I cannot say zis," she cried one day, "except in Europe something beeg will soon happen! Zumzing nobody dares to talk about … a great event, not revealed to anyone. Yet I know, because I have friends there. They tell me these things. *Il est vraimont!* All true!"

Her excitement was so intense all of us felt inexorably drawn in.

Even as she tried to teach us the language, (in my case, not very successfully), Mrs. Combs could not hold back frequent references to the war secret she knew but couldn't reveal. Right in the middle of a lesson she'd stop to wave her hands and exclaim, "Zees beeg happening … Mon Dieu! Today I hear about it again, on short-wave radio. From my friends. You will know soon. Zis month! Mr. Roosevelt knows already."

With difficulty, she'd get herself under control and go on.

The effect on us was palpable. We felt as though we were on the European front ourselves, on the verge of having war secrets whispered into our ears by Eisenhower. Each new class with her was a singular adventure, accompanied by the wild hope that one day she'd forget herself and spill the secret that consumed her.

Just before school let out in June, we found out what she meant. That morning of June 6 she stood before the class, waved her arms, and shouted "D-DAY!" Her eyes were alive and she was laughing and talking all at the same time. "Zee landing at Normandy! My friends … zay live near the beaches. They've heard the talk, always in whispers. They've seen the guns. Zat's how I know!" She clapped her hands.

Clearly she'd been privy to a host of Allied secrets. "Eees called D-Day!" she repeated. "I heard it. I knew it! For months I knew!" Her black eyes gleamed with suddenly-released excitement. She could hardly collect herself to continue our studies. "So now you know too!"

So now we certainly did.

As Odette Combs had promised, it was very beeg.

For Allan and me, Denver's South High remained a school of modest neighborhoods and clanking streetcars, while inside our house Mother had created her own miniature United Nations.

Occasionally she'd disappear for a few days to visit Hans, leaving her friend Mercedes Taliaferro in charge. We all assumed Mother was happy; at least she wasn't crying.

Happy or not, in late June of 1944, at the end of our school year, Mother made a decision that would affect us all. "You kids," she said, "are going back to Mount Shasta."

Allan asked in surprise, "We are?" His face changed as he thought it over. In his slow and solemn way he said, "I like it there. I like having us all together on the ranch."

Caught off guard, Mother paused to look at him, then slowly she shook her head. "Honey, we won't be together." She said it sadly. "I'm dropping you off."

"On the ranch?" I asked, hoping she'd once again enlisted Mammy.

She must have read my mind. "I'm afraid Mammy is too sick now to help out. Since we saw her last she's had a heart attack. I've had to make other arrangements."

Allan and I exchanged quick glances. Neither of us felt like asking what those other arrangements might be.

Within the week she had loaded the two of us and Hilary in the car and, as we looked out the window, Denver dissolved before our eyes like a fadeout on a movie screen.

And then, rather more rapidly than we might have imagined, came the Fade-in once more, back to our familiar town at the foot of our familiar mountain. Except this time, mother made a few comments that gave her away.

She hadn't exactly cemented the family, taking us back to our former home. As Allan and I suddenly realized, he and I would no longer be living together.

CHAPTER THIRTY-ONE

Mt. Shasta, Fall 1944

TO OUR MOTHER, ALLAN AND I MUST HAVE BEEN LIKE SUITCAS-es you can't keep carrying indefinitely. Eventually you simply must put them down.

Whether she needed to be free to jump in a car with Hilary and follow Hans to another state, or merely free to make passionate love when he was able to come home, our presence in the South Denver home must have become inconvenient. As luggage we'd grown too heavy.

I sensed she wanted us safely stashed back in Mount Shasta, a place we all knew. But at least for this move she'd waited until the school year was over.

As we arrived in town, with our ranch tantalizingly close but unoccupied, she'd obviously run out of people she could wheedle into living there as substitute parents. Always a problem-solver, and charming when her private candles were lit from within, Mother kept her machinations outside our hearing. Allan and I never heard her beguile people into altering their lives—never saw the process as they wrenched their roots out of the ground and came to wherever she beckoned; we just saw the beckonees after they arrived.

Perhaps it was just the times, when parents didn't pretend to be their children's buddies, but instead made decisions for their offspring without calling a Democratic Family Council.

While Mom never bothered with the small details of our lives … Allan and I knew we had to wake ourselves up, scrounge breakfast, pack our lunches, and walk to school (and also entertain ourselves *after* school)—on the bigger decisions Mother flew solo.

Within a few days she'd arranged for Allan to board at the Deetz's, whereas I was to be dropped off in an area I scarcely knew, to live with a woman I'd never met.

Marie Stanley was a working woman—an administrative secretary who rented an apartment somewhere behind the main street that ran through the town of Mt. Shasta.

She was probably a friend of a friend, and doing my mother a huge favor, yet with a personality our family would have called stiff and inflexible (flexibility being essential in all dealings with Mother). It was hard to imagine her as part of anyone's bizarre plans.

Yet there she was, pulled into my life as a substitute parent, an amazing feat. It seemed that Mom was able to manipulate even the Barely Willing.

My first view of Marie Stanley was not encouraging. Mother and I waited on her doorstep, I with a typewriter, Mother with a suitcase, until finally after a long minute Marie Stanley answered Mother's knock—and then only with a quick backwards step and the coolest of smiles. She reached up to tuck a strand of taffy-colored hair behind her ear. "Yes?" she said.

"Here's my daughter, Maralys," Mom said, "she's been dying … looking forward to meeting you."

I threw Mom a quick look, relieved that she'd changed an obvious lie into half a lie.

"Oh. Of course," Mrs. Stanley said, and only then thought to gesture us into the room. She had one of those all-business faces, not irritable, but not overtly friendly either. As I walked in, she looked me over diagnostically, and it felt like Mom was presenting me as a new maid.

I'd never been appraised before with such a lack of emotion.

As we all searched for seats, Mother gripped my one suitcase as though unable to let go—but at last realized she had it, and parked it next to an overstuffed chair, then quickly sat there herself.

For what seemed an eternity we looked past each other without speaking.

"Have you discussed what she should call me?" Mrs. Stanley finally asked, as though I wasn't there.

"Well … no." Mom looked confused. "It's never come up."

"I was thinking Mrs. Stanley, which is how I'm addressed at work. But then, since I'll see her every day, perhaps Marie would be better."

"Honey, would you like to call her Marie?" Mother asked, as though giving me a choice, but more because she couldn't think how to respond.

I shrugged. "I ... well, if that's what she wants." *To me she feels more like a 'Mrs. Stanley.'*

It occurred to me that the two of us had yet to say one word to each other.

"I'm fifteen," I said abruptly, deciding to look her in the eye, "and when I go to Mt. Shasta High I'll be a Junior, and I like to write and I've got my own typewriter and I write all the time ..." I'd run out of breath. Still, I wouldn't release her gaze. "Where do you work, Marie?"

Her face finally softened, though her voice was still crisp. "Just downtown, a few blocks away. I'm prepared to drop you off at school. If that's what you'd like," she added.

I nodded, and a long silence followed.

"I guess I'll just go," said Mom, visibly relieved.

Now that she'd finished with me, her second and last chore, Mother disappeared, leaving me unsure of where, exactly, she'd gone ... besides the fact she was nowhere to be seen in Mount Shasta. Had she been a different sort of person, she might have left a trail of letters; I cannot recall receiving even one.

With Mom gone, I looked around, fighting feelings of being lost, a stranger in a strange land. Why was I here, anyway, and for how many months? Like a rowboat that's come loose from its mooring, I'd once more drifted away from my family and into deep ocean.

Making an effort, I forced myself to see what I was seeing.

The apartment was what some might call realtor-ready (all surfaces cleared), with so little color I thought of it as having no color at all.

Marie led me to the back, where I had my own small bedroom and desk. I would soon learn that Marie didn't mind my hanging up pictures of Mom, Allan, and Hilary. Outside my window a dry-cleaner's sign was perfectly framed—ironical, I thought; those of us who lived square at the foot of the mountain couldn't see it. Still, I liked knowing it was there.

When I went to bed that night, I felt both abandoned and angry. *You wouldn't want to be here, Mom. Why have you done this to me?* I wondered where she'd gone … and how she'd come off if I wrote the story. *You won't look good.*

The next day my natural optimism surfaced. I awoke thinking, *I'll have to make Marie my friend.*

At breakfast she said, "I've got a few house rules, Maralys, so we should get them established." She paused, lowered her rimless glasses. "Do you have a boyfriend?"

"No." *How could I? I've only been in town one day.*

"If a boy asks you for a date, you must be home by 10:30. I can't wait up past 11:00."

I nodded. *I'd love to have that problem.*

"You must help with the dishes—and sometimes the cooking, too."

"All right."

She consulted a list. "Don't leave your towel on the bathroom floor."

"I won't."

"Be quiet on Saturday and Sunday mornings. I don't sleep well most nights, so sometimes I catch up on weekends."

"My mom doesn't sleep well, either. I'm used to being quiet. I read a lot."

"We may get along fine, then," she said without smiling.

And then abruptly she asked, "What are your plans, Maralys? How do you expect to spend your weekends?" With an intent look, she again studied me through her glasses.

"Weekends?" I was baffled. *How do I know what I'll be doing weekends?* "Well, I …" This was a topic I'd never encountered before, nor frankly even considered. Until now, weekends did their own thing; they simply crept up on me and *happened*. Having no answer, I found my gaze sweeping the apartment. *Maybe I'll sit in the living room.* A stupid thought. *I had no plans to be here, either.*

I shrugged. "What do *you* do on weekends? I'll do whatever you're doing." Before she could answer, I asked, "Do you ever go to movies?"

"All the time."

"Can I go with you?"

"Of course, Maralys. I expect you to go."

After that, she gave up on Weekend Advance Planning. Yet I discovered new House Rules she'd never mentioned. Marie Stanley did not like bright lights. As fast as I turned them on at night, she flicked them off, and I found myself sitting under a single light bulb, gazing into a room that was dark everywhere else. She didn't like the telephone, either, so most of the time she simply let it ring. Curiosity would have killed me … but not her.

LIKE THE NUNS WHO LONG AGO WATCHED OVER ME IN THE Catholic Boarding school (now forgotten by everyone but me), Marie started off as decent but distant, not the kind of person Virginia Luginbuhl would have chosen as her own companion.

However, Mother wasn't living with her; I was. Lacking the warmth of either Mamie or Kotsie, Marie was so naturally cool I had to work to make her smile. Yet somehow I didn't mind; I sensed a vulnerability in her, a need for my companionship, so that eliciting a smile became an interesting challenge. Softened with a smile, her stern features became more attractive.

Before long we found ourselves sitting together in the small dinette, chatting companionably over sandwiches, or sharing store-bought spaghetti (she cooked only slightly more than Mother), with Marie asking as she heated it on the stove, "Did you hear the latest with the Bartolini family?"

"No, what?" I knew they had several kids and lived in the Italian community south of town.

"They may be Wops," she said, "but the oldest son just got accepted to Cal Berkeley. He's leaving next week."

"The Bartolinis aren't Wops," I said quickly, not sure what the term meant, only that it sounded derogatory. "The youngest girl, Julia, used to be one of my best friends."

"Don't take it personally," she said, and brought dishes of steaming spaghetti and sat down across from me. "Wop is just an expression. I didn't mean anything by it."

It sounds like you did.

"Well, if he can go to Berkeley, so can you." She picked up a fork and began eating. "The town thinks the Bartoloni kid is a genius, and maybe he is. Imagine! His getting accepted at Berkeley, from this wide place in the road."

I gave her an evil smile. "When my brother and I go to Berkeley, we'll tell everyone we're from Mt. Shasta."

Within a few weeks Marie had become less a disciplinarian and more like a sorority sister, sharing the stories she heard at work. Eventually we did a lot of sisterly chatting, and never again did she use the term "wop."

SOON I WAS BACK IN MT. SHASTA HIGH, AND ONCE MORE AT the top of my class. As in my other schools the teachers required homework, but an amount you could accomplish without ulcers.

That fall the school put on a war play, for which I tried out and won the leading role. I was so surprised I said, "You mean me?" and one of the faculty said, "You're so nice and tall," and another said, "We think you have the right personality."

I wanted to jump up and hug someone, but held on to myself. "Thank you," I said. *Oh, my God, tall is finally paying off!*

I was to be a WAC—one of those soldiers distinguished mainly by a khaki skirt—a woman who is funny and then falls in love with a Corporal, whom I actually kissed on stage.

Chuck, the boy they chose as my love-interest was good enough looking—any girl would have thought so—with thick curly hair, moony eyes, and full lips. But understandably he hadn't auditioned for kissing, meaning that only I knew about his fatal flaw; like Clark Gable, he had horrible bad breath. The odor at kissing distance would have repelled the most determined insect.

During our clinches on stage I was so focused on trying to hold my breath, or at least taking in the least amount of air possible, that my womanly desire for this soldier must have come off as thin to nonexistent.

The play was supposed to be a comedy. The first time through, we six actors kept blowing our lines because we'd come across a bit of carefully-crafted dialogue that was so hilarious we couldn't stop laughing. The best parts could have been written by Neil Simon.

After a few rehearsals the comic aspects began to wear thin, until by dress-rehearsal a month later, we wondered what we'd ever seen in those lines—which now struck us as mostly dull and not the slightest bit humorous.

The night of our performance everything changed. To our amazement, the audience reacted as we had during our first reading. They laughed so hard we had to hold back before delivering certain lines, and we all felt like stand-up comics, the hilarious darlings of the Mount Shasta stage.

In later weeks, Chuck shyly invited me to be his girlfriend. "Surely, Maralys, you'd like to go to the movies," he said, treating me to his doe-eyed gaze, while a familiar vapor escaped and wafted my way.

Driven to fan my face, I forced a smile and edged back. "I'm sorry, Chuck, I ... well, I've got too much homework. I can't." Our stage encounters had disqualified him. You can't spend up-close time with someone whose breath requires an air freshener.

My junior year in Mount Shasta was distinguished by three phases, which in retrospect seem mutually exclusive, and possibly remembered in the wrong order.

Most surprising was my dressing up in high heels and a flattering dress and being dropped off by Marie at the Junior Prom. Since I was well-known at school and had meanwhile learned to dance, I was comfortable with showing up, all smiles. I knew I'd have a great time.

Having gone without a date, I quickly found myself alone and leaning against a wall ... for what felt like a week. In that large gymnasium, I was basically alone. No one shared my wall, and I was never asked to dance.

Not once.

I forced a smile, gazed absently at the dancers, studied my bright red fingernails, and pretended I didn't care.

But I did care—right down to the tips of my strappy pumps. Other girls were dancing and I wasn't. Other girls were popular and ... it was agony. The term wallflower took on new meaning: you feel as though you're literally painted on the wall.

Never mind that my high heels had made me the tallest girl in the room.

Nobody else would have stayed the entire evening, and I wouldn't have, either, except for the stubborn streak that sometimes invades my personality and refuses to leave ... *Surely, surely, I kept thinking, someone will ask me to dance.*

The mortification of the event lingered for years: the sense of finding oneself, even for such a brief period, so thoroughly rejected. I could almost feel the scar left on my ego.

Yet my Reader's Digest Mother said, *This will never happen again. You'll make sure it doesn't.*

And it never did.

AFTER THAT, THE SCHOOL YEAR BECAME EVEN STRANGER, though in ways that had nothing to do with dancing. Mother could not have predicted the myriad events that a vulnerable girl with no visible parents can get sucked into ... including a lifestyle she would have hooted right out the door.

CHAPTER THIRTY-TWO

Mt. Shasta, Spring 1945

I NEVER SAW IT COMING.

The next phase of the Mount Shasta saga was so antithetical to my earlier experiences, it's hard to imagine they occurred within the same school year.

With Chuck's advances repelled but not replaced, my days at school became ordinary. But soon they weren't. Marie was concerned that I was now dateless, and decided I ought to meet a male relative who lived in Weed. With that, she introduced me to her young nephew, Archie Stanley. The distance between cities was ten miles, but Marie, or sometimes her sister-in-law, was willing to make the drive.

Quicker than I would have guessed, Archie and I became a couple.

Archie Stanley had a light and agreeable personality, a kind of Alfred E. Neuman look, with tawny, fly-away hair and a fetching grin. He was instantly attracted to me; I was instantly attracted to his uncomplicated devotion. "When we're married ..." he murmured from time to time.

Though I couldn't picture myself spending a lifetime in Weed as Archie Stanley's wife, there was a certain leftover desperation inherent in having been such a recent, flaming social disaster.

Perhaps marriage to Archie wouldn't be so bad, I found myself thinking. *Especially if I'm stuck up here away from everywhere.* In Archie's company the world narrowed to the bucolic pleasures of small-town living and a circle of friends whose intellectual growth would doubtless not expand beyond high school.

Thanks to Mother I'd become adaptable; no longer imbued with her affirmations about "rising above this town" I took what I saw around me as the limit to my possibilities. If your world is small you begin to think small.

For awhile it was easy to understand how prisoners adapt to prison … even more, how citizens of certain countries, like China and Russia, conform to the everyday indignities of a totalitarian regime.

BECAUSE OF ARCHIE'S MOTHER, MY WORLD CHANGED EVEN FURther. A big, smiling tank of a woman, Mrs. Stanley rolled into view, deciding it was time to introduce me to the realities of eternal life.

"If you and Archie hope to find happiness in the hereafter," she declared one day, "you need to come to God." Unable to persuade Archie to accompany her and save his soul, she worked on me instead.

Driven there by Mrs. Stanley, I began spending Sundays in the town of Dunsmuir, where we attended a small but spectacular hillside church—a haven for Holy Rollers and parishioners who spoke in tongues.

At first I was merely baffled and emotionally distanced by what I saw around me. Kneeling on the floor among hard wooden pews, I heard fervent praying. Tears. Words spoken aloud in languages so foreign they were incomprehensible.

As I peeked through supposedly-closed eyes, I saw people in front of me waving their arms above their heads as they shouted "Amen!" and "Halleluiah!" This was nothing if not an out-loud kind of church.

Since theirs didn't resemble any behavior I'd ever seen before, I began to envision them as part of a story. Did Dunsmuir even know about its freaks on the hill? The shouters? The kneelers? The buckets of tears?

How about my mom's friends? What would they think? I couldn't wait to run this scenario past my mother.

Week after week, following his impassioned lectures (with each phrase punctuated by fervent cries of "Amen!"), the pastor implored us to come forward, to kneel before him and be "Saved."

For a long while I resisted. Yet the message was slowly seeping inside. Did I really want to end up in an eternal hell?

Eventually, feeling a pull as strong as an undertow, I crept down the aisle—to kneel and be blessed with the pastor's hands-on-head, to declare my allegiance to Jesus, and thus to be "saved."

Immediately, and perhaps not so strangely, I did feel a new peace, with the threat of death suddenly removed, along with fears of what eternity might hold. It was a joyful experience.

Yet I still looked askance at my fellow churchgoers who were driven to keen and wail ... and I regarded as curiosities those who had apparently found a new language in which to cry out their allegiance to God. Was this really a sacred dialect delivered from Biblical times, or merely the outpourings of a self-inflicted trance?

As a new convert, I took to heart the church's other dictates—that dancing and movies were earthly sins to be assiduously avoided, lest they undo that new, fear-free "saved" condition. For the rest of my stay in Mount Shasta I eschewed all temptation.

"You won't go to the movies with me?" Marie asked plaintively one afternoon.

"Oh, Marie. It's a ... well, it's a sin."

She shook her head and muttered under her breath, "Archie's mother... shouldn't have let you meet her."

Instead, when she wasn't around, Archie and I merely snuck away to exchange kisses in his bedroom or mine, where presumably no one was looking. "You know we'll be married someday," he said dreamily, and I nodded. Of the two of us, only I struggled to believe I was actually in love.

When Mother finally arrived in Mount Shasta, she found her two children living in wholly different environments: Allan had become a farm boy, helping with the very earthy chores of a dirt-poor existence, which included hearty guffaws over farts, belches, and animal propagation ... whereas I now existed in a deeply spiritual world that scorned everything Mother stood for—while imagining I would soon settle for a dubious marriage.

Which is what you get when you dump your children with people you don't know well or in situations you can't control.

My boyfriend, Archie, in his hometown of Weed.

CHAPTER THIRTY-THREE

Denver, 1945

WITH NEARLY DESPERATE SPEED, MOTHER GATHERED US UP and prepared to whisk Allan and me away from Mount Shasta, leaving us scant time for good-byes. While Archie and Marie stood at her front door, waving, Mom quickly backed down her short driveway. From a distance I waved in return and yelled out the window, "I'll write! Soon!"

I suspect Mother now regretted her decision to leave us there, wholly beyond her influence. We may not have subscribed to her ever-changing kaleidoscope of homes and communities, but now neither of us bought into her quiet, understated tolerance for all human behavior.

As we drove toward Denver, I felt aloof when Mom spoke of recent movies. I vowed I'd never go to another dance. No soul-damaging events for me!

Mother could not have known she was chauffeuring a child who, like the Puritans, saw sin in the most innocuous pursuits, and all because a Holy Roller preacher said so. In an earlier age he might have convinced me women could be witches.

Sitting beside her, I nursed my private thoughts. *I used to worry about my health; now I've taken charge of my soul.*

As for Allan, he'd become so quiet he was almost catatonic. We were nothing if not a couple of silent rebels.

WE ARRIVED IN DENVER TO A BLEAK SITUATION. TO ALLAN'S and my surprise, Mother no longer had a home. Instead she picked up Hilary from a babysitter and installed the four of us in a motel.

With her usual dearth of explanations, Mother implied that motel living was to be our new norm. "And now that we're here,

Maralys, I want you to get a summer job."

"Working where?" I asked. "Why would anyone want me?" I looked out the motel window and saw nothing but a single tree and another motel across the street. The four of us were confined to two bedrooms, and now Mom was acting as though our living here would be permanent. The overstuffed chairs emanated a lingering aroma of Lucky Strikes, but worse was the overlay of Evening in Paris perfume, which I'd sniffed once without enthusiasm at the dime store. I felt like we were displaced persons. The newly rootless.

A familiar queasy feeling began to form in my gut. How well I remembered the sensation, a stomach-deep insecurity that visited often in the days before Mt. Shasta.

In dreams, the best parts of my life came back—how we'd once had a home on a ranch. A home and a family, five of us, plus land. In every direction, land that we owned.

Ever since the fire, Allan and I had been on a slow, downward slide. Except for one brief year in South Denver, (and yes, my fresh-man year with Aunt Kotsie), we'd lived in a boarding house or we'd lived separately, neither of us with a home, neither staying with any-one connected to us by blood.

Often, in the middle of the night, I woke to a sensation that we'd become wanderers, a family without foundations—four vagrants momentarily confined to two rooms.

Those summer months became a nadir, the lowest point I could reach.

Yet still Mother insisted that I go seek outside work. "I'm sure you can find something," she said.

"But I'm only sixteen."

"Lots of sixteen-year-olds work."

"Where, Mom? Where?"

"Dear, I really don't know. But you can figure it out. You don't want to hang around here all day."

I thought, *I don't want to hang around here at all.*

In a glance I took in the motel room. Our walk-around space confined to the distance between Allan's bed and mine. And then over to the bureau.

Mother had found us a prison.

"I'll get a job," I said.

CHAPTER THIRTY-FOUR

Denver, 1945

DOWNTOWN, TRAVELING BY STREETCAR, I FOUND A RESTAU-rant with a "Help Wanted" sign in the window. "I've come for the waitress job," I told the manager.

She looked me over. I was taller than she was. "Can you start tomorrow morning?"

"Whenever the streetcars run."

"Oh dear. The first one doesn't arrive until about eight. We need someone to start at seven."

She fell into protracted silence. "You don't drive?"

I shook my head. *If I had a car I wouldn't need a job.*

"All right, then, be here at eight."

And thus, traveling by streetcar and wearing a pink, striped apron, I became a very bad waitress.

MY HEART WAS NEVER IN IT. I DIDN'T PAY ENOUGH ATTENTION to what my customers ordered. I was haphazard. I never figured out that the manager had actually done me a favor.

Deep in my private self-evaluation was a return of the snob that mother had long ago created. "You will rise above this town. You will be somebody." Though Mom's sympathies were all with the down-trodden, with the common man, she never saw her children becoming one of them. To her, we'd never been common children.

So why should I work at being a good waitress?

Within a few weeks of motel living, something about our non-home made me sick. I ran a low-grade fever. I was actually demon-strably ill. "I'm taking you to a doctor," Mother said with grim deter-mination, but he could find nothing wrong.

I returned to work and for a week continued to be a feverish, but ever more indolent waitress.

Finally I became sick enough that I couldn't move well among the tables. The manager noticed. "Maralys," she said one day, "you look ill. I think you need to stay home."

"I do have a fever." Reaching behind me, I untied the striped apron. "Thank you for giving me a try."

I'd lasted a whole four weeks.

Back in the motel again, I went to bed and stayed there. At least in bed there was no sense of the walls encroaching on the room, no further need for more space. Dimly aware that family members wandered in and out, I lay in bed wondering what was wrong with me.

AND THEN, ABRUPTLY, WITH NO SOUND OF TRUMPETS, MOM changed all this. She drove the three of us through a dignified part of town and up to a curb and parked. Off to one side was a huge house, but what I saw first was a two-story, brass-handled front door, big enough to claim the word Palace.

Mother asked, "What do you think, kids?"

"What are we supposed to think, Mom?"

"I've bought this house."

"Are you fooling us? Really?"

She said nothing, merely smiled.

Allan and I gaped and Hilary giggled. This time the home was vintage Mother. It was an enormous wedding-cake of a place that rose up and up, layer after elegant layer.

"It's got a full four stories, kids. Three for living plus a basement. Plenty of room for all of us. I think Hans will be home soon." She paused, deep in thought. "Russell told me to get it, so I did."

"Wow!" cried Allan.

"Wow!" I said—an echo. I could hardly believe what I was seeing. "I like it," I said. "It's ... it already feels like it belongs to us."

"That's because it *does*." She gave my shoulder a quick, affectionate hug. "I think this is what you needed, Maralys. I could sense it. Some children need homes more than others, don't they? Well, now we've got the home we've always wanted. It's special, don't you think? Like Mount Shasta."

192

Nothing like Mount Shasta, I thought, except it's old. I turned to glance at houses across the street, then back to ours. Common to all the homes on Lafayette, great elm trees spread protective arms over and around the house, and silver maples marched forever along the sidewalks. I would soon discover that driving down Lafayette felt like making one's way through a cathedral.

From that moment on, my illness disappeared.

Within a few weeks I'd be starting East High, now with my health and sense of security restored. Only later did I grasp that the illness was psychosomatic, though I'd never have imagined anyone could succumb to a fever simply for lack of a home.

In late afternoon on the first Sunday after we moved in, I happened to be outside when I heard strange, beautiful music wafting through the elms and right up to our front door.

Violins. A harp. A soprano's lilting vibrato. I recognized the tune: "Oh, Sweet Melody of Love," and thought I'd once heard the singer on the radio. I ran inside.

"Mother! Mother!" I cried. "There's music outside. Lots of it, coming through the trees. Hurry!"

She followed me out and stood on our sidewalk, head cocked. "Honey, I do believe that's Jeanette McDonald. Where on earth would this be coming from?"

"I thought you'd know."

"We've only been here a few days. Nobody mentioned Sunday concerts. A park, maybe?" She listened intently, then during a pause added, "My, they do have an excellent record, better than anything I own. Professional amplifiers, too."

The music started again, this time a tenor warbling through the branches. "Nelson Eddy!" she exclaimed. "Goodness! He sounds like he's two blocks away!"

As it turned out, Nelson Eddy *was* two blocks away, in Cheesman Park. And so was Jeanette McDonald, the two of them singing in harmony, accompanied by a full Denver orchestra. They'd come to town to entertain the troops, and while they were here, the City fathers had grabbed them for an hour's broadcast in our nearby park.

We would soon discover that light opera, professionally amplified, was a regular summer feature of our venerable neighborhood, and if you happened not to be sitting in the park itself, the music felt like an otherworldly experience.

SUDDENLY, JUST BEFORE SCHOOL STARTED, VJ-DAY WAS DEclared, meaning the war was officially over. All our local newspapers sold out, including one copy to Mother, who managed to obtain her own and raced into the kitchen holding aloft a sheet with huge headlines, waving as she shouted, "They've quit! The Japanese have surrendered!"

For a few minutes, Allan and I and our cook and mother danced around the kitchen, held hands and cheered while we skipped in circles. "We did it!" Mom cried. "We did it!" Like all the adults we knew, she took it as a personal achievement. Furthermore, Hans would now be coming home.

WITH THE WAR OVER, A NEW GIRLFRIEND FROM THE NEIGHborhood rang our doorbell. Betty Asher stood there beaming, her loose, wavy blonde hair framing a beautiful face, but with a body that spoke of too much white bread, too many cakes. She said, "Maralys, let's go downtown."

"Why? What do you want to do?"

"Nothing special. I just want to go and see."

"See what?"

"See who's there. See what's happening. Wanna go?"

"Yeah. I guess. Wait a minute, gotta get money for the streetcar."

"No, no. We'll walk," she said. "That way we'll be right on the sidewalk, viewing everything."

And so we set out. The mad celebrations had tapered off, but the Denver streets were still full of exuberant servicemen, whooping it up before they returned home. We hadn't walked three blocks before two soldiers began following us, whistling the universal whoo whoo under their breaths.

Betty turned around, smiling. "Hello, there, fellows," she said.

"Good news, eh?"

"Oh, honey … let us take you out for a drink," the taller one exclaimed. "Come with us, gorgeous. We'll show you what good news is all about. What's your name?"

Skinny me. I must have been invisible.

To her credit, sixteen-year-old Betty merely giggled. She gave them nothing else, no name, no promises. They cajoled and begged, but after awhile they gave up the chase and wandered off.

"Wasn't that fun?" Betty gushed. "Let's keep going."

"They acted drunk," I said.

"Of course they were drunk." She turned to laugh at me, then picked up the pace.

Deeper into downtown, we were followed again, with the same results. A soldier panted after her, but ignored me. Betty's last name might as well have been Grable.

This little trek had stopped being fun. I could understand about her beautiful face … but what about that cupcake figure?

Our jaunt added several new items to my private store of People Information; men prefer the amply-endowed, at least the ones topped by a movie-star face.

"Shouldn't we just get to the theater district?" she asked. "Study the marquee and see what's playing?"

"You know, Betty, I don't actually care what's playing. I'm not a fan of movies." I noticed three sailors approaching from the end of the block. "Lend me twenty cents, please," I said. "I'm getting on the streetcar."

"Aw, Maralys." She watched the trio coming closer, a threesome who lurched and gestured and seemed ready to chase us—or anything else. Hunters on the trail of a fox. The men had spotted us and were now waving and calling. Mesmerized, I watched them stagger as they came … three guys I could do without. They made me nervous. Betty could stay if she wanted.

Close at hand was a streetcar. Money or no money, I meant to escape. But then Betty wheeled around so suddenly she nearly knocked me over. "Get on, Maralys, quick." The doors squeaked open. "Hurry, I'm with you."

I rushed up the steps and so did she. For an overweight girl she was amazingly nimble, a miracle of stair-climbing speed.

While that day didn't end our friendship, it seemed prudent to me in the coming months to veer away from certain activities, like anything involving men. I simply couldn't compete with a cupcake.

Chapter Thirty-Five

Denver, 1945

Knowing stairs were of little consequence to a girl of sixteen, Mother had assigned me a third floor bedroom. "Now that it's freshly papered, honey, I think you'll love that eagle's nest of a room. It'll be your own kingdom."

She was right. I did love it. The wallpaper was a bright orangey-yellow, giving my garret the ambiance of a patch of poppies. My single bed was snugged up under the eaves, and from my desk under the dormer window I could peer out past shingles and through the tops of elm trees, and view half of Denver, like Harriet the Spy.

Nobody could be bored up there among the treetops. Except for me tapping on my typewriter, the room was quiet, only one of two bedrooms at that elevation. In a way, the third floor became my writer's hideaway.

A few weeks after the war ended, I started my senior year at East High, where the miracle of professional entertainment flowed nonstop, seemingly straight from Cheesman Park, or possibly Hollywood, onto our school's spacious stage. On a regular basis, East High's entertainment committee brought us a variety of famous performers, like Danny Kaye, Betty Hutton, Charlie McCarthy, and Martha Raye. We saw a lady contortionist who sat on her own head (the audience squealed and gasped), heard gifted pianists and marveled at precision tap dancers. Soon I began to anticipate assemblies as the stage equivalent of a hot fudge sundae.

Someone on the assembly committee must have had a direct line to Hollywood; certainly none of my other three high schools had ever come close. (Only think—in Mount Shasta High, *I* was once the entertainment!)

Yet movies and dances still presented a problem, a worrisome pathway that lingered in my subconscious as a certain route to hell. The first time I entered a movie theater I thought, *You're doomed, Maralys. God sees you, He knows what you're doing. Jesus knows. You've toppled, you've become one of the fallen.* I hesitated at the door.

Then I went anyway.

Hell backed off a little.

That year i joined East High's a cappella choir as a determined alto, one of the unaccompanied voices that sang everything from Gregorian chants to Beethoven. Our choir director was so impressed with our sound that she sometimes clapped.

In English I parsed sentences and felt I was playing a game, not working at all, but merely solving a puzzle that contained logic, challenges, and charm—all the charm that numbers lacked.

Sometime in the fall a boy in my senior class invited me to accompany him to the local amusement park, the famous Elitch's Gardens. A real date … while sweet Archie Stanley in Mount Shasta faded from memory, in a way as though he'd been part of a distant dream. I felt sad for him because he wrote me often. But now that I'd left (well, escaped), from the rustic town of Mt. Shasta, I wouldn't have to marry him after all.

Jim Parkson showed up at our door driving his own Chevy, a mustard-colored vehicle, elongated like a hot dog, something of a rarity in our high school. Most of us arrived at East High by walking.

With the confidence I'd once observed in electric-train-David, seventeen-year-old Jim talked as he drove. "Ever been to Elitch's?" he asked.

"Not recently," I said, then wondered how I'd managed to blurt out a lie. *I haven't been there at all—so I guess that's not recently, either.*

"You'll love the rides. Best in the country. Now take the roller coaster—"he threw me a quick sideways glance, "you gotta admire the speed. The drop. My Dad says it's like the jerk after you parachute from a plane. He did that, you know, in France."

Never mind France, I thought. "Your dad has ridden the roller coaster?"

"Sure. Bunch of times. Guess he wishes he coulda come today."

I was beginning to wish I hadn't come. Speed. Jerks. Sudden drops. None of them fit my notions of fun.

"You're gonna love this place," he crooned; he'd obviously forgotten my mention of a prior visit. "I come all the time."

"You do?" I was unimpressed but tried not to show it. "How all the time is all the time?"

"Dunno. Maybe two, three times a month. Gotta yearly pass, even."

"You must have taken other girls."

"Oh, sure." He caught himself. "But you're the one I've been … uh … I've had my eye on you."

Good boy, Jim. Quick Thinking. I glanced sideways, saw his playboy profile—just as good-looking as he thought it was, the sculpted nose and chin, the casual, wavy brown hair. Too good-looking, really. I'd never be his type.

I hoped I'd like the roller-coaster a lot.

Of course Jim knew his way around, and for a while was content to hold my hand and lead me past the crafts—the ceramics, the quilting, the paintings—then past the food booths, where he paused long enough to buy sodas and popcorn. Focused as he was on the rides, he didn't seem to notice that in every direction lay small beds of petunias and violets, even a ring of impatiens circling one of the elms. For a short time he was willing to sit on a bench tucked under a silver maple and share the popcorn.

"It's a beautiful park," I said.

"You betcha, but the best is still ahead." He paused, threw me a quick glance. "Through with the popcorn?"

When I nodded, he jumped to his feet and a few minutes later we sampled the Ferris Wheel. "A warm-up ride," he said as we rose toward the sky. "But for you, I won't rock the seats."

"Oh. Well thanks." Rocking the seats hadn't occurred to me. I leaned closer, gave him a grateful smile.

The Ferris Wheel finished, he grabbed my hand again and led me away at a quick pace.

Suddenly there it was. And so big. I looked up. And looked up more. The feeling was like standing under the Empire State Building. The ride, with its vertical steel struts, was tall beyond belief and spread out over acres—or so it appeared. The cars moved at incredible speed, and the riders, in high-pitched voices, screamed continuously.

The thing had a name, something akin to Satan's Death Trap.

I'd never seen anything to equal it; but how could I? I'd never been to an amusement park.

I could almost feel Jim salivating.

"Come on," he said, pulling me toward the ticket booth. "Hurry. The ride'll stop any minute."

"I don't want to," I said suddenly. "I don't like the look of it."

"Oh, come on. It's nothing. Really. You're gonna love it!"

"I don't think so, Jim." I felt like a reluctant dog, jerked along by its leash. "I think I'll hate it, the whole thing looks terrible, I'm—"

"Trust me," he broke in. "It's not as bad as it looks." He tugged my arm harder. "Hey, even the sissies love it. Nobody's afraid of this ride."

"People are screaming."

"Screaming with delight." He quickly bought two tickets. "If I'm wrong," he said, laughing, "I'll eat the program." He held it out, making his promise real.

The ride stopped, the screaming stopped, and white-faced teenagers staggered off. A girl leaned sideways and threw up.

That would be me.

Minutes later, Jim pushed me up a couple of stairs, plunked himself down beside me and eagerly buckled a small strap across our laps. He threw me a sideways smile. "Boy, will you enjoy this!"

I shook my head but couldn't respond. My words simply didn't come fast enough to beat the slow climb that had already begun. I had to concentrate, needed to get a better grip on the bar.

Bucking and jerking all the way, our little compartment chugged to the top of a very steep hill.

Suddenly hell poured over me. Our bucket dropped. I lost my grip on the bar. The thing dropped farther. And faster, surely breaking the sound barrier. Any minute the car would fly off the rails and catapult into space.

I thought I'd die.

But that was only the beginning. I regained my grip, but then came another sharp hill, even steeper, then an even more precipitous drop. A gale blew into my face, sent my hair whipping. I never dreamed we'd be shot out of a cannon. It was agony. Beyond agony. So awful I couldn't scream, couldn't make a sound. I simply waited to expire: soon my heart would explode out of my body.

More hills, more dropping. I'd never been in such misery, never hated being anywhere as much as I hated being right there in that horrible car. I might as well have been strapped to an electric chair.

I thought it would never end. Even as I tried to retreat within myself and submit to death, Satan's plaything jerked to a stop.

It was over.

Jim got out, beaming. He didn't even reach back to offer me a hand.

I jumped out, hating him with a white-hot anger. "How could you lie like that?" I shouted, "How could you! That was the worst thing I've ever done. The worst. I hated it!! Every minute, every second. I hated it so much I'll never go on another roller-coaster. Never! Ever!" I glared at him. "Start eating the program!"

The silence around us grew profound.

Hardly speaking, he and his great profile led off toward his ugly Chevy, where he quickly got in and drove me home. This time when I glanced sideways I could swear his nose had grown, like Pinocchio.

That was our first and last date.

HANS CAME HOME AND PEACE SETTLED OVER OUR HOUSEHOLD.

Before Christmas another boy, Hank, took me to the movies and back to his nearby house. The place was dark, meaning his parents were gone. We necked a little on his living-room couch, and then he began trying to reach under my dress. I pulled away: the necking had gone too far.

Standing, he unzipped his pants. What I saw scared me to death. "Hank, no," I said. "I'm not ready for this."

"Okay," he said abruptly, and re-zipped. "Sorry about this, I …

well, you've got such a great body."

He was basically a nice guy. As he walked me home he said, "No hard feelings?"

"No hard feelings. Let's just stick to the movies, okay?"

"I'll try. With you it won't be easy."

THE NEXT DAY I FOUND MOM IN THE DEN. "I NEED TO ASK YOU a question about boys," I said, and she nodded and said, "Well, let's talk, honey. Right now."

She led me into the living room and indicated a spot beside her on the red velour couch. *This is the first time in years,* I thought, *that she's had enough time.*

I leaned into her, more or less whispering. "How far can a girl go with a guy before she ... you know, before she gets in trouble?" I felt embarrassed even asking.

Lucky for me, Mom wasn't surprised or even slightly chagrined. "In trouble, honey? I presume you mean getting pregnant." Her calmness was steadying.

"Well ... any kind of trouble. My girlfriend at school says petting can be a problem."

"Petting," she said. "Let's go into this further. Let's talk about the things that boys and girls actually do. And then we can sort out what's dangerous and what isn't."

From her fund of knowledge, Mom calmly led me past the scenarios that usually occurred between young people. In a calm and unruffled way she explained what I should expect, and when it was important to be in control.

"Girls have the major responsibility," she said toward the end. "Because sexually, most of us aren't as driven as the boys. Myself ... I think I'm a bit more driven than most women, but even so I've known when to hold back." She smiled at me. "You'll come to understand your own feelings, honey, your own drives. And you'll know when it's best to ... well, to put on the brakes, to change the subject."

I relaxed, feeling relieved. Mom wasn't judging me at all, just trying to impart what she knew. By the end of the afternoon I felt armed with all the girl-type information I needed.

Only when she was sure I was satisfied, did Mother at last stand. "Come to me whenever you have doubts," she said, "or even the smallest questions. I've always been glad you've been my child, Maralys." For a moment she looked off in the distance. "I know we've had some scattered, confusing times. And I'm sorry for that. Perhaps now your life will be better."

As I stood beside her, she embraced me in a warm hug. "I haven't said this often enough. But you're a daughter to be proud of. And proud of you I certainly am."

That conversation and others like it took me past the most itchy parts of becoming a woman. As a Mother, she'd come through in exactly the right way and at the right moment.

CHAPTER THIRTY-SIX

Denver, Winter, 1945

THE STRANGE CALLS BEGAN IN JANUARY.

"Hello, is this Miz Klumpp?" It was always a male voice, usually with a southern accent.

My immediate reaction tended to be, *How lovely! A man is calling me!*

"Umm ... Yes," I'd say before asking, "Who is this?"

"Aahm Billy-Bob Swenson, Miz Klumpp, and I got your name from a friend 'o mine. Thought I'd give you a ring, justa see what you're doin'."

"What I'm doing, I guess, is talking to you." At first I thought, *Maybe he'll ask me for a date.* Soon I began to think otherwise. Since one of us had to say something, I'd ask, "What are you calling about, Mr. Billy-Bob?"

"Honey, ah jes wanted to talk. Thought I'd pass the time o' day. How y'all been? Huh?"

"Well, fine." By then the light had fully dawned. "Are you in the service?"

"Yep. Army. My unit's fixin' to ship back home. Leavin' in a few weeks, prob'ly. Got me some time on my hands. Denver's a purdy town, isn't it?" Then, with no pause, "Wanna talk to my friend, Harry-Jo? He's a right nice fella."

Before I could say *Well, I am kind of busy,* the phone would be passed along and the whole going-nowhere conversation would start over. Guessing they were just lonely, I couldn't be rude to these men who, after all, had recently fought a war.

Still, from author William Faulkner I knew that Southerners were noted for being good storytellers, and now I was surprised that this bunch had a knack for saying nothing but saying it slowly.

204

As always the new encounter would have the same speed-of-molasses quality as the old. Plus, when I wearied of trying, our tete-a-tete would suffer frequent conversational lapses where my phone pal seemed to fall in a hole—actually ran completely out of communicable thoughts. After awhile, the best words became "good-bye."

To my surprise, the calls kept coming. My phone number must have been passed around to a very large unit that was taking forever to be repatriated back to Georgia, or Mississippi, or Alabama.

For months after that, well years, I couldn't think of a good thing to say about the intelligence of tongue-tied Southerners.

WINTER IN DENVER WAS SOMETHING OF A MIRACLE. THE DAYS were crisp, the nights predictably cold, but the air was so dry we kids never felt chilly. An extra sweater under a jacket was all we needed to stay warm. One day Mom said, "Honey, did you know the city floods the tennis courts and at night they invite everyone to come and skate?"

I looked at her, dazzled. "I've always wanted to do that! Ever since I had those roller skates? Remember? I've been dying to skate on ice!"

"That's what I remember, too. Well, let's go out and find you some ice skates!"

Right then she took me shopping. But the man at the sporting goods store measured my feet and shook his head. "I'm very sorry. Ladies figure skates don't come in your size."

"Show me a picture of your men's figure skates!" Mom demanded, and when he did, she said, "What's the matter with these? They look exactly the same."

"I'll have to order them."

"Please do. As fast as you can."

Thus, within a week I had my own figure skates, and Mom was dropping me off at the nearest frozen-over tennis court.

For me those nights on ice were enchanting. Music issued from a wind-up victrola, skaters waltzed around the court, and I began, wobbly at first, learning how to ice skate.

Soon Mother stopped driving me to the court because it was no longer necessary. Within a few blocks of home was a bus that went right by the "rink," and all winter, as homework allowed, I threw the skates over my shoulder and hurried off to lose myself in another world.

To prevent daytime melting, rags were strung over the tennis court, and the shade they provided meant the ice remained intact. With a ceiling of floppy rags, the court appeared less than glamorous, but nobody minded. The tips of our noses turned red in the sharp night air and our hands required mittens. But nobody minded that either.

In no time at all, skimming across the surface to Strauss waltzes, I was transported. The skates became my wings, sent me flying across the ice, gave me a sensation of floating. Each lilting sweep of violins spurred on my blades, so the music and I became one. I leaned into the turns, swung around to skate backwards, recovered an edge to sail on effortlessly.

For a few hours every week I became Sonja Henie.

THAT WAS ALSO THE WINTER I LEARNED TO SKI. HANS accompanied me to a sporting goods store and pointed out some very long wooden Groswold skis, each adorned with a figure of a skier. "Zis will be right for you, Maralys," he said. "Made here, in Denver, by a skier from Norway. Not as long as my old skis in Switzerland. Styles change, even in skiing." He measured them against my body.

"They're longer than I am," I said, but he said, "Ze length gives you stability."

Though he never found time to accompany me or my friends to the mountains, Hans demonstrated proper technique in the living room. "You bend your knees—like zis. Lean into the hill, but keep your shoulders over your legs. Knees together. Okay. Turn by shifting your weight. Now try it."

After several attempts, I was more or less able to imitate his motions. Together, for several nights Hans and I skied across the living room rug.

Soon parents of friends drove four East High students, including me, up to Winter Park in the Rockies, where we unloaded equipment that seemed to weigh more than we did: skis and bindings, boots, poles, parkas, heavy gloves. With my body fully outfitted, I felt like a lumbering bear—a bear with ankle restraints. I could hardly walk.

I thought, *This can't be much fun.*

To my surprise the slope absorbed all the pounds, and once again my body felt weightless. After a few graceless runs, I became reasonably good at the beginner's slopes.

"Race you down the hill," said one of the boys, but I threw him a smile, shook my head, and let him whiz on down ahead of me, a neat track left in his wake, the snow spraying sideways as he skidded to a stop. *You guys can do the racing,* I thought.

For me, skiing was beauty, not speed, it was long, swooping turns, gliding first one way then another, soaring down a slope as though with wings, barely connected to the earth. It was wind in the face, a body as light as a butterfly, an effortless journey through endless, quiet space. Skiing was ice skating propelled along by gravity.

Most days I rarely fell down more than once.

UNTIL THE DISASTER WITH HILARY, LIFE IN DENVER WAS AN idyllic respite, a happy time that Allan and I had yearned for but experienced only in scattered years—some in Mount Shasta, one year for me in Rochester, and finally, now, the years in our big home on Lafayette Street.

Sadly, the accident changed everything.

Chapter Thirty-Seven

East Denver, Spring, 1946

"You know, Maralys," Mom said to me one day, "however vague the memories I have of my early years, I remember every cruel word my dad ever spoke. It's too bad, isn't it?" She gazed into space, musing. "Of all the things i don't want to remember ... yet some of his words still cut, still haunt me."

We sat together at the kitchen table. "Russell once said to me at a party, 'Virginia, you're the loudest person in the room. Do you want people thinking you're a hussy?'" She sighed. "Oddly, it was my enthusiasm that Dad loved most. But I noticed, only when it applied to him."

"I remember some pretty bad stuff, too," I said.

She patted my hand. "There's a truism I've observed over the years," she said, and now her tone was philosophical. "The words most apt to be imprinted in memory are those attached to an overlay of emotion. Any emotion will do it, I've discovered. The stronger the feelings, the deeper and more powerfully the words sink into our subconscious." She ticked them off on her fingers: "Fear, pride, anger, horror, embarrassment, love, despair, excitement. They all make certain statements indelible."

"I know," I said. "You'll think I'm crazy, Mom, but way back when they were taking out my tonsils, I still remember the smell of ether as the doctors covered my face with that awful-smelling cloth. I remember what I said, too."

"You remember your tonsillectomy?" she asked. "But you were only six."

"True. But I still recall it vividly. The cottony texture of the ether ... that thick stuff that creates the sensation of suffocating. It was horrible, Mom. Terrifying. I remember yelling into the cloth,

'I'd rather DIE than breathe this stuff.' Those were my exact words."

She smiled. "Really! The doctor mentioned that you tried to rip off the mask."

"And while we're on the subject," I said, "I still remember the words of the fat doctor at Jones Beach who shared my near-drowning experience ... you know, the Sea Puss. After we reached shore he grabbed my arm and dragged me away. He kept shouting, 'No publicity! No publicity!' I hated him for that no publicity stuff. After all I'd been through, I *wanted* some publicity."

Mother laughed. "Let's remember this conversation, honey. Even if we forget everything else."

MOTHER AND I COULDN'T HAVE GUESSED I'D SOON HEAR NEW words that would haunt me forever—the most heart-rending thoughts a child could express.

It was only a few weeks later, one afternoon in 1946, that I came down the winding staircase of our Denver home and happened to be standing in the front hall when my six-year-old brother appeared. Hilary had just climbed up from the basement. His young face was white, a mask of surprise and shock, but that was only the beginning. Glancing down I saw that his trousers were gone, and instead he stood half naked, with strips of skin hanging from his legs and drops of liquid seeping out around them and falling onto the floor.

"What happened?" I cried. "Hilary, what's wrong with your legs?"

"I got burned," he said.

"Burned?"

"With gasoline. The fire went up my pants."

"Oh, Hilary! Hilary!" I wanted to take him in my arms and comfort him, but the legs looked so bad it seemed wrong to even touch him. I would only make them worse. So I stared, horrified, not knowing what to do, yet aching to wrap him up and pull him close.

For long seconds Hilary didn't move, he simply stood there, noting the expression on my face. Finally he said in a voice so matter-of-fact I was devastated. "I'm pretty badly hurt for a little boy, aren't I?"

Oh God, yes! Oh, yes! His grasp of the situation, his deadly calm, his perfect grammar at a moment like that only added to my sense of shock.

Oh God, Oh, dear God, you are badly hurt. I nodded, numb and speechless. "Hilary, honey—where's Mom?"

"She knows," he said. "She's coming. She's taking me to the hospital."

Within seconds Mother appeared in the hall carrying a quilt. As I stood there in all my uselessness she wrapped the quilt around my brother's legs and carried him to the car. She said nothing, but the devastation on her face mirrored mine.

She was instantly gone, and didn't reappear again for three days. While she slept in the hospital, and Allan and I fended for ourselves, Hilary underwent burn treatment, then surgery, all the while fighting for his life.

He'd always been Mother's love baby, and now her love was tested to the limit. "I thought he was going to die," she said later. "I'll never get over this." She paused. "If he lives a long life he'll never get over it either."

IT WAS ALLAN WHO TOLD ME WHAT HAD HAPPENED. "I was making something down in the basement," he said, "using a blow torch. Hilary was standing next to me, watching. A can of gasoline sitting on the counter caught fire and tipped over, and the flames went up Hilary's pants. I ripped off his pants and put out the fire, but it was too late. He was already burned."

Allan was the most devastated of us all.

To Mother's credit, she never blamed Allan for the accident. But she didn't need to. He never stopped blaming himself.

The consequences for all of us worsened. Hans never responded to the calamity as intensely as Mother thought he should. He wasn't at the hospital much, didn't pull his weight, she thought.

As just another child in the house, leaving for high school each day, I wasn't aware of how much or how little Hans actually did. But it was never enough for Mother.

The aftermath of Hilary's accident ended their marriage. Hans disappeared from the Denver house, and from then on, though he was in frequent touch with Allan, he played no further part in my life.

FOR MOTHER AND HILARY THE ACCIDENT CHANGED EVERY-thing. My brother's legs were months recovering, with scar tissue building up so deep and so restrictive of motion, he was forced to return to the hospital over and over for additional corrective surgery. Even so, he was left with grotesquely scarred legs.

Through it all, Hilary remained remarkably stoical.

As it turned out, the burns didn't ruin his life. In the end, the harm that came to him was mostly because our mother stopped being a mother.

Allan and I with Russell and Grandma Alice.

Chapter Thirty-Eight

Denver, Summer, 1946

ONE DAY AT BREAKFAST MOTHER SAID ALMOST GAILY, "I'M NOW free to marry again. I wonder who it will be." Allan and I both stared at her, felt the looming sense that she was once again looking. The presence of yet another man, we knew, would be a notable shift in our family's seismic plates.

Without Hans we'd once more become a matriarchal household with a mother who was on the prowl … our gypsy mother.

IN JUNE, 1946, AT AGE 16, I GRADUATED FROM EAST HIGH, WITH good enough grades to gain easy acceptance at Denver University. My aunt Kotsie sent a telegram: "We're so proud of you, dear. Keep it up. All our love. Kotsie and Pauline." Suddenly I missed them both acutely.

That summer Mother hired a student from Boulder to accompany us back to the ranch for a month of outdoor repair work. Never quite sure how she'd found him, I soon gave up caring. More important to me was Chuck Massion himself, a pre-med student at Colorado University.

I soon realized Chuck was everything the boys in high school were not. He was mature, serious, intellectual, purposeful about his career, and handsome enough to set any girl's heart astir. "I've got to earn some money to go on with school," he said. "Your mom is making it happen."

That June, as we all headed for Mt. Shasta with Chuck driving one of our cars, I sat beside him in the front seat of our Plymouth and studied what I could see of his face in the rearview mirror. I couldn't get enough of looking at him, though I wondered from time to time if he knew I was staring.

"What kind of doctor will you be?" I asked.

A shrug, then a sideways glance. "Too early to know. Can't make that decision yet. Right now it's my grades that count."

"So what courses are you taking?"

"Everything that's hard." He laughed. "You name all the tough ones—Organic Chemistry, Advanced Anatomy, and they're on my list."

"Any math?"

"Of course. Analytic Geometry. Differential Equations. That sound hard enough for you?"

"Yeah," I said. "For me they'd be impossible." My thoughts drifted back. "In fourth grade I flunked long division." *Well, almost.*

I thought he'd laugh, but he didn't. Instead he glanced over at me, said gravely, "You'll need some serious math for college, you know."

I shrugged. "So far Denver U has accepted me practically math-free. Algebra and plain Geometry, that's all. Anyway, I got an "A" in Geometry." I fell silent. After a pause I said, "That's it for math."

He shook his head. "I'll help you plan your fall schedule if you'd like."

"Would you?" I hadn't the heart to tell him my courses were all decided. I just wanted to sit closer to him and talk. Yet now I found myself drying up, unable to think of witticisms that might entertain him; he was so serious and I was so anything but glib.

I hadn't done well so far.

Chuck must have figured out that I was smitten by him. But except around my Aunt and Pauline, who'd made it easy to conjure up the humor in everyday life, I was no good at small talk, which to me was talking about nothing.

While I could chat with girls endlessly, boys or men—and especially this man with whom I suddenly realized I'd fallen in love, created a whole new world of halting speech. "I'll tell you a story," I began one day, and was well into the tale of my eighth grade dance with an imperious squirt of a boy when I suddenly forgot the punch line. The ending dropped into storyteller's hell, but my face provided its own ending. I reddened up like a pomegranate.

Naively, I assumed Chuck would catch my vibes and automatically love me back. I imagined we'd sneak off to exchange kisses behind the barn.

But it never happened. As eagerly as I looked for opportunities, somehow they never appeared. Was he just being careful around my mother? I was never sure.

After four weeks of his working on the ranch and me occasionally following him around like a hopeful puppy, Mom put us both on the train back to Denver. I could see I hadn't won him over.

Desperate to inspire his love, in the middle of the night I crept down the train aisle and into his lower bunk, hoping to entice him with the oldest device available to young girls.

Even that didn't work. Though he kissed me briefly, he—mature man of 20 that he was—resisted my offerings. "This isn't a good idea," he said gently.

After a time, knowing I was beaten, I slunk away, back to my own bunk. All I'd done was add shame to failure.

Back home in Denver once more, Chuck Massion did indeed come down from Boulder periodically to take me to the movies. But there was one especially disastrous moment when he arrived at our door and, as the two of us stood together in the foyer, I was suddenly obliged to introduce him to one of mother's friends.

For a ghastly moment stage fright overtook me and his name flew right out of my head. Today I might have said with a laugh, "Okay, whatever your name is, introduce yourself."

Instead I fumbled and stumbled, turned a bright red and finally turned to him. "What is your name again?"

He stared at me, dumbfounded. Having supplied the missing data, he continued staring, then shook his head. He never thought it was funny.

Clearly, while I needed a cooler head in an emergency, he needed a better sense of humor.

AFTER THAT OUR RELATIONSHIP FADED. ONE DAY BEFORE THE end of summer he was kind enough to call me and report that he'd met someone else, and "she makes me feel like a little kid in a candy store."

As he spoke, the floor dropped out from under my feet. *That's how you make me feel,* I thought. I could barely respond, only just managed a mumbled good-bye.

As I hung up I knew I'd never recover; for days I moped around the house like a ghost, too shaken to cry, my whole interior as dry and desolate as Death Valley, my appetite so diminished I could hardly swallow food.

"Now that Chuck is gone," I confessed to Mom, "life is no longer worth living. How will I go on?"

She reached out to stroke my hair. "You'll get over him, honey. Trust me, you will. It'll happen in its own time, little by little. Next year you'll hardly remember him."

Oh, yes, I'll remember him, I thought, staring into space. With an inner ache as big as the Rockies, how could I not?

For weeks my despair was the same emptiness I'd felt after my father disappeared from our ranch. Eventually I realized the reasons were nearly identical. Like no young man I'd ever known, Chuck Massion was more than just a boyfriend, he'd been a father figure as well. A man who fills two roles will always be doubly hard to get over.

In the fall of 1946, probably because she felt unable to cope with three kids and no husband, Mom sent Allan to the Colorado Military school. Of all the boys who were self-driven and not at all militaristic in temperament, it was Allan. I couldn't imagine how he would fit there.

As it turned out, he didn't.

CHAPTER THIRTY-NINE

Denver, Fall, 1946

NOW NEWLY SEVENTEEN AND RECOVERING FROM MY BROKEN heart, I began commuting back to the south part of town (where I'd once lived), to attend Denver University. Again I traveled by streetcar.

Thanks to a hefty influx of returning veterans now on the GI bill after the war, the campus sported two faces: the dead-serious vets, intent on getting a fast education, but equally intent on luring co-eds into dark corners and as quickly as possible into bed; and the eighteen-year-old playboys who'd missed the war and were busy sampling the whole college experience: girls, drinking, fraternities, and, if there was still time ... studying.

Within a month I went on two or three dates with veterans who had the same "get to the point" mentality, driven to move fast because they'd lost too much time. They stared into my eyes with their hungry expressions; they lusted. "You know you want it as much as I do," one of them said, imagining he spoke for both of us (and for all other girls as well). Some simply tried, in the dark back rows of a movie, to reach up under my dress. As with most of the girls on campus, all younger than the ex-soldiers, we found ourselves not so much "going out" with these men as playing Dating Defense.

The contrast between the two male groups was fascinating. It was heartening seeing the serious intent to study and become educated displayed by the older men; they really cared about every aspect of learning. In class they were downright inspiring.

Not so nice was trying to keep their pressure-cooker bodies safely away from ours.

AT CHRISTMAS BREAK, ILL WITH RHEUMATIC FEVER, ALLAN came home from military school and was ordered to go straight to bed. Studying with tutors from the Randall School in Denver, he remained in bed until late spring. In a sense, Allan had been a captive for most of the school year—first with the rigid military, then with his illness. I thought, *Mother has not been as good for Allan, lately, as she's been for me.*

Ironically, when we discussed this in later years, Allan said, "I always felt Mom wasn't as good for you as she was for me."

My GRADES AT DENVER U, WITH CLASSES NOW MORE CHAL-lenging than ever, nevertheless rose and rose. Over the course of my Freshman year I took 15 units of chemistry with a tiny, birdlike teacher named Dr. Essie Cohn, who reminded everyone of Madame Curie. She was so brilliant in the way she made basic chemistry come alive that her students reveled in her lectures. With her I studied hard because I loved it, and by the end of the year my 15 units of chem were all A's.

For the first time I took general psychology, and found it fasci-nating—in a year that also included biology and English.

In many ways my Freshman year at Denver became a heady introduction to college, in some ways unsurpassed later—especially when my English teacher took me aside and said, "Maralys, you have a way with words. You should consider becoming a writer."

Her opinion brought to the surface my dormant determination to do exactly that. For all the years that followed, when I kept sub-mitting manuscripts that gathered only rejections, her encouraging take on my latent writing skills rang in my head. The strong rush of pride that accompanied her comments made everything she said burrow deep in memory.

LIKE THE REST OF THE CITY, DENVER UNIVERSITY WAS INTENT on making us love our school. On winter weekends the school provid-ed buses to transport Ski Club members to the mountains for whole days of skiing ... and even the bus rides themselves were heady and full of laughter.

Occasionally, parents of friends drove us to mountainous Evergreen Lake for nights of ice skating. Magic empowered my skates once more, sent me skimming along on the lake's glasslike surface, swaying to classical waltzes. As I danced, I waited to be "discovered," either by a man or the movies. Though this never happened, I was happy enough twirling and gliding in my own universe.

In one of my university classes I met a girl who became a lifelong friend, Verna Moriarity. As serious and steady and contemplative as I was, she seemed to find equal compatability in me, and we hit it off so well that Verna instantly became my campus chum. She was a classical pianist, beautiful, and with a keen sense of humor.

Verna was also president of the Alpha Xi Delta sorority and persuaded me to join. Often, as we sat on one of the benches strewn around campus, we engaged in philosophical discussions about Life and Men. Or we made comments that were all surface, utterly superficial. "I don't want a man to ask," she said, "I just want him to take me in his arms and kiss me."

"Forget the man who needs permission," I agreed. "The guy has to take charge, to woo me because he's strong and knows what he's doing."

"But not like the veterans."

"God, no, not like them." I made a face. "They don't woo, anyway. They just grab and go."

Often on weekends, as the weather warmed up, we donned our cutest shorts and posed outside our homes like budding Rita Hayworths, while a third friend took photos. Though we considered ourselves intellectuals and several lofty layers above the pin-up girl mentality, we weren't too uppity to memorialize our lovely bodies for … well, we weren't sure for exactly what.

Toward the end of my first year at Denver U, Mother moved a young man into our house. He was about 26, a sensitive and intelligent college graduate named Phillip, who probably became her lover.

I was never exactly sure. But then, on some occasions he also began to woo me. It was an altogether strange situation, with Mother and I more or less sharing the same boyfriend.

We did and yet we didn't. Phillip and I, with more of a platonic relationship than any other, sometimes drove around in his car and discussed our peculiar situation. He knew it was strange. I knew it was strange. The two of us were never quite sure what Mom thought.

Eventually he left to attend Princeton seminary. For a while his biology had obviously outstripped his theology.

For years Phillip wrote me occasional letters.

As SPRING BLOOMED AND WITH IT THE END OF MY FIRST COL-lege year, Mom brought me a new idea. "Honey, I think you can do better than this streetcar school in Denver. Why don't you transfer to Boulder? Or Stanford?"

"Stanford, Mom? Stanford?" I shook my head. "You know I can't get into that school. It's impossible. They take three men for every woman."

"Still. You ought to try."

"I'd never make it. So few girls are accepted."

Mother shrugged and let it drop.

Which is when my Readers Digest mother chimed in. *You're going to give up without trying? How do you know you can't get in—if you never make the effort?* I could almost see the inspirational story headlined on a Reader's Digest page: *"I'll never make it,"* the young co-ed said. *"But she refused to give up."*

Thus began the start of an intensive two-and-a-half-month campaign aimed solely at getting me into Stanford.

My yearbook photo, a Freshman at Denver U.

Best friend, Verna, also at Denver U.

I couldn't resist a few cheesecake photos.

CHAPTER FORTY

Denver, Late Spring, 1947

THE TUTORING AIMED AT STANFORD BEGAN WELL BEFORE THE end of the semester. Mother found Miss Andrews, God knows how, who knew exactly what vocabulary words I ought to study. Once a week we met in a library and discussed words. I tried them out in sentences, worked at getting the subtle connotations, explored the contemporary context. Miss Andrews was patient and happy to explain the differences between words like *Arcane. Abstruse. Recondite.*

"You're really getting a handle on shades of meaning," she said one evening after we'd finished going over the week's list. "That's going to be a big help."

At the end of each session she'd hand me a new list.

Mother never pressed me to keep going. I did it on my own, the stubborn German joining forces with the Reader's Digest mother.

Actually, it was fun.

Mother also found me a tutor for math. As good as he was, Mr. Clark could not make up for years of neglect and disinterest. I did try. Sort of.

Knowing I had a beginning-of-summer deadline for taking the Stanford Aptitude test, I hung out in my third-floor garret and worked assiduously and nonstop. The surprising feature to me was the complexity and variety of our language—that English offers half a dozen distinct ways of saying almost everything.

Yet subtlety enters the picture too; so many of our words are almost alike ... except in actual usage they aren't. For instance, *a virago* is not exactly like *a termagant* nor the perfect equivalent of *a shrew*.

For someone endowed with faint creativity but an abundance of logic, studying vocabulary words dovetailed with my ... well, *propensities*.

That is, all but one. I was hopeless in math.

ALL TOO SOON THE TEST DAY ARRIVED. WITH OTHER APPLI-
cants I reported to a large, downtown Denver hall and was handed
a multi-page booklet. At the beginning bell we all opened it to the
English section. And there I sat staring at a page full of vocabulary
questions: subtle comparisons; appropriate use in sentences; logic
drills. My first look was simple curiosity … then a dawning excitement. I was in a familiar land; I knew most of its people.

With heart pounding, I began filling in blanks, or choosing
among multiple choices. You can't respond to a question that begins,
"This is to This, as That is to blank?" if you don't know the meaning
of the "This" or the "That."

Miraculously, thanks to my tutor, it turned out those words were
indeed my friends; I understood the meaning of nearly every one. It
was the greatest fun I've ever had taking a test.

NEXT, OF COURSE, CAME THE SECTION ON MATH.
A disaster.
With the dwindling energy of a deflating balloon, I began trying
to work problems. A few I was able to figure out. But there wasn't
enough time; I was always flailing, constantly running behind. I soon
gave up. Instead I found myself muttering, *Well, I haven't had a "C"
answer in awhile, guess I'll mark "C".*

And thus I threw away any chance of entering Stanford. They'd
never accept a dodo who couldn't work simple math.

HAVING DECIDED IN ADVANCE IT MIGHT BE EASIER TO GAIN
entrance as a summer school student, I'd marked that preference on
my application. To my amazement, within a couple of weeks, my
admission letter to Stanford arrived.

I was in!!

I stared at the letter, hardly able to believe it. I could already see
the school mascot, the feathers of a Stanford Indian, and me dancing
around a symbolic campfire. I ran to show my letter to Mom.

Slowly she studied it. "Honey, I always thought you could do it!"

"You did?"

"Didn't I tell you, you could rise above this town?"

"You were talking about Mt. Shasta."

"Well, one town or another ... what does it matter, dear, you've risen and that's what counts." She gave me a quick peck on the cheek. "Early this year I was thinking, If I can go to Smith, Maralys can surely go to Stanford." She paused, gazed off into space. "I figure Allan for MIT."

Never quite sure that a summer admission meant acceptance to the fall semester as well, the moment I arrived at Stanford I went to the admissions office to check my status. And there I learned an astounding fact. My application had landed in the highest possible category: Group I!

From that revelation came an odd, but inevitable conclusion: In that era of 1947, Stanford University must not have cared a whit about a woman's abilities in math.

Saying good-bye to my best friend, Verna, and promising I'd write was difficult.

More difficult still was saying good-bye to my family. Hilary, with his injured legs, was now only seven, and in second grade. He was a cute little boy, but I sensed a loneliness in him. Mother seemed unable to give him the close, personal attention he needed. And his father, Hans, now courting another woman, seldom saw him.

Allan, finally recovered from rheumatic fever, was out of bed and working in a bicycle shop. I knew I'd see him again, but I wasn't sure when. He'd been an excellent student in Junior High, and good as well in the half year he'd spent at East High. As I'd expected, my brother was skilled in all the subjects I wasn't. Math and science were his shining topics. None of us were surprised. Allan could remember numbers without even trying. And he'd soon spend a summer wiring Mom's whole ranch with electricity. Allan would surely become a scientist.

As for Mother, her personal life was ... well, sketchy. As I left she was dating sporadically, not always suitable men. She'd been a good mother to me in the last two years. Now she needed to be a good mother to herself.

With Mom, it wasn't clear that would happen.

What I couldn't have known as I left was that I'd never come home again.

CHAPTER FORTY-ONE

Stanford: Summer 1947 – Summer 1948

WHEN IT CAME TO STANFORD, MY MOTHER AND MY READER'S Digest mother had agreed: *You can make it,* Mother said ... *if you try hard enough,* my Digest mother added.

Apparently it took two mothers to get me there.

Now I was on campus and part of yet another, utterly different world. In all directions, beautiful Spanish Mission architecture harkened back to California's beginnings ... and I sensed, almost from something in the air, that here was an amalgam of inherited wealth and heady intellectualism.

Feeling a newcomer's elation, I walked down paths that wandered past palm trees and led to pink-tiled buildings. Around them, deep green lawns spread out and gave the structures breathing space. The air was cool, even for summer. As students passed, their talk mirrored what I felt, a kind of rippling animation.

To me, everything about the school was either exciting or utterly foreign.

In 1947, before Affirmative Action, before the leveling influence of Student Activism, Stanford was almost entirely Caucasian. With today's eyes I would be aware of this uniformity. Back then I never noticed.

Without expecting trouble, I remembered reading about Stanford's reputation for snobbery. An article in a leading magazine described the disruptive effects of sorority "rushing" on numerous campuses, how it sometimes provoked breakdowns and suicides among rejected women. The story pointed to Stanford as a school that felt it had no recourse but to abolish its sororities. With the men less apt to be traumatized by rejection, they'd let the fraternities remain.

That first day on campus I happened to notice a girl who would have been swept up by any sorority. Stunningly beautiful, she had long hair and tanned arms and face ... not to mention perfect clothes and figure. I first saw her down at the Admissions Office, then immediately afterwards at the Women's Gym. I was startled by her ability to transport so quickly from one spot to another.

That night at dinner in our dorm, Casa Naranja, I was amazed to discover that two tables away sat that same gorgeous student. Except there were two of them!

A girl at my table whispered that they were rich San Francisco debutantes, and that everyone on campus knew about our twins because they modeled clothes for magazines.

The next morning, in fact, the two made themselves known to all the girls on my floor: in a saccharine voice one twin called down the hall to the other: *Olive, what are you going to wear today?* And then by return-voice, a long-distance, hall-echoing answer back from Olive.

Luckily for the rest of us, this whiff of snobbery wafting along the upstairs hall didn't make any of us feel diminished. Behind closed doors we were apt to ask one another in mocking tones, "Olive, what are you going to wear today?"

Nor did most of us care about rumors that quite a few of the Casa Naranja girls went home to San Francisco during the Christmas holidays for their own extravagant coming-out parties. For me, and the girls I felt closest to, the classes were what mattered most. Oh ... make that the classes and the boys.

Before we arrived, we were all aware of Stanford's reputation for rigorous courses and brainy students. Once there, most of us were inordinately proud of our label as a "Stanford Indian," and among us was the long-standing joke, "If you flunk out of here, you can always go down to USC."

Of particular interest to me, though, was the school's famous Honor Code ... partly, I suppose, because who would value an honor code more than a Miss Goody-Two-Shoes?

On day two we newcomers were told to assemble in the Student

Union. There we heard the first of several admonitions. "As a Stanford student you are expected to understand the Honor Code," the lecturer said. "We trust you to uphold our standards, to pride yourself on maintaining the integrity of our classes." The lecturer spelled out expectations beyond what we'd ever heard about at other universities. At exams we were expected to bring only our pens and pencils (nobody would check), to keep our eyes on our own papers, to eschew any and every kind of cheating.

As exams began, the proctors often tested us by leaving the room.

The Honor Code was drilled into us so thoroughly that most of us came away with the mindset of missionaries. *I wouldn't cheat for anything.*

If we happened to observe cheating, we were supposed to report it. But the behavior of other students is not something you notice when you're hell bent on keeping your eyes on your own paper.

Nobody ever talked about Stanford's dorm food; I might have been the exception.

After all my years with Mother, I was thrilled that back in our dorm's kitchen, *somebody was actually cooking.* Unlike the few spoiled girls who glanced down at their dinner plates and squealed with disdain, "Eieuw, I wouldn't eat that," I sat there thinking, *Oh wonderful, here comes another great meal!*

Day after day we gathered at long tables with white tablecloths, where we were served fresh fruit plates, crispy salads, homemade rolls, chicken in a creamy sauce. Around us, eager fraternity boys dashed among tables setting down plates, while a few girls giggled and called out to the men, "Are you putting saltpeter in our food?"

The thought kept returning, *We're all being treated like queens. Am I the only one who notices?*

For me that first quarter, Stanford was a four-star hotel, a brainy environment, and a high-minded moral climate all rolled into one.

Summer quarter ended, and with it my single-minded focus. I was getting tired of so much studying and all the papers and exams that lurked in the wings, staring me down. With only a nominal break, Fall quarter began. I realized I was no longer springing out of bed.

As Fall quarter drew to a close, even the thrill of being in that celebrated environment began to fade. All at once I started thinking as I cracked a book, *I can't do this any more. I can't take another test.* From somewhere came the pressure of classes dating back to the beginning of Denver University. *I haven't had a break in a year and a half. How can I keep this up?*

Often I sat on my bed, dazed and unwilling to work. But I wasn't the only one; my roommate, Tina, wasn't studying either.

About that time Mother stopped by briefly to visit the campus, which is when she met this latest roommate. The minute Tina was out of sight Mother said, "I don't like that girl."

"Why, Mom? Why not?"

Mother gave me one of her looks. "I sensed something about her. A character defect. You should stop rooming with her, Maralys, she won't do you any good." For dramatic effect she stared into my eyes. "Tina is evil."

"Evil? Oh, Mothuuur. How do you know?"

"Don't ask me how I know. I just do."

I didn't like her telling me that, had never responded well to Mom's dump-truck manner of unloading drama onto my head.

Yet in this case I knew her snap judgment was right. No, more than right. Uncanny. In that short few minutes she'd sized up my roommate perfectly. What she didn't know was that for an entire quarter I'd been under Tina's spell.

Tina: who decided the two of us should ignore all the other women at school and be a separate unit unto ourselves. "The other girls are inferior," she said. "They're beneath us. We don't need them."

Once she said, "I'm smart; I can get grades without studying." She gave me a sharp, probing look. "So can you. Why are you spending hours with those books? Why? When you can get by without them?"

Tina: who spent her weekends in San Francisco sleeping with an endless variety of men.

"But most of them are married," I protested.

She purred like a cat. "I'm giving them pleasure, which their wives can't. I'm making them happy. They're grateful—every one is endlessly grateful." She fingered her new gold necklace and turned her strange look on me. "Come with me, Maralys. We'll make it a menage a trois. Three of us in one bed, all pleasuring each other. You've never experienced anything like it."

Nor do I want to, I thought.

"You aren't living," she insisted, "spending your weekends here." As I watched, she began shaving her legs, then her arms; I suppose she also shaved other areas. "Come with me, Maralys. Why don't you?"

"I can't," I said, which wasn't the truth. What I meant was, *I don't want to.*

FOR ONCE MOTHER WAS RIGHT, THOUGH SHE HAD NO IDEA how right; I sat with her in our bedroom and couldn't help listening to her. "You should take a break, honey. Find a job. And return to Stanford rested."

"What if I never come back? What if I lose my drive?"

"You'll return, dear, I'm absolutely sure you will."

Again, Mother had sensed the truth.

I couldn't have guessed this would be the last advice she'd ever give me.

BEFORE CHRISTMAS I TOOK TWO QUARTERS OFF FOR A RE-prieve from the classroom and moved to a boarding house in Berkeley. From there I commuted to a job at Hills Brothers Coffee in San Francisco. Determined to remain informed, I read *Time* magazine coming and going on the bus. At Hills Brothers I learned to run a vari-typer, the most boring machine ever created. In my spare time I wrote stories. Sometimes my personal writing drifted into my working hours; clearly I would never be Employee of the Month.

When I returned to campus early the next summer, Tina was gone and once again I roomed with a normal woman.

But my fall quarter with that off-kilter girl had not been wasted;

I'd discovered how quickly a sinister person can manipulate your ego with assurances that you are superior and part of an elite group, how cunningly evil can invade your psyche when you encounter it unprepared. I'd always wondered how Hitler managed to hold sway over so many presumably reasonable people. After rooming with Tina, I began to understand.

My first Saturday back, I watched my new roommate as she sat before a mirror applying mascara. "Are you getting ready for the Jolly-up?" I asked.

Elaine swiveled to look at me, her lips tight with scorn. "Oh … those get-acquainted dances," she said disdainfully, turning back to give her lashes another touch. "They're nothing but a meat market." Another glance in my direction. "You're nearly a Junior now. That stuff is for Freshmen. What girl wants to be part of that?"

I do! I thought, without answering. *I'll go to anything where I meet men.*

I walked toward the closet, began looking for the right dress. *I'm nineteen now. My dating years are getting away fast.*

Leaving my roommate behind, I walked over to the get-acquainted dance. That Jolly-up became the most important dance of my life.

CHAPTER FORTY-TWO

Stanford: 1948 – 1949

I'M GLAD I DIDN'T LISTEN TO MY STANFORD ROOMMATE THAT Saturday night … that I ignored her look of derision and her dismissive words: "Those Jolly-Ups are nothing but a meat market."

You can stay glued to the dorm, Elaine; *I'm going anyway.*

Still, I thought as I walked toward the dance, *I'm not expecting much.* I began musing about past dates, how so far the campus men seemed to fall into two categories, the nerds or the party animals, and those who didn't spend our date lingering on the mysteries of subatomic particles, were apt to squander it instead guffawing with friends over last weekend's drunken bash at Rosati's. (Never mind that to those who held such hi-jinks in high esteem I was one of the nerds.)

That night, as always, the flirting I did with the men observing from the sidelines had a kind of high-water mark, based on the fact that I was so tall, over five-ten, and resolutely never made eye contact with anyone shorter than six-foot-two. All my little smiles and coy glances went to the men who towered above the rest.

Thus Rob Wills, the man who would change my life, first saw me at the Jolly-Up and I never saw him at all. It's faintly possible that sometime during the evening my eyes flicked across the top of Rob Wills's head, but I certainly never saw his face.

The truth was, I didn't know he existed until he cut in on me.

He introduced himself, and when he took my hand to begin dancing, I saw at once that he wasn't up to my height standards, his eyes being only slightly higher than mine. Yet I noticed other things: his lively expression as he engaged my eyes, his dazzling smile. He drew me in with his energy, his obvious life force.

To my surprise, he bored in quickly as though in a hurry to get acquainted: "Where did you go to high school?" he asked. And almost before I'd finished answering, "What brought you to Mt. Shasta? Is the rest of the family as tall as you are? Who's walking you home tonight?"

I was taken aback by his blunt questions, found myself stumbling over the answers.

At the end of the dance he asked, "What are you doing tomorrow?" Before I could answer, he held up his hand. "I withdraw the question. How would you like to go to a beach party?"

"A beach party?"

I was beginning to sound like a parrot. But how else to slow him down? Surely he meant a fraternity party, where there'd be other men, probably some who were taller and didn't ask blunt questions.

He nodded and said, "Tomorrow. One O'clock."

"Well ..." I finally said. "I guess I'll go."

THAT NIGHT ROB WILLS LEFT A NOTE IN MY DORM MAILBOX, a message so personal and embarrassing I considered backing out. The note began, "I feel drawn to you, Maralys. You remind me of someone I once loved. I was watching you at the dance, waiting for you to spot me, but you never did. You have great legs, and an energy that made me want to know you better." The note went on, grew even more intimate.

"Egads," my roommate said, "I'd be curious enough to go. But I wouldn't bring a bathing suit, not with what he's thinking."

Another surprise. Rob's "beach party" turned out to be an acquaintance with a Model A who stood ready to drive the two of us to the beach. "This is Hudson Bowlby," Rob said as I squeezed into the narrow black seat. The man nodded, and I noticed at once that he was stiffer than a flagpole, reminiscent of a proper English chauffer. I imagined he wouldn't be saying much. Which he didn't.

Happily, Rob never mentioned his late-night mash note.

"You call this a beach party?" I asked as we sat there all squashed together while the Model A chugged down Memorial Lane.

"Sure," said Rob. "I've brought grape juice and cheesy crackers. It's a party. And we're going to the beach."

I simply stared at him.

As he explained after the man dropped us off, "Hudson Bowlby had the only car I could get my hands on."

THIS WAS ONLY THE BEGINNING. WHEN ROB ARRIVED AT MY dorm he never entered the lobby, never rang the bell to my room. Instead he stood under my window and whistled, as though calling a puppy to come out and play.

With the first three notes of "Over There," every girl on my side of the building knew that Rob Wills had arrived. When I looked down, he'd be staring up at my window expectantly, like an eager Tom Sawyer, with shower water still dripping off his brown hair.

But then I'd already figured out he was the most unusual man I'd ever met, nothing like the others I'd dated. I also guessed he was brilliant—and only partly because one day he offhandedly mentioned his army AGCT score.

On our dates, traveling to the movies on bicycles, or just sitting somewhere under a tree, we discussed things that mattered: racial problems, money issues, world events, politics, and students who smoked.

Sometimes we went to the library and made a stab at studying. But with all the notes we passed back and forth across the table, our homework merely limped along.

Our choice of courses that summer couldn't have been worse. He was taking Organic Chemistry and Quantitative Analysis, each of them a year's worth of work condensed for the summer, and I was taking a demanding course in Creative Writing. As my classmates wrote furiously, trying to turn out literary novels, I gave the writing only passing thought; surely inspiration would swoop down from the clouds and send me to my typewriter. I'd yet to learn that this rarely happens, that creativity begins when you sit down to write.

Anyway, I was too busy with my new boyfriend, too happy now to be darkly creative.

Suddenly the semester was half over, and Rob was saying, "Maybe you'd better write *something* for that class," so I managed to eke out a story about poor people in a bar. I gave it some time, thought I'd done well with details and dialogue, even imagined I might have created a masterpiece.

With the return of my manuscript I came thumping down to earth. "Not bad for something of its sort," the professor wrote, "but its sort has been overdone." Somewhere in his comments lurked the word "hackneyed." Unfortunately, I knew what that meant.

As I reviewed the story in detail I recognized other deficiencies: I'd never been in a bar. And, except for the Deetzes, I didn't know any poor people.

THAT SUMMER ROB AND I RUINED EACH OTHER'S ACADEMIC standing. By applying for an incomplete in Creative Writing, I managed to rescue myself. But Rob didn't fare as well. With a "C" in one course and a "D" in the other, he was told by the Dean, "You can go down to San Jose State, bring up your grades, and come back."

Rob's answer, conveyed to me in private, resonated harshly. "I'll go down to San Jose State, all right, but I'm not coming back." I was only beginning to recognize the hard metal stratum, the pride, that lay beneath his mercurial outer self.

A few weeks later we were in different schools, separated by a length of Bayshore Highway and a 40-minute commute in Rob's newly acquired but almost prehistoric roadster, a munge-green Lafayette dubbed the Turtle because of its low-slung, stumpy-looking rear end.

"This drive is hell on wheels," he said after many weeks, "it's getting more grinding by the day."

And then one Saturday afternoon when we were having a late lunch at Manning's Coffee Shop on Market Street in San Francisco, Rob leaned across the Formica table and said earnestly, "You know, Babe, I'm tired of this every night routine, running up and down Bayshore Highway. I spend half my life in that car." As an afterthought he threw in a comment never intended to set me aflame. "We might as well get married."

There it was. All of it.

Perhaps I should have waited for more. Something bigger. Something closer to my dreams. The two of us riding an Alpine chair lift up a snowy mountain, and Rob pulling me close. "I could go on skiing with you forever, Babe."

Instead, my heart thumped in my throat and I gazed at him with a rush of warmth mixed with excitement, and I said at once, "Why don't we, Rob?"

He smiled. "We could, you know. With a little money from our folks, we could." And so it was decided.

He might not have meant his offhanded comment as a proposal, but he's never said he didn't—and anyway, four weeks later we were married.

In the short space between Fall and Winter quarters, we transferred as a couple to San Jose State where, with the commuting ended and our stress minimized, we both earned straight A's. But San Jose wasn't to be our last school.

Rob was the prime mover behind our transfer to UCLA.

"Let's go back to Stanford," I said, but his jaw got *that look* and I knew it was hopeless. Women who aren't married to flinty husbands say things like, "You should have made him go," or "You should have gone without him." But frankly, I'd just acquired this man and wasn't ready to push him to an ultimate test.

So we transferred to UCLA, for a reason that now seems flimsier than dust. "The surfing's terrific down in Los Angeles," Rob exclaimed, and he wore that same bright expression and exuded the same air of breathless excitement that once made me imagine a "beach party" would consist of a significant number of people gathered on the beach.

"Babe," he exulted, "the sand everywhere is broad and clean. And the water's warm," and then he added as an afterthought, "and UCLA's an excellent school."

That part was true.

Before long, though, I learned that the Santa Monica version of the Pacific Ocean was only slightly warmer than the water that lapped across the shore at Santa Cruz, which, by the temperature registered on my toes and legs, left it pretty frosty as oceans go.

But that never mattered much.

We were soon so busy with all the homework piled on us by UCLA ... and making new friends ... and coping with the nausea that accompanied my first pregnancy ... that we hardly ever saw the beach.

I GRADUATED FROM UCLA WEARING A MAN'S GRADUATION gown, trying in vain to cover a pregnancy so ample that my doctor shouldn't have been so surprised that our baby turned out to be eleven pounds, two ounces.

The hospital nurses kept teasing me: "Does Bobby know how to read?" "Is he going to walk home?" I forced a laugh, but I was embarrassed about his size, thought perhaps I'd eaten too much ... that I'd created a monument to piggery. *I can't wait to get him out of here.*

Days later Rob filled in Bobby's baby book. When he got to a section titled "Special Problems," Rob paused. Then he wrote in his inimitable, strong-minded hand, *"This baby has no problems."*

How we wished, later, he hadn't invited the fates to anoint our son with a problem—a life-long struggle with asthma.

Within ten years Rob and I had six children, five boys and a girl. The two of us were quickly immersed in the multiple activities of young children. School. Homework. Music Lessons. Ten different sports.

Yet I never stopped yearning to be a published author.

And, lucky for me, Rob never stopped trying to help make it happen.

My always-imaginative husband, Rob Wills.

CHAPTER FORTY-THREE

Mother's Path: 1948 On

BECAUSE I HAD BEEN AT STANFORD AND EMBARKED ON A TRA-jectory away from my family, I lost track of where everybody was, especially my mother. No letters came to me at school-at least none that I remember. Yet somebody, forever unseen by me, was paying my bills there, probably Grandmother Alice. Ultimately, of course, the money all came from my grandfather Russell.

AFTER MOTHER SAW ME OFF AND I WAS NO LONGER ONE OF her appendages, her less anchored life followed an erratic course. Only because my brother Allan had long ago created his academic timeline, did his records later explain what happened to Mother once I left for Palo Alto.

Within a few months, according to Allan's notes, Mother took her two sons back to Mt. Shasta, where Allan entered Mount Shasta High School and Hilary, the elementary school.

Nowhere was Denver ever mentioned again. As though our good memories and strong feelings for that town and that home meant nothing to her, Mother sold our glorious house on Lafayette Street.

For the next two years Allan's summary of Mom's path reads like a gypsy's itinerary: partial years spent in Mt. Shasta, several addresses in Berkeley, then back to Mt. Shasta, and once again to Berkeley. Allan was at the mercy of a mother whose peripatetic travels resembled the wanderings of a minstrel.

Only someone with an Allan-type memory would have managed to keep the record straight.

Meanwhile, Mother was falling apart. In her own handwriting—a few sentences added to Allan's timeline—she states without explanation that in the spring of 1948 she spent three months in

Berkeley's Livermore Sanitarium, the first of her many psychological breakdowns. Grandma Alice, who still lived nearby in Berkeley, must have committed her. With few real options then available for the mentally ill, Mother received several electric shock treatments.

Did Grandma Alice care for Hilary? Probably not. But who did?

As though following her pre-stated destiny, once Mother returned to the outside world, her proclivity for finding new husbands continued. For a while she lived in Bend, Oregon, where, for perhaps a year, she called herself Mrs. John Carter—though some of us learned much later that the Oregon husband's name was actually Otto Lett. Obviously Mother considered herself several social notches above anybody named Lett, so she blithely re-named him.

However Mr. Lett felt about Mom's unique fondness for re-labeling, her added stamp on his character was relatively short-lived. Probably mercifully so.

Only Grandma Alice could have known much about Mother's subsequent marriages, of which we heard there were at least two. The first of these, so the story goes, was to a man on parole. The minute Mother learned the details of his background, she fled.

Whatever hapless fellow became the next addendum to her life, none of us were ever specifically informed, beyond hearing from Grandma Alice that there was yet another Mr. Somebody.

As a young married woman, for awhile I had two mothers—my own and Rob's mother, Ruth. Yet my sense of having a caring parent came more from Rob's mother than mine.

In 1949, with the ties to my mother and Mount Shasta still relatively intact, Rob and I, as newlyweds, went up to the ranch. It was our first summer together and Mother had promised him a job. For two months Rob worked with her crusty hired hand, clearing old fire stumps.

After that interval, Rob said, "Your mom does have verve and vitality. And a robust sense of humor. I can see why she's been able to alter so many people's lives."

Sadly, as Rob's and my family grew, my contacts with

Mother became ever fewer. By the time I had several kids, we almost never saw her, never heard from her except at Christmas.

Yet one visit stands out—an event so startling the details are still vivid. I was long finished with college and settled into our tiny home in the San Fernando Valley, by then the mother of three boys. Mother called one day and begged me to come for a visit to the Durant hotel in Berkeley.

As I left the taxi and began walking toward the hotel's front entrance, I noticed someone waving—a fleshy, white-haired woman leaning out an upper story window. Hesitantly I waved back, but only to be polite. If a stranger wanted to extend a friendly greeting, what harm was there in responding?

To my astonishment, the white-haired person turned out to be Mother. "Oh, Mom," I said as we met in the lobby. We fell into each other's arms.

But even up close I didn't recognize her. Mother had always had brown hair and a trim figure. Now, with white hair and an extra seventy pounds, she was impossible to identify. Except for the timbre in her voice, the person leading me to the elevator was a stranger.

And thus began two of the oddest days of my life.

By then her father Russell had died and Mom had hired high-priced lawyers and was embroiled in a contentious fight over her father's estate—with her brother and sister on the other side.

"Maralys," she began dramatically as we settled into her room. "I'm so glad you came, dear. You need to know this. You won't believe what is going on."

"What, Mom? What?" I squirmed in my chair, feeling an old, gut-deep reaction. Over the years during Mother's worst moments, I'd endured too much of her heavy emotionalism.

"My brother and sister have hired lawyers, and they've also hired people who are tracking my every move."

"You mean spying on you?"

"Yes, honey. That's exactly what I mean." Her voice dropped into a familiar, darkly-dramatic range. "And they've got burglars, too. Many of my important papers are missing."

"How could they be missing? Are you sure?"

"Of course I'm sure. My safe-deposit boxes at the bank are empty."

"Maybe you removed the papers yourself and just forgot."

"I did not forget. They've been stolen. I'm under attack." She looked at me with widening eyes, with an expression of horror. "Don't you think I'd know when I've been robbed?"

"But it's a bank, Mom."

Her voice dropped into something of a hush. "The bankers have been bribed. They're in on this too."

"Oh, Mom—"I began.

"Listen to me, honey. You need to know the whole story. Somebody on my side has to hear the details. That's why I brought you here. If I die, nobody will ever be the wiser. This story can't go untold."

I found myself glued to a nearby chair, now beyond protesting because I began to see her as disconnected from reality, perhaps even mad. I listened as Mother unloaded a fantastic tale of deception, fraud, thievery, and ongoing skullduggery … always with the hovering but unseen presence of a burglar.

The longer I listened, the more absurd her story became.

Yet I couldn't leave. She gave me the sense that somewhere in the morass of details there'd be an explanation that made sense. I was looking for reasons why her family was attacking her, a clue as to why Russell left her share of his money in trust. Mother gave an hypnotic performance.

Meanwhile, she kept at her side a bottle of 7-Up and a glass, from which she occasionally took long swallows. "The sugar keeps me from sinking into hypoglycemia," she explained. "I need this, or I'd have an attack." Only later did I learn she was treating her blood sugar problem in the worst possible way. The sugary 7-Up also accounted for the extra seventy pounds.

For endless hours Mom's dramatic tale of being victimized kept me under her spell. If we slept, I don't recall it. My memory centers entirely on her breathtaking descent into the wildest sort of fiction, with that continuing overlay of discouragement, of helplessness. Yet even in her distress she was still a compelling raconteur.

Toward the end I shut down emotionally. Then mentally. Nobody sane could respond to such an outpouring of evil deeds, while feeling they couldn't be true, and worse, that she couldn't be helped.

At last, on the second day, I did have a train to catch. I simply had to go home.

I rose to leave.

As I headed for a corner to grab my small suitcase, Mom asked plaintively, "Where are you going, Maralys?"

"Home, Mom. Home. I have to get back to my kids." I was hovering in the doorway, wondering if she'd even stand to kiss me good-bye.

From her chair she asked, "How are you? And your children?" This in the last minute-and-a-half.

"We're fine, Mom. Everybody's okay."

Only then did she finally stand and give me a brief hug. "I hope you can help," she said, but I knew I couldn't. "Please call or write."

"I will, Mom. I will." *Please let me go.*

With that event I lost my mother; she'd become a stranger.

As I left in the taxi I looked back. There was nobody at the window.

In time I would learn the story behind my mother's "stolen," or rather restricted funds. For years, Grandma Alice, who lived to age 99, paid scant attention to her son and daughter in the East, but did all she could to take care of my mother, Virginia, her first-born child. When Grandma died, to make up for Russell's un-fairness, she left all her money to Mother.

For me, and for my children, only three more encoun-ters with Mother remained. The first was my visit to the ranch many years later to find a thin, subdued, emotionally drained woman wan-dering around the old house, paying scant attention to her cook, in fact hardly speaking at all.

To my amazement, she finally looked up at me and said in a near-whisper, "This is my husband, Maralys," and she pointed across the kitchen to her latest live-in: Wayne Small!

244

"Hullo," he muttered, and I stared, dumbfounded. Wayne had been the youngest of the Small children who, years earlier when I was ten, had poured onto the bus at the Four-corners. I simply could not imagine how Mother had retrieved him from his falling-down house ... how she'd brought him to the ranch to work. And then married him!

"Does he ... uh ... share your bedroom?" I asked in an off moment.

"No," she said dully. "Most of the time he sleeps in the living-room. Under the piano."

At the end of my visit she insisted on writing me what was then a generous check, a gift of $300. I watched as she wrote. Slowly. Painstakingly. Her once bold handwriting had vanished. To match her shrinking personality, her writing had evaporated into the tiniest of unreadable scripts.

THE OTHER OCCASIONS WERE DESCRIBED BY TWO OF MY SONS. One of them, Chris, tells about working on the ranch for a few summer months and viewing Mother's display of gold bars "So you can all come up here," she explained, "to live on the ranch when the Russians take over the country."

Chris, now an orthopedic surgeon, claims to this day that the gold bars were real. "If only we'd managed to retrieve them," he says.

To me, since I never saw any such thing, they've remained a fantasy.

THE LAST VISIT, PERHAPS THE MOST VIVID OF ALL, HAS BECOME part of the family's folklore about my mother.

With his best friend, Bobby Weinberg, our fourth son, Kenny, made a summertime trip up to the ranch. As the two boys alighted from their car, they saw Mother sitting on the front porch in a wicker chair.

Clearly unaware of who they were, she stared as they walked up the path. As soon as they were close enough Mom asked, "Wanna buy a bull?"

The boys turned to each other in surprise, then shook their

heads, trying their hardest not to laugh out loud.

But that wasn't all. What they saw was a woman with some kind of tinfoil hat over her head and a layer of tinfoil covering her knees.

They wanted to ask about her strange get-up. But they never got that far. Mother quickly explained. "The burglar is up on the hill, sending down rays. The tinfoil is to ward them off. As long as I keep this foil around me, the rays can't penetrate."

The two boys nodded as though believing her tale. Since both were basically respectful, Kenny and Bobby merely listened politely but decided not to linger.

They knew crazy when they saw it.

DURING HER FINAL YEARS, MOM'S LOVE CHILD, HILARY, RE-turned to the ranch to take care of her.

When I muse about my mother, I think of the salmon that swims upstream to spawn, and after spawning, with its essence gone and its mission fulfilled, sinks to the bottom of the stream and dies.

In a way that's what happened to our mother. Having produced Allan and me, and then Hilary, and raised us haphazardly but as best she could, her goal in life was accomplished.

The best of Mother's zest was over, the rest a blank page with nothing on it except tracings of misery.

Chapter Forty-Four

Hilary's Path: 1948 On.

For me, Hilary's journey is a nearly blank page, a mystery. He is my baby brother, ten years my junior, yet what I remember best about him are his younger years, those moments in his babyhood when Allan and I hovered over him ... a darling little boy, adored by both of us.

The first breakup of our core family in 1942, with the war raging, meant a splintering that sent Mother and her love baby off to follow Hans from one Western army camp to another, while I joined my aunt in far away Rochester. Only Allan stayed in the area, now living with the Deetz family.

For mother, following Hans to his earliest deployments did not prove worthwhile; she and Hilary rarely saw him. And of course Allan and I almost never saw Hilary.

Later, for two different and widely separated years, while Hans taught skiing to soldiers in the Rockies, the four of us were in Denver, once more together. But by then Allan and I were in different schools, each with our own circle of friends. Hilary had become merely the little boy who was always underfoot.

Hilary's tragic burn accident in the basement of our Denver home, when he was six and I was sixteen, made him the focus of our family—for him an era that ended badly in every way; Mother's fury over Hans' inattention to his son meant she banished him from our lives forever.

In later years, after I married and had my own children, I received only scraps of news about Hilary. In one letter I learned that he'd become a sad and frightened twelve-year-old in a boarding school. "Sis," he wrote, "I'm so lonely. Come see me."

I didn't know how to respond. My heart broke for him, but he was a day's trip away, and going there by myself was nearly impossible. I was stuck at home with a husband in law school and two little boys.

Our paper-cut-out home, a tiny tract house in the San Fernando Valley, was already crammed to the brim with our own children; we couldn't take another. So I wrote Hilary expressing my love and sympathy, which surely wasn't enough. In odd moments I worried about him and felt chagrined. Oh, the guilt you feel when a family member cries out and you fall short of doing anything useful.

Only later did I become privy to Allan's assessment of Hilary's growing up years—the few that remained while Allan was still at home. "My most vivid memories of Hilary after you left, Sis, were Hilary sitting in front of a television and smoking. Some days not even going to school." He shook his head. "And Mom letting him do it." He paused for long moments. "Mother would never have allowed that with us."

ONCE OR TWICE MY HUSBAND AND I MET WITH THE ADULT Hilary in Berkeley. At the time my youngest brother was running a repair shop for expensive foreign automobiles—a losing business, we learned, supported largely by Grandma Alice and Mother.

As we sat together in a restaurant, I was dismayed to find that I didn't really like the grown man. He drank too much. He smoked. He used foul language. He smirked and laughed like a vaudevillian—all insincere, all theatrical.

What had Mom done to him? Hilary had taken on what felt like a false façade, trying too hard to impress us. To impress everyone.

In subsequent years we heard about one, then two, then three marriages and several children. I met two of his wives and liked them both.

Yet above all, Hilary had one outstanding talent, never fully developed; he was a great actor. Allan saw him once, in a town north of Mount Shasta playing Tevye in "Fiddler on the Roof."

"He was the best Tevye I ever saw," Allan reported back to us. "He should have stuck to acting." As a postscript Allan added, "He was completely real as an actor, playing a role on stage. I can't figure out why the real life Hilary was such a phony, when the acting Hilary wasn't."

Toward the end of Hilary's life, when he returned to the ranch to care for our mother, he became somewhat real again. His airs had subsided—perhaps into illness. "I think I've got cancer," he confided to me.

"Oh, no," I said. "It can't be, Hilary. You look so good." Once again, in a rare visit to my old home, I found it possible to like him.

What I didn't like was that our ranch home was now full of guns, or that Hilary wore a vicious-looking knife strapped to his ankle.

In that final chapter, lonely once more, Hilary put an ad in the paper for a wife. Describing himself as "fecund," he found a woman who was willing to join him on the ranch. For several years they lived as a couple in the old house, tending as best they could to my mother.

At age 83, Mother died.

Hilary lived on for another three years. But then one day he went out on a small All Terrain Vehicle to tend the fences surrounding our property.

He never came home. Out there on the fence line, Hilary himself died.

My feelings about my baby brother can be summed up in two words: sadness and regret.

Once our Mother deteriorated, in a variety of ways, so did he.

Chapter Forty-Five

Allan's Path: 1948 On

ALLAN WAS SO UNLIKE HILARY IN EVERY WAY, IT'S HARD TO imagine they were even half brothers.

Allan has never been anything but "real", and at times so high-minded, so Lincolnesque—almost like the Abe who supposedly walked miles to return a penny—that the rest of us shake our heads and decide that sometimes a little compromise of principles isn't so bad.

Happily for everyone, his crazy upbringing by a gypsy never seeped in, never came close to altering his persona. In spite of Mother's dragging him around as her personal rag doll, at times trying to imbue him with mysticism and fairy tales, Allan silently disagreed and never believed any of it.

"One time Mother explained reincarnation to me," he says in his own memoir, "and I didn't believe it, but I would never speak about my disbelief at that age." He must have been about six. "Another time she told me about extra-sensory perception, which I didn't believe either. Then she said she knew what her brother Sam, who was a continent away, was thinking at that very moment. I thought she had lost her mind."

As much as my own school years were scattered in all directions like the beads of a broken necklace, Allan's schooling was worse … all thanks to our peripatetic parent. His academic timeline reveals that before graduation from high school he changed schools 17 times, often switching back to the same school he had left earlier that year.

During the academic school year of 1949 to 1950, Allan notes that he was a student at San Jose State College—coincidentally trailing me and my new husband there by half a year.

After the miracle of two whole uninterrupted years at Claremont

Men's College in California, Allan describes what happened in 1951. "Mother suggested that I spend the summer with my father, saying, 'Ted is a good man.' I was stunned because it was the first positive thing I had ever heard her say about Ted, aside from his brilliance and professional eminence."

Allan adds, "I had a great time with Ted and his family that summer. The next summer Mother made the same arrangements—and that time it changed my life."

During Allan's second visit on Long Island, a young woman named Sue Wing was staying nearby, enjoying a girls' slumber party. Allan arrived at the party uninvited, and as he stood in the doorway, Sue remembers, "Here was this tall, good-looking guy. My friends were too snobbish to talk to a stranger, but I decided I would be friendly."

For Allan, Sue was exactly the girl he'd been looking for—in a way since First Grade. Attractive, serious, and intelligent, Sue had been fortunate enough to grow up in a family that encompassed all the stability that Allan's own childhood lacked.

The only girl among three brothers, she was never intimidated by men. She was light-hearted and flexible in areas where Allan was serious and rigid, and invariably able to see the humorous aspects of their relationship.

In 1954, Allan and Sue were married.

From the moment I met her, Sue Wing became the sister I'd never had. Whenever we got together, Sue was apt to grin and say something like, "Allan just hiked part way up Mt. Wilson with rocks in his pocket. The only way, he says, he'd be going slow enough for me."

"You're more of a hiker than I am," I said. "For me he'd have to drag an anchor."

She laughed. "Explain that to him, please. When Allan decides to climb a mountain, he seems to think it's possible for everyone. Wait 'til we have kids … !"

Happily for Allan and Sue, Grandma Alice pulled some important strings and secured his admission to the Massachusetts Institute of Technology—a perfect fit for his serious and scientific bent.

Eventually, after earning a Master's degree there, Allan and Sue and their four children, three boys and finally a girl, moved out to California. Luckily for me, they were only an hour's drive away.

Now an engineer, Allan was hired by Jet Propulsion Laboratory to work on the Space Program. It was Allan who designed the computer program that guided the Astronauts' Lunar Landing module from the Mother Ship to the moon.

SOME TIME AFTER HIS MOON-LANDING DAYS, ALLAN DECIDED to drag me into his rarified world. "Maralys, you're a writer," he said, "You should be using a computer," and never mind that most authors still pecked away on typewriters.

"I know nothing about those machines," I said, and he said, "Leave it to me," and soon he arrived at my house laden like a mule, carrying half a dozen large and small boxes, and what appeared to be 5,000 pages of instructions.

"You want me to read all that?" I whimpered. He'd just thumped down three of the world's thickest manuals.

He threw a glance at the obese notebooks. "Nah. They just came with this stuff," he said. "I'll teach you myself."

And a good thing he did, because in those days the literature was incomprehensible. Every third sentence contained words I'd never heard of. Obviously, PhD's from schools like Cal Tech had drafted the instruction manuals—all intended for other PhD's from schools like MIT.

Instead, with Allan coaching me, I composed my own manual—a full seven pages: "To Print: Type Control P."

Soon I found myself complaining to Sue, "When Allan tries to teach me things, he keeps wanting to explain the science behind my mistakes. I swear, he'd like to start with Leonardo da Vinci. A simple question takes us an hour. All I want to know is, which button should I push?"

She laughed. "He does that to me, too. I finally said, 'Allan, it's fine that you know how they work. But honestly, I don't care. Just accept it. The women in your life are computer dummies.'"

At a later time she said, "I try not to get into mechanical

explanations with him." She made a face. "He finally figured out I'd never understand the details of how men made it to the moon."

"I gather he's given up on all of us," I said. "I don't hear the science behind moon travel, either."

"In some things he's thrown up his hands," she said. "But he'll never quite accept it—that the rest of us are techno-phobes, that we care a lot about buttons and not a whit about theories."

Now a retired engineer, Allan still enjoys a certain amount of notoriety from his old colleagues at Jet Propulsion Lab. Those who don't remember him for anything else recall his pedaling to work every day on a bicycle ... not to mention his astonishing size 15 shoes. Or that sometimes they were tennis shoes. And red.

We have movies of him hiking up a steep hill—shots taken from above. All you can see are those great, moving patches of red.

But Allan is only retired in principle. He still works on a daily basis, writing essays and giving speeches about the perils of Global Warming ... or mailing off treatises about a planet in danger of running out of water.

Sometimes he tells personal stories. But he's too thorough to win any prizes as a raconteur. In all seriousness he recalls the time he decided to shore up a very expensive San Francisco hotel bedroom in case of an earthquake.

We learned how he prepared the windows with towels, about the dimensions of the mirror taken down from the wall above the bed and its careful placement in a far corner ... then his final discovery that the nearest stairwell was made impassable by the storage of bins of dirty linens.

He mentioned the vanishing of time into hours past midnight as he called the hotel management about the blocked stairwell, and the explanations given to a startled security guard on patrol. Among the things he said to the man: "This is an earthquake town. I had to take down the bedroom mirror; our bedroom isn't safe."

The guard replied, "Sir, I'm sure by now it is."

"Look at this—people trying to escape will die on this stairwell."

"Maybe we won't have an earthquake tonight."

"I'm calling the front desk again."

By the time the stairwell was unclogged and his room fully earthquake-proofed, make that dismantled, Allan's listeners had heard too much; they also knew Allan had left himself and Sue almost no time to sleep.

With Allan, a casual story can become a scientific treatise on earthquake preparedness.

DESPITE HIS ENGINEER'S QUIRKS, ALLAN PROVES THAT EVEN our mother was not able, ultimately, to ruin a basically sound son.

Mostly from a distance, I watched the way Allan and Sue raised their children. I swear, they sprinkled their kids with some kind of fairy dust because the kids all became remarkable adults. And yes, avid hikers. And they all admire their father.

In every way … with his choice of a wife, his stellar career in the Space Program, his comic aspects, his rock-solid sense of decency, and the marvelous raising (with Sue, of course), of their four children, Allan is one of the most successful men I know.

Allan receiving an award at Jet Propulsion Lab.

CHAPTER FORTY-SIX

My Path: From 1949 On

HOW DO YOU KNOW WHEN YOU'RE DESTINED TO BECOME AN author?

Perhaps it's when, even as a child, you begin seeing all of life as a book. Simon & Schuster editor, and now agent, Betsy Lerner, says most of the authors she's worked with began writing as children. And that was certainly true of me.

What I never expected, had never really thought about, was that I was also destined to become a mother. And oops ... a mother six times over.

First came Bobby, then Chris, then Eric, then Kenny. With the arrival of Kenny my obstetrician confided in another patient, "I've got to go tell a woman she's just had her fourth boy!" Frankly, I thought he should apologize.

When our fifth child was a girl, I couldn't sleep for the excitement, and later it seemed the gifts for Tracy would never stop coming. Last came Kirk, a curly-haired boy.

Friends assumed that Rob and I were Catholics, when in truth we were just ardent Presbyterians. We soon discovered it was like creating our own club and housing it under one roof, with a variety of personalities we supposed we could control.

Except, of course, we couldn't.

Eventually a group that large becomes an army, and somehow Rob and I imagined we'd be the generals and we'd march off and all the kids would fall in behind us. But that's not how it worked. Suddenly the army scattered and we found ourselves running behind, racing to catch up.

We soon discovered several kids, including Tracy, were out in the orange groves behind the house, staging orange wars. Bobby was in the garage designing a double-decker bicycle that he and Kenny pedaled around the neighborhood—with Bobby reporting offhand-edly, "You should have seen all the double-takes." We learned that two sons were up in the hills shooting oranges out of a carbide cannon. Meanwhile Chris, ever exuberant, was out on the blacktop building a tow-plane. And those were just the activities we were aware of.

All six were deeply involved in sports. It would have been nice if they'd all chosen the *same* sport, but instead some swam, some played tennis, some rode motorcycles, and others flew.

And I was thinking, *My Lord, I never planned any of this.*

Sometimes I looked back, musing, Who needs to write about poor people in a bar? When I've got a circus right here, under my own tent?

IN SPITE OF ALL THE CONFUSION AT HOME, AND THANKS TO Rob's support, I churned out short stories, poems, essays, words of advice, humorous pieces, whatever inspired me at the moment.

With each new piece I sent to magazines or publishers, I imag-ined as I sealed the envelope, *This one's going to get published.*

And every one of them came back—sometimes with little notes, most often with a few perfunctory sentences of regret. I stopped reporting to Rob, "Another rejection."

In the earliest years, while some of my children were still spend-ing nursery school mornings at our church's Little Red Schoolhouse, Rob offered, "That's one place, Babe, you could go where it's quiet," so he encouraged me to hire a babysitter for the chaotic dinner hour and use my keys to take over the schoolhouse and write.

Later I escaped into the nearby, still-empty hills, where I parked with my typewriter in my lap and a copy of *To Kill a Mockingbird* on the passenger seat. With my usual German doggedness, I studied Harper Lee's words, hoping some of her skills would rub off on me.

Along with shorter pieces, I also began a memoir, "*Rough Around the Edges,*" a collection of humorous letters written to Verna, my Denver girl friend, all about my crazy early years with Rob.

Soon my father, Ted, was involved. As he'd once promised, he read my mailed manuscripts and offered suggestions. "Study *Onions in the Stew,*" he began, "it's by Betty McDonald. She's exactly the kind of writer you're trying to be."

Ted showed my early drafts to his secretary, to friends. As my writing improved he showed the book around again. "My secretary loves this latest version," he wrote. "And so do my friends." With Ted encouraging me all the way, I began sending the completed work to publishers.

Only in retrospect do I realize that several positive rejections meant I should have kept re-writing and polishing, continued sending it to editors, that publication was closer than I imagined. Instead, after three rejections I gave up. (Decades later I borrowed most of it for another memoir, *A Circus Without Elephants.*)

In an old, ratty shoebox I saved all my rejection slips for articles and the book—not because I was a masochist, but only because I saw myself as eventually published. (Hadn't my Reader's Digest mother promised I'd make it?)

In daydreams I imagined myself speaking to a fascinated audience, heard them gasp as I opened my shoebox and dumped all those rejections on the floor. For me, the important word about publication was never "If."

It was "When."

THERE CAME A TIME WHEN MY WRITING EFFORTS STALLED LIKE a grumpy old car. In 1973 our two oldest sons, Bobby and Chris, became champions in the burgeoning sport of hang gliding. "Come watch us!" Chris cried. So Rob and I drove out to the Southern California hills to see them fly. We reveled in their enthusiasm and the sheer wild exuberance that permeated the atmosphere. Even more, we were caught up by the beauty, by multi-colored sails that masqueraded as butterflies. Like our sons, Rob and I were soon hooked.

BEFORE LONG I WROTE ARTICLES ABOUT THE EXOTIC NATURE of silent flight, about the miracle of young men becoming airborne without an engine. Nearby, a friend took photos, and I sent out several packets, including, as Rob suggested, to United Airlines' *Mainliner Magazine.*

One day a letter arrived, an envelope too small for the return of my manuscript. I opened it and gasped. "A check!" I yelled to Rob. "They're paying me $350!"

At that moment I was no longer a mother-with-a-typewriter; I'd become an author.

With Rob watching, I dumped out my shoebox. "A hundred and twenty-seven rejections!" I cried. "Maybe now I'll stop getting them."

"Let's hope so." He grinned. "That check will get us to Honolulu, Babe. Pack up. Let's go."

After that I sold a dozen more articles on the sport.

IN THE SPRING OF 1974, OUR FAMILY WAS RENT BY TRAGEDY. Our third son, Eric, who was never a champion, went out in the San Bernardino hills to fly. Suddenly he, too, was caught up in hang gliding. Imagining he could emulate his older brothers, he experimented mid-air and attempted a 360, which he'd never learned to do.

Now trapped unexpectedly in a diving maneuver, Eric crashed into a hillside and died.

As a family we were devastated. None of us could believe it. This couldn't happen to us, the family with two champions who, at Chris's insistence, also ran a hang glider manufacturing company. Bobby kept moaning, "I should have showed him how. I should have taught him better."

We had no idea what to do next.

In my mind I kept seeing him: Eric, who sat beside me in the Wills Wing office. Eric, with his engaging eagerness to buy carefully and save us money. Eric who always knew which young men would purchase something and which wouldn't. I couldn't imagine returning to the office without him.

Suddenly all our lives were on hold.

We held a rare family conference in the living room, a sad hour in which nobody could think what to say. Rob asked, "What shall we do?" and glanced at Bobby, who sat on the fireplace hearth, head down, his long legs stretched out in front of him. Bobby couldn't answer.

Rob turned to Chris. "You're planning to be a doctor, Chris. But what about Bobby?"

Finally Chris said, "You know, Dad, hang gliding is pretty much Bobby's whole life."

Rob sighed. "I guess we have to go on."

IN AUGUST, THREE YEARS LATER, BOBBY WAS DOING A COMMERcial for Willys Jeep, and in a few moments of careless flying, the filming helicopter caused an accident. At first Rob and I didn't know what had happened.

From here on, as I recorded in my memoir about our sons, I learned what it meant to "let go" and commit your deepest feelings to paper—and thus find a way to live through them.

AS I WORKED IN THE WILLS WING OFFICE THAT DAY, I REceived an urgent call, and now Rob and I paced the hospital lobby, stonewalled by the staff. "How is he?" I kept asking at the desk, but nobody would tell us anything. "Please fill out this form," a clerk insisted, but instead I glared at her in fury. "I don't care about that form. how is he?"

She shook her head and scurried away, a scared rabbit. To my amazement, Rob took the form and began filling it in.

I left him, went off to pace. After a long while a nearby door opened and a nurse came out. I ran to her. "How is he?" I asked.

She shook her head. During a terrible hour she was the first caring human I'd seen. "He's critical," she whispered. And with that I knew.

Bobby is dead. And now I will die too. The pain is too great. Any minute, I thought, my heart will stop beating. No mother can survive the loss of two sons.

The door opened again and a man came out, followed by a different nurse, who indicated we should follow him. Rob fell meekly in line, but I couldn't.

She gently took my arm. "Please come," she said.

"No," I said, "I can't. Let me go outside and run." I shook my head, watched the others walk away. "My husband will tell me." *I can't go down there and hear what he's going to say.*

"Please," she said, pushing me along. "You have to come."

I tried to pull away. *If I hear it, I'll die too.*

She gave me no choice, tugged me down the corridor into the "blue room."

I was vaguely surprised to find that I arrived there still standing. Across the room, Rob sat calmly in a chair. *Oh God, he still doesn't know.*

The doctor turned slowly, looked at us both. "If he'd lived," he said, "he would have been a vegetable."

Out of the corner of my eye I sensed the nurse staring at me. But for me the doctor's words meant nothing; they came too late.

Rob's face crumpled. Simply caved in. *Oh Rob,* I thought, *You didn't know. You never figured it out. Oh, Rob.*

I ran across the room to hold him. *Oh, poor man. Oh, poor Rob.*

Together we staggered out of the room and somehow made our way back along that corridor, where hang glider pilots now lined the walls. They called out to us, "How is he?" and Rob shouted back, "He's dead!" and somebody cried, "Oh, no!" and the rest fell back, groaning.

Outside the hospital a man waited. I stared at him, for he was openly crying. He said hoarsely, "I loved that man. I only knew him a week but I loved him."

CHRIS COMES HOME FROM MEDICAL SCHOOL TO ORGANIZE HIS brother's funeral. *How can this be happening? That one of our sons is memorializing another?*

In our church social hall Chris shows movies of Bobby flying.

We all watch, mesmerized.

Bobby flies across the screen in front of us, turning abruptly to face us head on, his butterfly kite with its red leading edges and large yellow circles on a blue field—beautiful, lyrical, and I feel better, suddenly. He is back where he should be, it is natural and right, the world is ordered again.

Chris has chosen his movies well.

Bobby does a three-sixty; he does it as though he were born knowing how. My pain eases further.

Every scene is about him, it is as though he is summarizing his life for us in the way he might have done it. Flying.

I think, What does the number of a man's days matter if he's lived a lifetime?

I watch him floating away serenely, the sail rippling in a whisper of sound, the sun splashing across the fabric. One hand rests easily on the control bar, the other in his lap. Up here, I think, he is perfect. Flawless. This is Bobby, and this is the way he'll always be.

Chapter Forty-Seven

How it all worked out.

Unlike Eric, Bobby was known world-wide, the current hang gliding champion of Britain, the United States, and Canada. People wrote us from all over the world. "If it could happen to Bob Wills," several of them said, "it could happen to anybody."

Weeks later, Rob gave me one of his looks. "The wolf has always been right outside the door, Babe. I've known it forever."

He'd sensed this but I hadn't.

"Thank God," we murmured to each other, "we have a large family." The loss of two children is never softened by the presence of others. It simply means that with six kids you still have four more to love. One child does not substitute for another. Never. But the love you feel as parents can still be lavished on other children.

After Bobby's death, our business became too cruel; I couldn't stay there any longer. Instead, I left my job at Wills Wing and went home to write books.

Thus in 1978 I began my second full-length book, *"They Could Fly a Brick,"* a memoir about Eric and Bobby, with Chris writing special chapters about his part in hang gliding.

But then we couldn't sell it.

I revised it, changed the title, changed the focus, took classes, had Chris do revisions, polished endlessly. Finally I re-wrote the story from the beginning. And then I re-wrote it again. But still, as if bedeviled, the manuscript found no takers.

With nothing to show for our efforts, I collected manila envelopes full of rejections—greater numbers than I'd once had in my shoebox.

Because an early rejection came from Prentice-Hall, my agent, Patty Teal—also a dear friend—said, "Why don't you offer to write them a different kind of book?"

"Oh no, Patty. I'm still working on my personal story. I have no interest in starting another."

"You might as well ask," she said. "What can it hurt?"

So I did.

After I'd sent out a wholly unprofessional book proposal for a factual book on hang gliding, I was astounded when Editor Saul Cohen, with his own imprint at Prentice-Hall, offered me a contract, complete with a large advance. How could an author aspire to more than that?

I soon finished *Manbirds: Hang Gliders and Hang Gliding* (with chapters by Chris), which landed on Library Journal's list of the year's hundred-best books in Science and Technology.

Surely I'd never get another rejection.

(Oh, surely I would!)

FOR THE NEXT EIGHT YEARS I WROTE—AND YES, SOLD—FIVE other books, including, to Harlequin, four romance novels co-written with Chris's wife, Betty-Jo.

Yet all that time, between completing other books—a volume on party games, a techno-thriller—I revised and polished the book of my heart, giving it one name after another. Ultimately titled *Higher Than Eagles*, the manuscript went everywhere I could think of, but kept collecting rejections.

Even I, the unquenchable optimist, began to lose hope.

Still, an editor at Crown Publishers sent a rejection so full of praise (even begging me not to give up), that his words could have been an endorsement on the book jacket.

One day on an airplane, Rob was thumbing through another airline magazine and found the article, "Small Presses Have Big Clout."

He passed it to me. "You might send *Eagles* to some of these, Babe."

At last, perhaps a hundred rejections later, and fourteen years after I began the first draft, Longstreet Press in Atlanta sent a letter.

Imagine, a letter!

That was the Saturday I'd forgotten to bring in the mail. At midnight, in bare feet, I ran down to the mailbox and minutes later opened a tiny white envelope. Out fell my small postage check. But more important, an editor had penned the words, "I've written your agent making an offer on *Higher Than Eagles*."

"Rob!" I cried. "Rob, listen to this!"

I read it to him, waved the letter around, whooped and yelled around the family room, screamed and clapped and danced. "Aren't you happy, Rob?" I cried, "Aren't you excited?"

Forever allergic to crazy displays of emotion, Rob said only, "I'll be excited when they send the check."

The next day I thought everyone could tell by looking at me that I'd been anointed and was now a changed person. After fourteen years of on-and-off angst, I felt I'd been touched by a scepter, by a magic wand, so that even my clothes gave off a glow. People would want to touch the hem of my skirt.

I couldn't believe it when my tennis friends said, "You sold the book? Oh, that's nice, Maralys. Now who's going to serve first?"

At last I reached my writing friends ... and they all screamed and yelled.

Within a month, reviews came in from everywhere, astonishing in their enthusiasm, better than I could have hoped. Five movie-makers (including Disney and the producers of *Northern Exposure*), took options on the story.

Though so far the movie has not been made, the book became a favorite among my readers.

Today another producer is once again hoping to turn *Higher Than Eagles* into a feature-length film.

One day in early 2012, after I'd published 14 books (the latest: two light-hearted memoirs, two writing books), Chris, said, "Mom, you've got to write the story about your childhood. It's incredible."

I thought about it briefly, then shook my head. "There's not enough to say, Chris. I wouldn't know how to begin. Or even what should be there. Those years don't have a plot."

"Just start, Mom," he said. "There's plenty of story. You'll figure it out as you go." He gave me a sly grin. "Write it, Mom. It'll be your best book yet. You'll see." He stopped to consider. "All the stuff you think you don't remember will come back to you. The plot is already there, in your head. Start writing and the story will come. It'll write itself."

I sighed. "Okay, Chris. If you say so."

And so this book began.

Sure enough, Chris was right. It turned out there was more to say about my gypsy childhood, about my mother and brothers, than I'd ever thought possible.

TODAY, I'M WAITING FOR MY READER'S DIGEST MOTHER TO point the way to a movie—to help our family see Eric and Bobby on the big screen as we once saw them in life.

In some inner corner of my soul, which I'm too superstitious to express out loud, which I hesitate even to put on paper, the operative word about the movie, *Higher Than Eagles*, has never been "If."

For me it's always been "When."

THE END

Selling the-book-of-my-heart, "Higher Than Eagles."

MARALYS WILLS HAS LIVED THREE DISTINCT LIVES: AUTHOR OF fifteen published books, teacher of college students, and mother of six children—five boys and a girl.

Educated at Stanford and UCLA, she is married to a retired trial attorney. She currently teaches novel writing on the college level, and in 2000 was named Teacher of the Year.

Her most challenging project, a poignant memoir titled *Higher Than Eagles*, became her biggest triumph, garnering excellent reviews and five movie options.

Wills considers public speaking the dessert for all the hard work of writing, and relishes every moment spent with a receptive audience. She welcomes readers' input.

Contact her: Maralys@Cox.net or www.Maralys.com